SEESAW
HOW NOVEMBER '42
SHAPED THE FUTURE

SEESAW

HOW NOVEMBER '42
SHAPED THE FUTURE

75th Anniversary Commemorative Edition

Stan Moore

© 2012, 2017 Stan Moore

All rights reserved. No part of this book may be reproduced or transmitted in any form or by any means, electronic or mechanical, including photocopying, recording, or by an information storage and retrieval system—except by a reviewer who may quote brief passages in a review—without permission in writing from the publisher.

Maps and design by Jack Lenzo

This book is dedicated to the anonymous workers, soldiers, and sailors of all nations whose toil and suffering is the true stuff of any story about World War Two

CONTENTS

A Note from the Author xi

Foreword: November 1942; The world in 1941 and in 1943 1
Who: Dramatis Personae 7
When: Setting the Stage: What Happened Before, During,
    and After November, 1942 15
Maps 17

CHAPTER I
November 8: Operation Torch;
    The world in the 1930's–1941 23

CHAPTER II
November 8: Logistics; The war, 1941–1942 39

CHAPTER III
November 8: Early Guadalcanal; The war, 1942 57

CHAPTER IV
November 9: Warriors and administrators;
    Russia; Technology 83

CHAPTER V
November 10: Submarines; Battle of the Atlantic;
    Intelligence 105

CHAPTER VI
November 11, Armistice Day: Pact of Steel;
Civilians in the War 125

CHAPTER VII
November 12: Throwing lightning bolts;
Training Pilots; India.. 141

CHAPTER VIII
November 13–15: Naval Battle of Guadalcanal;
intelligence 161

CHAPTER IX
November 13–15: Russia; the Home Front;
New Guinea 181

CHAPTER X
November 16–19: North Africa; Cactus; Stalingrad............... 197

CHAPTER XI
November 20–29: Burma; Tunisia; Land battles;
What if? 211

CHAPTER XII
The Future Defined.. 219

Bibliography... *227*
Glossary: Who Is Raj and What Is a Tin Fish?.................... *229*
Daily Breakdown *233*
Discussion Questions... *237*

A NOTE FROM THE AUTHOR

I grew up on World War II stories, movies and books. My lifelong fascination with the conflict finds expression in this work. It is intended to be interesting and informative and as you read it, I hope you will not be disappointed. This book has some unpublished, new personal material. Even so, it is not intended as a groundbreaking, definitive work of military history. Rather, it is an overview of an important time in the war focused on certain critical places. The audience aimed for is the reader interested in what makes history.

People who have helped are too numerous to mention. Thanks and thanks again to the many who have encouraged, given ideas, loaned materials, proofread, and generally supported me in this effort. Special thanks to Bill Stevenson, Betty Beckett Arnold, and Carolyn Henderson Tinkham, and their families.

This book covers events in just about every time zone on the planet, so to keep it simple, all times cited are local time, the time at the place of action. Clock times are noted in military time, that 0600 is 6:00 AM; 1830 is 6:30 PM and so on.

Despite best efforts errors may have crept in. They are mine and mine alone.

Special recognition should go to my beloved wife Kiki, for everything.

FOREWORD
November 1942; The World in 1941 and in 1943

It has been seventy five years since November 1942, the watershed year of World War II. The countries that seemed to be winning were knocked from their perch by actions in that month, and they became the war's losers. Countries which had been losing started winning.

During this month campaigns were initiated and other ongoing campaigns had pivotal battles. These took place with backdrops of each country's long developing home front plans and preparations for war. Some of these measures were at last coming to fruition and helping the war effort. Some countries had made early decisions which went sour. Those decisions ended up hindering, not helping the war effort. Physical, logistical and manpower preparations were starting to have their effects. Some countries made preparations and measures but cut them short or abandoned them as ineffective, too expensive, or not important enough to pursue.

Early war plans, tactics and materials developed by the Axis nations worked well for them early on. But early in the war, the Allied nations had learned much at the hard school of defeat and retreat. These skills and tactics were hard come by and bought by many valiant dead soldiers and sailors. Their use was starting to counter the early Axis successes.

There were five broad theaters where the pivotal campaigns reached balance in the summer and fall of 1942. The term "balance" means that both sides were fighting as hard as they could but neither could deliver a knockout punch. In fact neither could really budge the other side. To use a playground analogy, both were on a seesaw but both ends were in the air. Neither side could get their side down to get their feet on the ground.

But this period, November 1942, saw movement in the balance. One side, the Allies, was able to start moving the seesaw, start gaining small wins and start gaining momentum. Then they began to gain real advantages, some big and some in smaller less evident ways. The Allies also gained the initiative, the ability to make the opponent react rather than act independently. There was of course action all over the globe in 1942, not just the areas this work will focus on.

This work will focus on five arenas. The first two were in Africa, in Egypt on the east end to the west end countries of Morocco and Algeria. This was two distinct theaters, Egypt and Northwest Africa. The third was Southern Russia centered on the struggle for the city of Stalingrad and the resources of the Caucasus region. The fourth and fifth were in the southwest and south Pacific. There were two distinct theaters: the Papuan peninsula of eastern New Guinea and the southern Solomon Islands some 500 miles east. A daily breakdown of operations in these theaters shows ongoing battles with results about evenly matched. Then one side gains a breakthrough victory.

Throughout history, each war follows a pattern of action, a formula. Wherever the battles are fought, the pattern holds. One side takes actions or steps and their goals are furthered. Then the other side acts, whether reacting or seeking to take the initiative. It takes its own steps and actions to counter the first's gains and to further its own aims. Action and reaction are played out over time and space. At some point each side has extended itself as far as it can, and the struggle is about evenly balanced, almost stalemated. This can occur fairly quickly, in weeks, or it can take months or even a few years to develop.

There are many cases where one side seemed to be near victory but the other side fought back to stalemate. Then that side goes on to prevail. One example is the Napoleonic Wars: they went on around the world, armies marching, fleets sailing, first the French ascendant, then the rest of Europe allying to ultimately prevail. In the American Civil War, Robert E. Lee and Jefferson Davis' Confederacy ran rings around the Union for about three years. It took that long for President Lincoln to identify, assemble and organize a team able to capitalize on Union strengths while hammering at Confederate weaknesses. The Union won the war only thirteen months after Lincoln assembled his team. In World War I: Germany came close to scoring a knockout in summer and autumn 1914 with its march through Belgium to northern France and its victories in Russia. But the Russians, French and English held on that fall and fought slowly back. Ultimately the western allies, with American help pushed them back.

At the point of stalemate, the outcome becomes a matter of grit, persistence and luck. The question revolves on who can hold on, who can slug a little harder, who can innovate and out-think the other, in order to win and impose their will. The sides perform a ballet fraught with death, violence, comebacks, determination, and ultimately victory and defeat. Of course it is not as clear cut as two men in a ring hitting each other. In war there are multiple nations pursuing their own national interests over time, with battles, raids, political offensives, economic efforts, and other actions taking place on the battlefield and round the world.

It is easy enough to start a war but not so easy to end one. Once a war starts no one knows who will win, how the peace will look, who will be the big winners and big losers. Every war is an attempt to create the future. At some identifiable time, in this case November 1942, the struggle is in balance and could go in favor of either side. But in order to recognize how the scales were balanced then, it is necessary to look back.

Consider how the world looked in November 1941:

Hitler had conquered and looted western and central Europe. His men were at the gates of Moscow. Nazis had occupied and were plundering the Ukraine and much of European Russia. His tanks were running free in North Africa. With Italy he controlled an empire larger than the Roman Empire of old. The Wehrmacht and Luftwaffe, his army and air force, seemed unstoppable. Nazi Uboats were running amok in the Atlantic. German surface raiders, warships and armed freighters, were sailing the seven seas looking for Allied freighters and tankers to sink. As they sank or disrupted freighters, they forced Allied warships and planes to divert resources. Ships and planes had to be used to search for and protect from Germans, not attack them. The British relied on imported food and materials. The Nazis were killing so many freighters that starvation was becoming a real concern for the Englishmen. German influence was growing in Syria and the Mideast. The Nazis enjoyed a friendly reception in Argentina, a foothold in the western hemisphere.

The Axis controlled the Mediterranean Sea, closing the Suez Canal. This meant Britain's chokehold on east-west trade, its very lifeblood, was endangered. Shipping had to be routed around Africa, an expensive and time consuming detour. And that detour increased the freighters' exposure to being torpedoed and sunk by a Uboat. Italy was fighting Britain in North Africa, diverting attention and tying up resources.

Japan was on the march in China. They already occupied Korea and part of Manchuria. Nipponese forces were consolidating their hold on French Indochina. It was apparent to all that Japan was readying for a Pacific War. Just how big and ambitious their plans were no one knew. The US was unprepared for global combat. Even so, it seemed almost certain she would be dragged into the war despite the public's strong opposition. American isolationist sentiment was so strong that even the President couldn't openly advocate helping Britain or Russia.

The USSR and Britain were reeling. They were only able to react, not attack, as they were pummeled by Germany. Their armies and navies repeatedly tried ineffectually to counter punch. The Russians were losing whole armies, surrounded and taken prisoner. "Governments in exile" were strung together by refugee politicians and monarchs from all over Europe. In London and Moscow they helplessly watched their homelands being raped and their people enslaved.

Now let's fast forward and look at the world in November 1943:

Roosevelt, Stalin and Churchill were the leaders of the US, the Soviet Union, and Britain. Already they saw the end of the war, victory of some shape, and they were ready to start shaping that postwar world. They met in summit in Teheran, Iran. Already they were negotiating on future borders, governments, and economies, and the fate of the millions of refugees.

In the year just finished, the Soviet Union's forces had captured and destroyed entire German, Italian, and other Axis Armies. The Red Army had cleared German invaders from much of Russia. But they were not content with throwing out the Nazi invaders. They were on the march west towards Hitler's Reich.

The German surface raiders, the surface ships looking to sink freighters were gone. Most were sunk, the survivors hiding in fjords and harbors. The Uboat menace was not eliminated but it was greatly diminished. The losses they inflicted were manageable. American and allied troops, supplies and food were reaching England and the Mediterranean with very little shrinkage.

Italy was altogether out of the war. The southern part of that country was in use by the Allies as a base to attack Germany. The rest of Italy, an ever shrinking part of it, was under German occupation. The two sides were fighting slowly and desperately up the Italian peninsula. The Wehrmacht was stubbornly contesting every yard of ground. The Allies were pushing with their British Eighth and US Fifth Armies. Both of these were coalition armies made up of troops from 15 or 20 countries from six of the seven continents. Hitler no doubt considered them a mongrel lot, but they were doing the job against the Germans.

Japan's fleet and naval air force were emasculated. The carriers left to its navy had only skeleton air forces manned by green pilots. The land based air forces faced a similar quandary, fewer planes and a dearth of experienced fliers. Its armies were pretty much whole and intact where stationed China. But this was not true elsewhere in the Emperor's new conquests. The army's troops were strewn across hundreds of islands and bases from the Indian Ocean to mid Pacific The owners of the Rising Sun flag had been tossed out of their toehold in Alaska and they struggled to hold on to New Guinea and the Solomon Islands. America was poised to start taking islands in big strides across the Pacific, towards Tokyo. The Nipponese forces were on the defensive on almost every front they chose to take earlier. From China, Burma, India, western New Guinea, the northern Solomon Islands, and the Central Pacific, the Japanese fought on but were no longer on the attack.

Now, take a look at the year in between these two, at November 1942.

As that month started, the Axis advances were at high tide, with conquests and occupied lands as big as they ever got. As the month wore on, the conquerors met the slowly unrolling but inexorable Allied response. For a short time, about three weeks, the War could have taken different directions and ended differently than it did. Each side desperately fought for advantage. To go back to the playground analogy, think of two children on a seesaw. Each is trying to exert enough weight and momentum to bring his or her feet down to touch the ground, leaving the other high in the air, helpless. In the eleventh month of 1942, the seesaw was level. None of the combatants were able yet to bring it down to their benefit. This was true whether looking at various campaigns or theaters, or looking at the global picture. This balance, obvious now, was not apparent at the time.

November 41 to 43, what a difference: from Axis ascendant to Allies on the move. This book will look at the global backdrop with an overview of the various countries' military and domestic situations. It will examine the strategic situation and how it came to be in fall of 1942. Events will be viewed through the prism of November 1942, especially how and why the outcome was in balance during the twenty one days from November 8–29. Lastly it will look at the dramatic results of early 1943 and beyond that resulted from those days.

DRAMATIS PERSONAE

The number before the name is the chapter where the person will first be mentioned.

SENIOR POLITICAL LEADERS:

1 **Churchill, Winston:** British Prime Minister and Minister of War. His moral courage kept Britain in the fight with Germany in 1940 when they stood alone in the world. He led Britain until 1945 when the British people threw him out of office. He died in the 1960s.

1 **Hirohito:** Emperor of Japan. Revered as a deity by Japanese citizens, he had great influence on going to and ending the war. He seems to have had little influence on the prosecution of the war itself. Died in the 1970s.

1 **Hitler, Adolf:** Supreme Leader (Fuhrer) of Nazi Germany. His personal prejudices and hatreds were taken on and given life by the German people. Committed suicide 1945.

1 **Mussolini, Benito:** Supreme Leader (Duce) of Fascist Italy. His "New Roman Empire" lasted less than twenty years. Killed by Italians, 1945.

1 **Roosevelt, Franklin Delano:** President of the United States and Commander in Chief of US Armed Forces. Managed the mobilization of the Country and provided strategic vision and leadership. He died in office in April 1945.

1 **Stalin, Josef:** Head of the Communist Party and defacto tsar of Russia. He was responsible for industrializing the nation in the 1930's. He was also accountable for killing outright or allowing to starve millions of his citizens before the war. With Allied material help and huge Russian Armies he drove the Nazis out of Russia and Eastern Europe. He died in the 1950s.

1 **Tojo, Hideki:** Prime Minister of Japan from the start of the Pacific War until 1944. He tried to commit suicide in 1945 but was saved by the Americans only to be tried and executed in 1948.

OTHER POLITICAL LEADERS:

6 **Darlan, Francois**: Admiral in charge of the French forces in North Africa in 1942. Against the wishes of his political masters, he signed a truce with the Allies in November 1942. He was assassinated shortly thereafter.

6 **Himmler, Heinrich:** German associate of Hitler. He gathered to himself the reins of the SS, the Gestapo, and other elements of tyranny which made him one of the most powerful and feared men in Nazi Germany. Committed suicide in 1945 in Berlin.

9 **Stimson, Henry L:** US Secretary of War. He was the senior civilian officer of the US Army during WWII. Had been Secretary of war and also held other cabinet offices for other Presidents. He worked with Roosevelt and senior military officers to manage the war. Died 1950.

SENIOR MILITARY OFFICERS:

4 **Marshall, George:** Chief of Staff of the US Army. Called by Churchill "The Organizer of Victory." Went on to serve as Secretary of State, Secretary of Defense and envoy to China.

2 **King, Ernest:** Chief of Naval Operations and Commander in Chief, US Fleet. His drive, strategic vision, and energy kept the Pacific War in the minds of the President and American public.

8 **Weygand, Maxime:** Senior General in the French military. As such he ordered the scuttling of the fleet when Germany tried to take it over in 1942.

2 **Yamamoto, Isoroku:** Commander of the Japanese Fleet and architect of Pearl Harbor and other early offensives. Commanded during the Guadalcanal campaign. Died by American plane ambush spring 1943.

THEATER COMMANDERS:

2 **MacArthur, Douglas:** Commanded Southwest Pacific Theater (ComSoWesPac). He personally took the Japanese surrender for the Allies in 1945. Went on to serve as Military Governor of Japan and UN commander during the early part of the Korean War.

1 **Nimitz, Chester:** Commanded Pacific Ocean Fleet and Area. (CincPac) Took the Japanese surrender on behalf of the US in 1945.

4 **Ghormley, Robert L:** First commander South Pacific theater. (ComSoPac). Relieved in October 1942. After that he held responsible but not senior jobs in the Pacific Theater.

1 **Halsey, William:** Named ComSoPac October 1942. Held that job until early 1944. Went on to command the 3rd Fleet which, with the 5th Fleet, swept the Pacific of the Japanese Navy.

GENERALS:

4 **Chuikov, Vassili:** Russian leader of the 62nd Army. He fought the Germans in Stalingrad to a standstill. Buried in Stalingrad.

1 **DeGaulle, Charles:** French general who fled to England as France fell to Germany in 1940. He called freedom loving French to him and rallied Frenchmen worldwide. He headed their government after the war.

9 **Eichelberger, Robert:** American commander at Buna-Gona in New Guinea. He held various training jobs in 1943 and 1944. He went on to command 8th Army in Philippines and Japan.

2 **Eisenhower, Dwight:** He was an aide to General MacArthur in Washington DC and the Philippines in the 1930's. Was named the overall commander of Operation Torch. Went on to command all Allied forces in Europe. First commander of NATO. In 1952 he was elected President.

2 **Groves, Leslie:** American in charge of building the Pentagon building, then given the job of overseeing the Manhattan Project. He had a budget of billions, a staff of thousands in this effort to build the atom bomb before the Germans or Japanese.

6 **Horii, Tomitaro:** Commander of South Seas Detachment, the Japanese Army's attempt to invade New Guinea. He was defeated by Australian militia in Papua. Died as his forces retreated, drowned while trying to ford a flooding river.

7 **Kawaguchi, Kiyotake:** Commander of 14th Imperial Japanese Army on Guadalcanal. He was repeatedly defeated by American forces there.

4 **Kenney, George:** Commander of air forces for MacArthur in SoWesPac.

4 **Kesselring, Albert:** German commander in the Mediterranean. He led the fight in Tunis and later Italy. He was actually a General in the Luftwaffe not the Wehrmacht.

2 **Montgomery, Bernard:** Commander 8th British Army in Egypt, victor at El Alamein. He drove Rommel out of Africa. Went on to be land commander at Overlord and led the British Armies in the conquest of Germany.

10 **Patch, Alexander:** Commanded at Guadalcanal after the Marines evacuated. Went on to lead the Seventh US Army in Europe under Eisenhower.

3 **Patton, George:** Commanded American invasion of Morocco. He went on to lead the Third US Army in Europe under Eisenhower.

4 **Paulus, Friedrich:** Commander 6th German Army in Stalingrad. He surrendered his survivors to the Red Army as a Field Marshal in the Werhmacht, the first German of that rank to surrender. He died as a police commissioner in East Germany in the 1950s.

2 **Rommel, Erwin:** Commanded the Afrika Korps. Later commanded the Nazi's D-Day beach defenses in France. He was implicated in the 1944 plot to assassinate Hitler and was given the opportunity, which he took, to commit suicide rather than face trial.

3 **Vandegrift, Archer:** Marine commander at Guadalcanal. He went on to command the Marine Corps.

ADMIRALS:

7 **Abe, Hiroaki:** Japanese who was to lead a bombardment of Guadalcanal on November 12.

7 **Callaghan, Dan:** American Admiral killed in the first night of the Battle of Guadalcanal. He had been an aide to FDR and had no battle experience. Nevertheless his forces turned back Admiral Abe's.

2 **Doenitz, Karl:** German commander of Uboat forces. Later he was made commander of the Kriegsmarine. After Hitler's Berlin suicide he was named the Fuhrer and sued the Allies for peace in May 1945.

7 **Kinkaid, Thomas:** American who was to lead a task force to Cactus November 30 but did not because he was transferred to Alaska. Later he commanded all naval units for MacArthur in SoWesPac. Brother-in-law to Admiral Husband Kimmel, the man in charge of Pearl Harbor Naval Base on December 7 1941.

7 **Kondo, Nobutake:** Japanese commander on the last night of Battle of Guadalcanal. He held responsible posts after that defeat but gradually faded from active seagoing roles into obscurity.

7 **Lee, Willis:** American commander at the last night of Battle of Guadalcanal. His grasp of radar gave him the victory which secured local sea control for the Allies.

3 **Mikawa, Gunichi:** Japanese commander at the Battle of Savo Island, early August 1942. He inflicted the worst defeat the US Navy ever suffered.

7 **Nishimura, Shogi:** Japanese Admiral who led a cruiser force that bombarded Henderson Field November 13–14.

DRAMATIS PERSONAE | 13

3 **Scott, Norman:** American Admiral killed in the first night of the Battle of Guadalcanal. He had battle experience but was junior to Admiral Callaghan thus ceded command of the force.

7 **Tanaka, Raizo:** Commander of Japanese resupply convoys. His forces repeatedly and successfully delivered thousands of men and tons of supplies. Died 1959.

8 **Wright, Carleton:** American whose forces were defeated at the Battle of Tassafaronga Straight, November 30. This was the last major naval battle of the Guadalcanal campaign.

OTHER MILITARY:

4 **Brookes, Major Al:** Ordnance officer, SoPac and Mediterranean theaters.

3 **Edson, Lieutenant Colonel Merritt "Mike":** Commander of 1st Raider Battalion on Tulagi and Guadalcanal. He was awarded the Congressional Medal of Honor for his leadership at the Battle of Edson's Ridge.

9 **Henderson, Lieutanant Frederick R:** Sonar training officer in the Aleutian Islands.

3 **Ichiki, Colonel Kiyono:** Commander of the 28th Brigade who charged fixed positions on Guadalcanal in August 1942. His Brigade was wiped out and he committed suicide.

6 **Negri, Staff Sergeant Mike:** Gunner on an A-20 airplane, 9th Air Force, Mediterranean Theater

6 **Rawie, Lt Commander Wil:** Navy pilot, flight trainer, and night squadron commander.

3 **Stevenson, Captain William:** Communications officer, 1ˢᵗ Raider Battalion. Awarded the Navy Cross for leadership and actions at Battle of Edson's Ridge. Joined a family newspaper in Pennsylvania after the war.

CIVILIANS:

7 **Bose, Subhas Chandras:** Indian political leader who gave allegiance and aid to the Japanese.

4 **Fields, Charles V:** Helped to develop radar working for Westinghouse Corp in Pittsburgh.

7 **Gandhi, Mohandas:** Indian political leader and independence activist.

9 **Harrison, John:** Civilian armaments worker, General Motors in Grand Rapids Michigan.

9 **Moore, Charles:** Civilian war products worker, Gates Rubber Company, Denver.

SETTING THE STAGE
Before and During November 1942

In the several weeks prior to November 8 there were battles and armies were positioning themselves for future battles.

In northeast Africa: The Battle of El Alamein started October 23 in Egypt. The Army there was British but had formations of troops from many nations attached. After lengthy preparations, it defeated the German Afrika Korps. That army started its retreat west towards Libya in early November.

In northwest Africa the US had put out diplomatic feelers to encourage French forces there to remain neutral or to come over to the Allied side should they invade.

In Russia: Hitler at the last minute took troops from his army invading Stalingrad. He sent those troops to the Caucasus. He insisted he must have petroleum from the Caucasus oilfields to sustain the war. This diversion had the effect of substantially weakening the Stalingrad force but reinforcing the Caucasus force too late in the year for it to accomplish its goals. In northern Russia the Germans held what they had. In the south, despite Herr Hitler's shuttling around of troops, both German forces were able to continue their advances deep into Russia.

In New Guinea: The Japanese Army's land attack via the Kokoda Track across the island was blunted. It would be turned back by Australian counterattack and pursued in retreat. Two US infantry divisions were marshaled to be sent to the island.

In Guadalcanal: Imperial and Allied forces had been fighting since August for control of an airfield on the island. The Japanese had given the Allied Navies several harsh defeats, at Savo Island, Battle of Cape Esperance, Battle of Santa Cruz Islands, and others. Plus they were able to bombard the field at night, at will. They had delivered more than a few punishing bombardments. On land, the Marines had repulsed repeated attempts to dislodge them, at Edson's Ridge, the Battle for Henderson Field, and numerous smaller engagements.

At sea, German Uboats continued to stalk and sink Allied freighters and troop transport ships. Every month they were sinking almost as much tonnage as can be built in a month.

MAPS

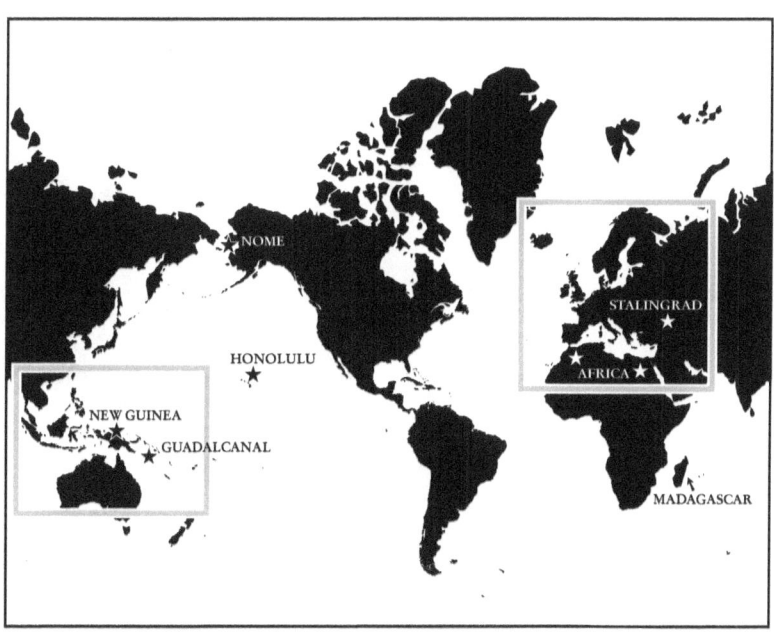

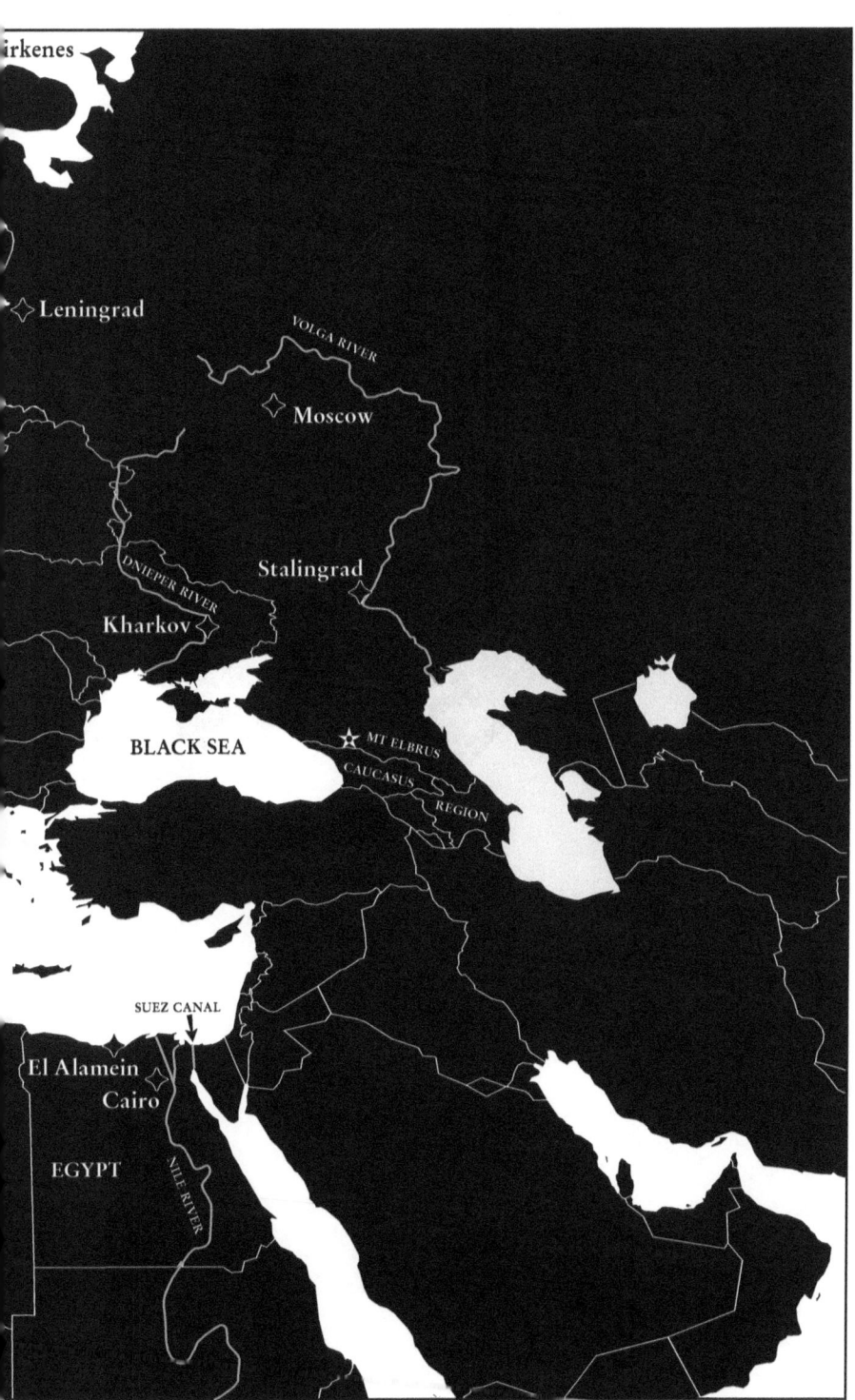

CHAPTER I

November 8

Operation Torch; The World in the 1930's–1941

By late autumn 1942 much of the world had been at war for years. World War II it was called, because countries all over the world were involved. The US and Imperial Japan were the late comers to this conflict. Even so, they had formally been at war for almost a year. Nations are always in search of power, security, resources, and riches. Sometimes that search boils up from negotiations and alliances into war, talk into action. The upshot is men killing or trying to kill other men. In modern times it also brings in civilians. Adults and children just trying to live their lives find themselves dying or running from the front. Immense amounts of property and knowledge are destroyed.

The morning of November 8 1942 is the latest chapter in this war. Off the Atlantic coast of Morocco in Northwest Africa a vast fleet bombarded and then sent troops ashore. Carrier planes swooped and dove, protecting the invading fleet. On land, pilots took to their planes to protect their homelands. Riflemen advanced, stopped, sought shelter, took and held objectives. The same was happening in the Mediterranean Sea, inside the Straits of Gibraltar. There ships and planes delivered their opening bombardments, raining death and destruction. They cleared the way for troops to land in Algeria. These invading armies were sons of America and Great Britain come to dislodge Germans under the Nazi flag.

This was a war between and among the US, Britain, Russia, Japan and Germany. So the question is, why were they fighting in Africa? It wasn't next to any of these belligerent nations nor was it central to their survival. The continent was not an industrial powerhouse. The northern part, the part being fought over, was not a place of easily recovered natural resources. It was not known for its skilled and learned workers. How did this land become a stage for the opening act of the fulcrum month of the biggest, costliest, most far reaching of wars?

To answer this question, consider the backdrop. Politically, World War Two, or WWII, was an angular affair: There were five major players: Imperial Japan, The Third Reich of Nazi Germany, The Union of Soviet Socialist Republics, The United Kingdom, and the United States. Call it a war pentagon. It was a fractured pentagon in that Japan was at war with the US and UK; Germany was at war with the US, UK, and USSR, but Japan and the USSR were not at war. (They had fought a brief battle at Nomonhan in far eastern Russia in 1939. It was a dispute over the Manchurian-Soviet border. The Japanese got their noses bloodied there, which may have influenced later decisions about whether to invade Russia or Southeast Asia.) The Soviet Union did, however, declare war on Japan in August 1945, honoring a promise to come in against them ninety days after Nazi Germany went down. For most of the war the two countries were not at war.

On the one hand, there were the Allies, formally the Grand Alliance, three nation-empires, the USSR, the UK, and the US. Their primary common interest was the defeat of Germany. Looking past the rhetoric to long term goals, the Soviet Union wanted to help the spread of communism, to advance their concept of the "workers' state" and steer trade and commercial benefits towards Moscow. The United Kingdom wanted to remain master and owner of India, Australia, Canada, Malaya, and numerous islands. Keeping them meant commercial and economic advantages and riches flowing to London. The United States wanted to foster the spread of democracy and the end of empires, with business and political power moving to Washington. So the Allies' first goal was to defeat Germany. Their secondary goal was to maintain and spread their own particular political-economic models. The three main nations brought along allies such as Brazil, Canada, Australia and China. These smaller countries contributed to the war effort but had little say in the overall direction of it.

On the other hand, there were the Axis. This was an assortment of aggressive nations which came close to conquering the world. Originally just Germany and Italy, the self defined group was later expanded to include Imperial Japan. Although Fascist Italy predated Nazi Germany, in reality Germany overshadowed Italy early on. Italy ended up German a vassal state much as Vichy France or Poland. It joined in the war only after Germany had conquered most of Europe in June 1940. Measured by the capability and willingness to make war, the Axis were really just Germany and Imperial Japan. Germany brought along allies such as Hungary and Romania. They attracted volunteers from many nations, from Britain to Turkestan, Arabia to Russia. These volunteers often had their own military units even if they did not represent formal alliances with other nations. Japan created and nurtured a stable of allied puppet states as well. Tokyo installed governments in Burma, Malaya, the Philippines, Manchuria, and other conquered states. But they were essentially for political show. None of the countries conquered by Japan sent troops to fight alongside the Sons of Nippon.

The 1930's were difficult everywhere. The economies of nations struggled. International trade dropped steeply and unemployment was high everywhere. Governments did what they could to encourage jobs and trade. Each took a variety of steps to help themselves. Some built up internally. The Soviet Union and the US both worked on domestic utilities, dams, roads, electrification, factories, and other infrastructure needs. The UK worked to stimulate trade within its empire. Germany built infrastructure and rebuilt its army, navy, and air force. Japan expanded its economy by taking parts of China, colonizing and industrializing them.

In the mid 1930s Japan was at war on the Asian mainland. They considered themselves the cultural and technological equal of any western power. Indeed they had come a long way from being an agrarian feudal state in the 1860s. In terms of industry, economy, and learning they were not a major power, but they were of respectable size and stature. However some time during the 1920s or 1930s their parliamentary government came to be controlled by the military. The heads of the Army and Navy sat in Cabinet of the Parliamentary government. In that form of democracy, if a Cabinet member resigned, it could cause a government to fall. The military heads could cause a government to be dissolved by resigning or threatening to do so if they didn't get their way. More than one government fell by this type of manipulation. In addition, senior civilian ministers who did not toe the military's line were assassinated by soldiers from time to time. The Army sent troops to China in the early thirties. They carved a puppet country out of Manchuria and called it Manchukuo, installing a puppet government answerable to the War Ministry. This quasi colony provided raw materials and jobs to Japanese. It also had a virtually inexhaustible supply of cheap labor, the Manchurian people.

The Japanese Army, or more precisely its senior officers and Cabinet ministers, decided to expand Imperial holdings in China. This decision was taken by the military without civilian input. In 1937, junior officers created a provocation, an excuse to invade more of the country. Called by some the Marco Polo Bridge Incident, a few shots were fired at Japanese Troops in Peking. Where the shots originated is disputed and it isn't certain if they were from Chinese or Japanese guns. In any case, the Army used the incident as a pretext for invasion. The Army and Navy invaded China proper without permission or even consultation with the government in Tokyo. In the coming years they would inflict millions of casualties and untold cruelty and barbarity on the Chinese people.

Their reasons were to gain natural resources and to project and grow power. They saw western countries with special treaties and communities in China. Those treaties had been imposed on China to enable exploitation of Chinese resources and population. Britain had been enjoying preferential treatment since they forced the Chinese to give it in the 1840's. Britain fought at least two

"Opium Wars" to force the weak Chinese government to open the country to British interests. The Nipponese saw no reason they should not do the same. Military leaders in Army and the War Ministry came to the decision that they must take land and resources for the Emperor. As time passed the Japanese Army and Navy became increasingly aggressive and savage in their conquest of China. The Japanese perception of being shut out of economic development by western interests fueled the effort.

Germany, like the rest of the industrialized world, had suffered through the Depression. It also suffered under the strictures and reparations imposed by the Versailles Treaty after World War I. In retrospect that treaty was harsh and vengeful. It required huge reparation payments from Germany for starting the war in 1914. Its demands were unworkable, indeed counterproductive. The postwar government of Germany, the Weimar Republic, struggled and failed to work with its requirements. There was tremendous unrest, fighting in the streets, and hyperinflation. Prices were at one point increasing so fast that people demanded to be paid several times a day so they could buy necessities before the price got too high. The Nazi party—the National Socialist Workers Party—started in 1918 and was inconsequential until a man named Adolf Hitler took it over. He made it his own personal vehicle of power and ultimately steered it to run the nation and pull the world into cataclysmic war.

The Nazis came to power peacefully. They ran a slate of candidates for the Reichstag, the German parliament. It took several elections but in 1933 they finally got enough members elected to form a government. They had run for office in opposition to the Treaty. When they came to power one of the first things done was to repudiate it. The Nazis seized total power, negating parliament, the judiciary, and any political opposition.

Hitler first intended to restore Germany's place as a Great Power. Secondly, he intended to take "lebensraum" or living space for Germans. His stated intention was to take it from countries to the east. He was explicit about his plans for Russia and for anyone but pure Germans in his book, Mein Kampf. He wrote this while in jail for trying to overthrow the government of Bavaria in 1923. As he said, along the way he also planned to "cleanse" the population to rid it of non Aryan and "weak" peoples. Starting about 1935, he retook provinces stripped by Versailles and given to France. Then he annexed Austria. That is, he invaded it and made it part of Germany. He helped a friend to power in Spain by sending "advisors" to help in the Spanish civil war. And in 1938 he took what he wanted of Czechoslovakia, the part with sophisticated arms factories and big forts he didn't want to have to invade. He got this by "negotiating" with the leaders of France and Britain. Czechs were not allowed even to sit in. Their country was carved up before their eyes. All of this territory Herr Hitler acquired with bluff and skillful political manipulation backed by growing military strength. No country made a real effort to stop him at any point until 1939. He took advantage of the willful blindness of the leaders of the western democracies. They dealt with him as if he were an honorable man, but he considered them weak fools and dealt with them as he was, a liar and a thief.

Italy had been busy as well. Benito Mussolini came to power in 1922 as a "Fascist." He too created a political party and took control of a nation. He wanted to create a "New Roman Empire" and in 1935 invaded Ethiopia. He used airplanes and poison gas against a country of nomads and herders. Again, no country in the international community stopped him from this aggression. Italy already had a colony in Libya in North Africa.

By 1939 it was clear that Japan was on the march in Asia and Hitler had aggressive intentions in Europe. Even so the western democracies were slow to react. France and Britain were reluctant to spend the money and political capital needed to rearm. They remembered the slaughter of a whole generation of young men in the trenches from 1914–1918, and wanted to avoid a repeat. Rather than put up a firm front, they had spent the 1930's trying to ignore Hitler's actions and threats. And they figured Japan was far away and not an advanced country so they had little to fear.

Hitler had taken and digested Austria and Czechoslovakia, and had Poland in his sights. He was building a fraudulent case that Poland was hostile and was mistreating ethnic Germans. His intent was to take and dismember it. Britain and France were waking from their sleep and finally guaranteed Poland's borders. That is, they made a treaty to come to Poland's aid, to fight for it, if it was invaded. Hitler was taken aback by this show of resolve. He doubted they would honor the agreement but didn't want to take the chance that they wouldn't

In 1939 Hitler made a non-aggression pact with Russia, Stalin's Soviet Union. He was about to try to bully his way to take part of Poland. He didn't expect a war with anyone. After all, he had gotten all he wanted so far by bluff, lies, and threats. Just to be sure, he wanted lock Russia up so it would not side with Britain and France if they did in fact step in to protect Poland. So he made a treaty with Stalin to do that. This treaty was a surprise to Britain and France who had their own teams in the Moscow trying to make their own treaty. They wanted Russia to come in with them in the event of war but were too slow in getting serious talks started. The German-Soviet treaty had a secret section which agreed Germany and Russia would each take and occupy a part of Poland after Germany attacked. They cynically distrusted each other and wanted a buffer zone to help protect them from attack. Less than ten days after the German and Soviet governments got the treaty done, the Wehrmacht invaded Poland. The west, Britain and France, had supinely and shamefully let Nazi Germany grow and take countries through much of the 1930's. At long last, the September 1939 invasion of Poland was one lie too many. France and Britain honored their commitment and declared war on Germany.

Hitler hated Stalin and communism. He viewed Russians as subhuman and communism as a vile creation of "International Jewry." Apparently that was his equivalent of black helicopters, the universal "they" who have your persecution and destruction at heart. He thought the Soviet Union was fit only to be wiped off the earth. By the same token, Stalin feared and loathed Hitler and the Nazis. The Nazi-Soviet non aggression pact was not a goodwill, let's be neighborly type of agreement. Rather, it was a cynical accommodation made by both sides for short term advantage.

The Soviet Union at the time was in the grip, literally, of Josef Stalin. He was an active Communist and enjoyed some small amount of political power when Lenin died in 1924. He consolidated and built that power and by the mid 1930's ruled Russia himself. One did not contradict Comrade Stalin. If one did, one would likely get a "Russian Nickel," a bullet in the back of the head. He stated his philosophy as "One death is a tragedy. A million deaths is a statistic." This man had ordered the elimination of his citizens by the million, whether by murder, exile, or forced starvation. And he had purged his military by show trials and executions. He got rid of most anyone who looked to be any sort of a threat, or who voiced their opinion, or who did not agree with him quickly enough. That said, there were jobs for the people. The country was industrializing quickly, with a population being educated and dams, power plants, factories, and steel mills being built up. The economic life of the country was improving, and the standard of living getting better. But what western democracies knew as personal freedoms were not improving for Russians. If anything they really did not exist.

In addition to Germany, Japan, and Russia, the two remaining sides of the war pentagon were the US and Britain. Neither had much stomach for war after the 1914–18 bloodletting. In that war the US lost hundreds of thousands of men, the British millions. Memories of men running towards machine gun fire made their leaders reluctant to contemplate yet another war. The US relied on wide oceans and a strong Navy to buffer it from European or Asian aggressors. American public opinion was strongly against getting involved in foreign affairs and especially foreign wars. Isolationists, "America First" adherents, were a potent and widely supported political force. Not until war broke out in Europe did America even think about starting to rearm. Both the army and the navy had been allowed to shrink to pathetic size. The US Army was the seventeenth largest in the world in 1939.

Nor were the United Kingdom's populace and government ready to face the prospect of war in the mid 30's. They were busy rebuilding their economy and tending to their Empire. The Nazis and Hitler were specific in saying what they intended to do. Most of it was so outlandish and terrible that most Englishmen and women simply did not believe them. British leaders were trying to work with the economy, encourage jobs, and improve living standards. Britain and France were the major European powers. Neither government took steps to rebuild their own military strength even in the face of a specifically bellicose Germany. Some steps were being taken, little and late, when war came on September 1 1939.

Poland struggled valiantly against Germany. It was a sad mismatch—the sight of horse cavalry charging Panzer tanks was symbolic of this "fight." And in mid September, as agreed, Russia took the eastern part of the country. Britain and France took half steps against Germany but did not invade nor bomb. They did send troops to man the French borders. Along those borders the French had built stout forts called "The Maginot Line" after the politician whose idea they were. They were strong but easily avoided by a motorized invader. Germany was content to let British and French soldiers loiter on the border while Poland was finished off. This period was called by many "The Phony War."

The US and the UK shared language, culture, and legal heritage. After Hitler took Poland he gathered his forces. In May 1940, he turned on the west and took France, Holland, Belgium and Scandinavia. He did not finish off Britain. On May 10, the British changed Prime Ministers, tossing out Neville Chamberlain who had sold Czechoslovakia out. Winston Churchill took over and promised that Britain would struggle on. England was alone. France was going and soon (by June) gone, Russia neutral by treaty, the US behind the seas.

Many around the world thought England was done for. There were two notable Americans who thought so. Joseph Kennedy was FDR's Ambassador to London and was very pessimistic about their chances. His family including sons, Joe Jr, John, Robert and Teddy went to school there. Kennedy was soon replaced as ambassador. The other pessimist was Charles Lindbergh. He had fame and aviation expertise and was shown around by Nazi insiders at the Luftwaffe. He was impressed and said so. Later he admitted he had been hoodwinked. Too late—FDR never forgave him and made sure he couldn't get in the military when war came. He did some civilian aeronautical "consulting." There were rumors of Lindbergh flying combat and shooting down Japanese planes, but he never did wear a uniform.

Most members of the Roosevelt Administration believed the British would hold and eventually win out. So the Administration and allies in Congress did what they could to help, and made plans. Even though US law prevented direct aid to any nation fighting, ways were found to circumvent these limits. President Franklin D Roosevelt was clear eyed and saw Nazi Germany as the real threat to his country.

Elements of the British and American governments, at subsidiary levels, had been meeting for several years in the expectation of having to fight another war. President Franklin Delano Roosevelt and Prime Minister Winston Churchill met at Argentia, Newfoundland in August 1940. This was the men's first meeting since World War I, when FDR had been Assistant Secretary of the US Navy and Churchill a Cabinet Member. At Argentia Roosevelt remembered that encounter; Churchill did not.

This secret meeting was held in a bay on the remote coast of Newfoundland in Canada. Roosevelt was supposedly on a "fishing trip" and out of reach of reporters. Churchill was operating under wartime secrecy. The meeting let the two leaders become acquainted (or re-acquainted). Later summit meetings along with ongoing staff contacts also yielded strategic decisions. The major decision, a basis for the entire war, was "Germany First." With greater industrial and war making capacity and its location in Europe, Germany was felt to be a real threat to the Allies. Japan was aggressive but was felt to be a lesser threat to the democracies. It was agreed that most of the two nations' resources would first go to defeat Germany. Japan would be fought with holding actions until it could be faced alone. The war didn't work exactly to this plan, but close. Also at Argentia, a joint council of each country's senior military leaders and ongoing staff conversations were agreed to.

Japan was on the move. It took another step to secure its future as self appointed leader in Asia. The Emperor sent troops in to French Indochina in July 1940. At that point, France was newly under Hitler's heel and could not stop the Nipponese. From there, the Emperor's forces looked hungrily south at resource rich Malaya and Netherlands East Indies. They had been moving troops inland in China, killing civilians and looting as they went. The US was uneasy with Japanese advances in China and Southeast Asia. The Roosevelt Administration took increasingly harsh steps to stop those advances. Finally the President signed an embargo on petroleum and scrap iron exports to Japan. This was viewed in Tokyo as an intolerable insult and the first step of economic strangulation. In fact at that time Tokyo had only about one year's supply of petroleum products on hand.

The US public was strongly against getting involved in any foreign war. People thought Germany's aggressiveness was strictly a European dispute. After all, the US had sent troops to fight in World War I, the "war to end all wars," the "war to make the world safe for democracy." Twenty years later, the same European countries were at it again. Many Americans simply did not want to see their sons, brothers, fathers, and husbands going over there.

President Franklin Roosevelt was acutely aware of the strong isolationist views. Ever the realistic politician, he made sure his reelection campaign promised no foreign wars. But he also saw that if Hitler knocked off his European enemies one by one, the US might later have to fight him alone. If the Nazis had the industrial, military and naval resources of all Europe, they would be a formidable foe. FDR maneuvered to help the European democracies as much as American laws and Congress would let him. Many members of Congress also saw the need to help the countries already fighting. Plus they wanted to buy time so the US could bolster its own defenses. Neutrality laws required that any belligerent country pay cash up front for any munitions, armaments, or other war supplies. Any country involved in a war the US wasn't part of was considered a "belligerent." No US entity, bank, corporation or government, was allowed to advance credit for such purchases. By late 1940, Britain was simply running out of money to buy arms.

Roosevelt took many steps. He had military officials consult with some of the belligerent (i.e., those at war with Germany) democracies. There was substantial planning for common action with Britain and others, although those efforts were downplayed. He negotiated a deal with Britain, giving them fifty surplus World War I era destroyers for them to use as convoy escorts. In return they gave the US ninety nine year leases on a number of military bases throughout the Caribbean basin. He lobbied Members of Congress and Senators and worked with Congressional leaders to enact legislation to reinstate the draft. The Selective Service Act easily passed the Senate but passed the House by just one vote in 1940. The Army and Navy immediately started to expand. One idea of someone in the administration had far reaching, positive results. It was the program for "lend-lease."

FDR explained the lend-lease program thus: "If your neighbor's house is burning, you don't sell him your garden hose, you lend it to him so he can put the fire out. You don't worry about getting paid, you worry about ending the emergency." The idea, nobly packaged, was to be able to help friends to fight Hitler even if they could not pay for the goods. And a major benefit was to put Americans to work building those materials and goods. On March 19, 1941, Congress enacted the Lend-Lease Act. Initial funding was for $7,000,000,000. In twenty first century terms, that is easily trillions of dollars. And the program was extended and re-funded a number of times.

Under the program, the US could (and did) "lend" trucks, locomotives, arms, ships, planes, and many other kinds of equipment. The first benefactors were Britain and its Commonwealth allies. Before long the Soviet Union was receiving materiel as well. By war's end, France, Brazil, Mexico, China, and many others did too. It started as a means to provide arms to beleaguered friendly countries. It was always that, but it also evolved to be a tool of power for Washington. In 1944 General DeGaulle was giving the US Army problems because in France he wanted to exercise power his way. He didn't care that "his way" obstructed the US Army's moving men and arms towards Germany. At one point the Frenchman was being particularly stubborn about some specific point. FDR told the Lend-Lease administrator to cut him off. After a few days, DeGaulle got the message, fell into line, and his deliveries were resumed.

Lend-Lease goods were moved from America to all points of the globe. Of course there were ship convoys delivering to Great Britain. There were also delivery convoys to Murmansk in the Soviet Union. These generally ran via Iceland or Britain. Germany had planes, ships and Uboats stationed in northern Norway. The Murmansk convoys ran near there, between land and pack ice not too far north. The cargo ships were easy pickings for the Nazis during long summer days. At one point summer convoys were put on hold for a short time. This was in response to the virtual decimation of one Murmansk bound convoy, designated Convoy PQ17. Shipments were soon restarted. The convoys did better in winter when long nights sheltered them to a large degree.

In 1941, Britain and the Red Army occupied Iran, taking the south and north halves respectively. The government there had been friendly to the Axis. Neither the UK nor the USSR wanted that kind of thinking near their areas of influence so they moved in. During most of the war, Iranian ports were used as a funnel for Lend-Lease goods. Supplies came via cargo ship from the US and were unloaded and assembled. From there the planes were flown into the USSR. The trucks, locomotives, arms, etc were driven or put on trains and sent north. This arrangement worked well. Uboats rarely molested the ships and much materiel was delivered.

November 20, 1942 saw the dedication of the Alaskan Highway. This road was hastily built from southwest Canada to Fairbanks Alaska. Initially it was to provide access should the Japanese somehow cut the sea lanes. That threat had disappeared in June with the American victory at Midway. But the Highway served another purpose. It became part of the AlSib (Alaska-Siberia) route for Lend-Lease goods. Goods were trucked up the highway to be sent on to Russia. Planes were flown by Americans from the lower 48 to Alaska staging at bases along the Highway. They were picked up by Russians and flown through Siberia to the front with Germany. Ships were transferred to Russian crews in Alaska as well. A tremendous amount of war materiel transited via the AlSib.

What happened after the war to the goods "lent" under this Act? Many items of course were destroyed in the fighting. The US generally forgave the loan on the items which survived. The benefactors kept all the trucks, guns, planes and ships.

By 1941, the war spread. In more modern terms, it went viral.

In the spring, Hitler's Wehrmacht invaded Yugoslavia and other countries in southeast Europe. It took the Nazis about two months to defeat and occupy the Balkans. They never did pacify the area. For the entire war they faced persistent and ferocious guerilla opposition.

Then in June, on the 22nd, he invaded Russia. This brought Russia into alliance, or at least common cause, with Britain. Churchill, a long time anti communist, took the lead. He was criticized in London for working with Stalin and his henchmen. In response, he said "If Hitler invaded hell I would make at least a favorable reference to the devil in the House of Commons."

Early December, Japan went on the offensive. There had been an internal debate. The Imperial Army advocated invading Russia for its resources and to help Hitler. The Navy wanted to take the Netherlands East Indies for resources. The Navy's southern approach won out. It is interesting to speculate how much the defeat at Nomonhan in 1939 drew the Imperial gaze south, away from the Russians who had defeated them. In any case, On December 8 Tokyo time, the Japanese unleashed their numerous offensives. The attacks on the US were timed to go in just after war was formally declared. The timing went off the track and although relations were tense, no state of war existed when Japanese bullets and bombs started hitting Americans.

Americans remember Pearl Harbor, the surprise attack and sinking of US Navy ships at peaceful anchor in Hawaii. But on that day, the Imperial Army and Navy also attacked: Guam Island, Wake Island, the Philippine Islands, the Allied garrisons in the Chinese city of Shanghai, and British Malaya. Within days they had also attacked Hong Kong, sunk a British naval task force sent specifically to overawe them, destroyed American air power in the Philippines, and were on the move throughout Southeast Asia and the Pacific. The speed, skill, and effectiveness of these attacks stunned the world.

Early 1942 held scant good news for the Allies. Germany was looting occupied Europe and was having its way in Russia and North Africa. Japan had conquered or held sway over an immense area. Stretching over one eighth of the globe, it ran from Alaska and Manchuria to Burma and the Indian Ocean, from below the equator to the borders of Russia. Most of these areas were taken on the pretext of needing the natural resources they held. Japan worked feverishly to exploit their newly gotten resources. These included minerals and agriculture, and the personal wealth of the conquered peoples. And the Emperor's men had conquered all of this with shocking ease.

There were a few glimmers of hope for the Allies in the first half of 1942, especially in the Pacific. In February Admiral Halsey led a force to bomb and shell Japanese installations in the Gilbert and Marshall Islands. The expedition did little damage but the effect on US homefront and fleet morale was positive.

In April Halsey again led a carrier force, this time towards Tokyo. One of the carriers carried B25 bombers, land planes of the Army Air Corps. The pilots had been trained in ultra short take off techniques. They bombed the home islands and flew on to land in China. Again, no heavy damage was done but they humiliated and shamed the Japanese military leadership. They were mortified that the enemy could approach and hit the Emperor's homeland. One result of this raid was the navy's scheme to destroy the US fleet, or what was left after Pearl Harbor. The Japanese admirals made a plan. The intent was to invade Midway Island, 1100 miles northwest of Honolulu. They figured that when the Japanese actually invaded the island the US fleet would come out to fight. Then, they assumed, the Imperial Fleet could finish the US Navy off. The operation was scheduled for early June 1942.

There were problems for the Japanese. Unbeknownst to the admirals, the Americans had cracked the naval cipher and were reading some of the Emperor's mail. The Americans were able to piece together the Nipponese Midway plan, and they decided to lay their own trap. Admiral Nimitz, commander of the Pacific Fleet (CincPac) sent his carriers to wait. He positioned them on the flank of where he anticipated the Japanese carriers would attack Midway. Through exquisite, unintended timing, the Japanese fighters protecting their carriers were down low on the water shooting up American torpedo planes, just as Yankee dive bombers flew in. Those dive bomber pilots were unhampered by the fighters and were able to put bombs on the decks of the Japanese. The Americans were able to sink all four (Hiryu, Soryu, Kaga, Akagi) of the main Imperial carriers that day. The trade off was one American carrier sunk, the USS Yorktown. The Japanese lost much that day: four capital ships, hundreds of pilots and air crewmen, and the strategic initiative in the Pacific. The Americans were not yet strong enough to take the offensive but they had forced the Japanese to give it up.

CHAPTER II
November 8
Logistics; The War, 1941–1942

FDR was ever the canny politician. He had a knack for seeing the political advantages and drawbacks of any decision, before it was made. So it is no surprise that he saw it was important that US troops be joining the fight soon. America had taken many shots and defeats in 1942 and needed some good news. Also he was looking at the Congressional elections scheduled for November 3. He wanted to keep a Democratic majority in the House and Senate. It was essential for public morale and favorable election results to have US troops in action by November. So early in the year of 1942, plans were made to invade Northwest Africa in early November. The target date was originally to be before the elections. Events elsewhere put Americans in the fight. It was politically feasible and militarily advisable to put the North African operation back a few days. The reasons for mounting Operation Torch, the invasion of North Africa, were military in origin. There were also very strong political considerations.

But back to the original question, why Africa? Why not mainland Europe, France or Germany? There were a number of reasons. France, while close to England, is also close to Germany, and Germany would contest any invasion. And that attack would have to be across water onto a beach bristling with Germans firing guns.

British Prime Minister Churchill had personal experience with the problems of invading a hostile shore. At the time, 1915, he was First Lord of the Admiralty, the civilian head of the Royal Navy. As such he was largely responsible for the invasion of Turkey at Gallipoli, near the Dardanelle Straits. The intent was to knock Turkey out of the war. Also, it would open southeast Europe for the Allies to attack Germany in the rear. Hopefully the struggle in the theater would become a war of maneuver, not trenches like in France.

That whole invasion was a poorly or mis-managed fiasco. No one had tried making an amphibious invasion with modern arms, and much was learned in the process. The waiting Turks imposed a bloody repulse, and it cost many Commonwealth and British troops their lives. To this day, Australia and New Zealand observe Anzac Day in remembrance of the Aussies and Kiwis lost there. Anzac comes from the Australian New Zealand Army Corps, Anzac. They made up a large part of the invading force and the casualty lists. Winston Churchill lost his Cabinet Post over the matter. He ended up commanding an infantry battalion in the trenches of northern France for a while.

So, later, in 1942, as Prime Minister he was adamant. He was reluctant to consider any invasion of Europe. He certainly would not agree to one unless overwhelming force could be brought to bear. In 1942 the Allies simply could not do that in or near France.

Using Canadian infantry, the British staged a "raid" on Dieppe in August 1942 as a test of invasion techniques. It was a costly disaster, with over fifty percent of the troops killed or captured. The lessons learned were applied to subsequent amphibious invasions. Churchill thought of and mentioned the fate of those Canadians often. Especially he would think of them whenever the Americans got enthusiastic about invading France in 1942 or 1943.

But Northwest Africa was a different story. There, the Germans were in the background. The French were in control. Nominally German allies, in truth they abhorred the Nazis. Individual French citizens felt a certain allegiance to their government. That allegiance could be honored with a swipe or two at their attackers. Then they would feel free to seek vengeance for their 1940 defeat at Nazi hands. In terms of determined and skilled opposition to the Allied landings, the nearest armed Germans were at the other end of the Mediterranean. There were good reasons for launching a campaign in Morocco and Algeria.

An effort there could also yield other political and military benefits. It would relieve pressure on British forces near Cairo. Axis armies had approached Egypt and the Suez Canal several times in the previous two years. Each time they had been driven back. In late 1942, the Axis had control of most of the North African coast and were again pounding on Cairo's door. The British needed to knock General Rommel's Afrika Korps and Italian allies back for good. They needed to take the war to the Germans, not fight on their own doorstep.

It would help to clear the Mediterranean Sea, opening it to Allied and friendly shipping. If ships could go through the Med, not around Africa, they would transit quicker and use less fuel. It would free up some ships for use elsewhere. The demands on shipping were immense. Troops all over the globe needed to be supplied and fed. Anything that freed up shipping was an advantage. By the same token closing the Med to the Axis would put strains on their shipping and logistical needs.

It could well knock Vichy France out of the war. The French government at the town of Vichy was allowed to exist by the Germans. Its job was to oversee the parts of France Germany did not occupy outright. French General DeGaulle had established the Free French in direct opposition to Vichy. He started when he escaped France to Britain in June 1940. There were many Frenchmen who did not recognize his authority, but grudgingly saluted Vichy. It was hoped a strong Allied showing would cause the French to unite and come in as allies.

It would blood, that is give combat experience to, green American troops. Torch was being planned in the spring and summer of 1942. At that time, nowhere were American troops in combat (except in retreat from the Japanese). The new big American army being raised would have no battle experience. Only a few senior NCOs and officers remembered World War I. Most of the men were drafted citizens whose only experience hearing gunfire was while hunting or at a shooting range. Senior military leaders thought starting the Army out fighting French and colonial troops was advisable. It would be a gentler introduction to the gruesome job of war than they would get from the Wehrmacht. The troops had to gain combat experience and this campaign would give it to them.

It would show the American public and the other Allies that America would pull its weight. It had been almost a year since Pearl Harbor and no Americans were fighting in the European area. American public opinion and support was vital to the war effort. Putting troops in the field would stoke public opinion.

It would show the Russians that the Americans and British were willing to take the fight to the Axis. Up to that point no American and few British had actually fought Germans on the ground. The Russians had been fighting them every day for over a year. Stalin was calling for a second front to relieve pressure on Red Army troops. It was important during negotiations during summit meetings to be able to point to battlefield efforts. The Allies' efforts against Germany, while substantial, had not been comparable to the bloodletting and destruction the Russians had experienced.

Political calculations underpin all the decisions, actions, and strategies taken by all sides. Witness how Roosevelt worked this aspect. He recognized the strong isolationist sentiment in US public opinion in 1940 and the need to get US troops into action before the 1942 Congressional election. Each nation, each leader had their national interests at heart. The perceived advancement of those interests drove Hitler to throw his weight and armies around. It was what caused the Japanese Army to invade Manchuria and China. It was what caused Britain not to rearm during the 1930's, and to stand by while Hitler did. It was what caused Stalin to decimate his officer corps in the 1936–37 purges. Political calculations and miscalculation had landed the world in another war. But this is not about how the world got there, but what happened after it did.

Once a nation has gone past the talking stage and into active war in pursuit of national interests, a new set of limits and tasks come into play. One obvious one is size of the army and navy, another public support for government actions. An element of warmaking that is critical but under-appreciated is logistics. That is the unglamorous business of getting troops, planes, and ships where they can do their job. Also, and this is absolutely essential, it is keeping them fed, armed, supplied, fueled, and reinforced, wherever they are. Modern armies and navies have six, eight, or ten people working to support and supply every one fighter at the front. When it comes to war, the adage is that the amateur talks tactics, the serious student talks strategy, but the professional talks logistics.

If you look closely at the various campaigns and battles, they all turned on this mundane, under played aspect. Whoever got their troops on site and then was able to follow up with "beans and bullets" prevailed. Some examples:

- The German Uboat campaign was designed to stop the flow of goods to Britain. Admiral Doenitz figured if he could stop the British from eating they could not mount a war against Germany. His submarine campaign saw the German Uboats do real damage to the merchant marine fleet. It helped to cause food rationing in Britain. Even so, it never came close to starving Britain and the British of food and goods.

- The American submarine force did play a huge part in isolating Japan. American subs sunk enough ships that Japan could not effectively exploit its conquests. Near war's end Japan couldn't supply the home islands with adequate food. Fuel was virtually not available. In 1945 Tokyo, the only taxis on the streets ran by charcoal, not gasoline. Many of Japan's island outposts were cut off and forced to grow their own food just to survive.

- D-Day in Europe was not staged until the Allies had adequate forces and supplies stockpiled in England. They made sure they had enough troops to send a stream of men and arms to follow up the invasion. And they made sure they had enough shipping and trucking to move and sustain them in France and beyond. Many of the early objectives in the Overlord plan were port cities in the area. Brest, Havre, Caen, and other harbor towns were to be taken and put to use as soon as possible. Moving supplies through a port with harbor, dock and crane facilities was much more efficient than bringing things in over a beach.

- Japanese Admiral Tanaka made a name for himself with his successful "Tokyo Express" destroyer runs to take troops and supplies to Guadalcanal. He loyally and ably delivered men and supplies. The Japanese logistical plan for Guadalcanal seems to have been "take it from the Americans." Tanaka did his part but the overall scheme, capture what you need, was not a workable one.

Looking again at the war pentagon, Japan-Germany-Russia-Britain-US, the five major players took differing logistical approaches with varying success.

The Soviet Union had the least complex problems to solve. They had interior lines. That is they could move men and supplies within Russia wherever they were needed. Thus there was no need for oversea movements. That said, the road network away from major cities was not robust. Paved roads were a rarity throughout the country in the 1940's. The Russians also had the industrial and agricultural means to pretty much feed and supply themselves. They got some food, supplies, arms, planes, and vehicles from Lend Lease. These came three ways, via ship from Britain, overland via Iran (after the goods came there by freighter from the US, either around Africa or through the Mediterranean), and through Canada and Alaska via Siberia. Their troops and citizens were fed and armed adequately. They fought a mechanized war. Most of the infantry, the guys who have to seize and hold ground, were on foot not riding trucks. The home front was totally mobilized with everyone working seven days a week. At the start of the war Nazis were taking big bites of the country. The Soviets responded to this in part by moving their war factories. Industrial plants of all sorts were dismantled and moved east. Hundreds of factories were literally taken apart, put on a train, moved east out of German reach, reassembled, and were back producing shortly. As the Red Army moved west, these factories did their share to supply them with armaments. As for food, the troops were given the basics—a sack of potatoes each. They were expected to supplement that by living off the land, that is, taking from the local populace.

In its initial European campaigns Germany too had little need for naval operations and enjoyed interior lines. Europe had a well maintained rail system. It reached virtually everywhere in western Europe. Using it, Germany could move troops and supplies quickly and efficiently. Use of this rail network worked well for the Nazis in their early campaigns. The further from Berlin the Nazis went the greater the demands on the system and the less efficient they were at delivering supplies. Distance is a harsh master in war: The further afield an army goes the more supplies it takes to supply those who are bringing supplies to the infantry, armor, and bombers at the front. Every mile you extend your lines means an extra two miles you have to cover to supply your army. For Germany, aside from sheer distance, poor roads and rail facilities made things more difficult. Then add to the mix guerilla attacks that made transport more dangerous and the roads worse. The Wehrmacht pioneered mechanized warfare, with tanks planes and artillery. Even so, it relied heavily on horsedrawn mobility. Over half of German transport was not moved by the internal combustion engine. Rather good old Dobbin pulled wagons, artillery pieces, ambulances, and of course carts full of hay, oats and horseshoes.

Logistics became a serious issue when Germany invaded Russia with its vast treeless steppes. Hitler anticipated a quick victory over Russia. His armies jumped off in June and he planned on it being over and done before the snow flew. He did not supply his troops with winter gear, nor did anyone ensure that stocks of winter gear would be available to send them if needed. To complicate things, the Russian rail network was of a different guage (width) than European rails. This was by design—the Soviets, and the Tsars before them, did not want any invader to be able to just hop on the rails and come faster towards Moscow. The combination of these factors affected all Nazi forces, not only the ground troops. The mechanized units and the Luftwaffe faced their own problems in addition to frostbite. The typical Panzer driver had to build a fire underneath his tank just to get it started in the winter. Airplanes had to be winterized and did not run particularly well in the intense Russian winter.

Wehrmacht troops were supplied from home but also were expected to live off the land. The Nazis purposefully and systematically stripped all occupied countries of food and treasure. They took everything from wheat and crops to machinery, gems, hides, most any form of goods or wealth. There was even a Reichministry for appropriating wine from the French. All this loot, foodstuffs and wealth were sent to Berlin or used locally to feed and support the occupying troops. The Nazis also used slave labor from conquests throughout their economy. Slaves mined, farmed, worked in factories, and logged. Slave labor in Nazi Germany kept the economy going every bit as much as it did in Imperial Rome. Without slaves little would happened and much less of everything would have been produced.

Britain endured the two edged sword of being an island. Invading an island is harder than crossing a land border, and defending an isle is correspondingly easier. But sending and maintaining troops from an island to points all over the globe is an expensive, complex task. It means using ships. To protect the ships means having a navy. Having a navy means having bases around the world to provide coal or fuel oil and supplies for the fleet. Having bases means needing to supply those bases. Supplying them was expensive and complex. For Britain, incoming ships brought foodstuff, troops and supplies to the home island. Outgoing ships served to supply troops in the Mediterranean and elsewhere. India contributed a large part to the British economy. It was largely self sufficient in foodstuffs and personal supply. It was not a producer of armaments, planes and fuel. It had own supply network which was loosely linked with that of Britain.

Japan too was an island nation. As it took the pieces of its short lived empire, the "Greater East Asia Co-Prosperity Sphere," it took steps to secure the conquests. Nippon planted military and naval outposts over one eighth of the globe, many of them on islands. The intricate timing and constant motion needed to supply and feed forts on scores of islands and hundreds of other bases posed a big challenge. Such a project would be a gigantic and complicated job in peacetime. Their having to do it while fighting a creative and aroused foe made the task ultimately insurmountable. Many Japanese island garrisons grew gardens or fished from 1943 until they were repatriated in 1945 or 46. They were forced to do so because Tokyo could not get supplies through to them. Some soldiers verged on starvation. There were instances of cannibalism. Some of it was apparently ritual, chiefly of prisoners, and some was of other Japanese, for survival.

The US was a maritime nation which sent troops to six continents and islands across the Atlantic and Pacific. Supplying these hundreds of installations proved a formidable challenge. Fleets of merchant ships were put to use most of which had to be escorted when away from home waters. Even when they got to their destination, merchant ships would sometimes have to line up and wait at anchor, fully laden, because there was not the capacity to unload them all at once. Once the goods were ashore, trucks and trains were used to deliver ammunition and food. In some roadless jungle areas mule trains, native porters, or even elephants were put to work. Likewise sometimes supplies were airdropped to far roving units behind enemy lines. Even submarines were occasionally used to deliver supplies, especially in the Philippines. Subs were also used to deliver troops for commando and reconnaissance raids and other specialized missions. The Army Air Forces' Air Transport Command developed and used a chain of bases which allowed regular round the globe flights. This route went through South America, Africa, the Mideast, India, Australia, and to islands across the Pacific.

The US Army set up a separate "Service of Supply" branch whose sole job was to build and maintain bases, and then supply the people on those bases. They had four basic areas of facility to build and maintain: lodging, shops and maintenance facilities, hospitals, and airfields. They developed shipping, air, and surface fleets to supply the hundreds of bases around the world. They had to supply and support the biggest hospital in the world in Calcutta, training facilities in Australia, air bases on islands across the Pacific and Atlantic, lend lease transshipping facilities in Alaska and Iran, and on and on. And of course the point of it all was to support the troops actually carrying a rifle or dropping a bomb wherever they were on the globe.

The US Navy developed a sophisticated program to refuel and resupply ships at sea. This was used to keep the task forces built around aircraft carriers at sea and hitting at the enemy. It was not uncommon for a task force to remain at sea for months at a time. The Navy too had bases all across the oceans and fighters to support.

Initially the US military struggled to supply it far flung troops. The first part of the war arrangements were done "on the fly." In the Pacific the Japanese held the initiative. The US and Allies were fighting rear guard actions in the Philippines, Malaya, Netherlands East Indies, and Burma. Often as not they were simply trying to extricate troops. Since they were retreating the Allies enjoyed interior lines, that is, the troops were generally retreating back on a base of supply. That is one of the few positive developments the Allies enjoyed in those campaigns.

As the situation stabilized the Allies started fighting back in New Guinea, the Solomon Islands, and North Africa. Supplying those forces involved shipping over long distances and in the Pacific, primitive facilities. Even after supplies were gotten to the general area, forwarding them to the front was another issue.

In North Africa, supplies came from the US direct and from the UK. Shipping and procedures for moving goods across the Atlantic were well established and understood. A large flow of supplies, tens of thousands of tons, was going from North America to the UK every month. Some of those goods were either diverted direct to North Africa or transshipped via the UK. This adjustment strained the system at first. By mid November of '42 the supply depots, transport battalions, and supporting units were in place and working well. Supplies were not short in the North African campaign, at least not for the Allies.

Troops had to be taken care of around the world, far from Africa. The sheer size of the Pacific and the isolation of the two campaign fronts presented real challenges for the supply efforts. MacArthur's New Guinea campaign was supplied largely from and via Australia. The island is only 100 miles from northern Australia. Ships and planes were able to sustain a flow of food, medicines, and arms. Once on the island, supplies were moved to the sharp end of the spear by jeep, mule, or porter.

The southern Solomon Islands are a thousand miles from nowhere. Supplies had to move from the US or Australia via Fiji to New Caledonia by freighter. The capital of New Caledonia is Noumea. For the south Pacific it is a large city, but its port facilities had scant equipment for unloading ships. There were just several docks, a few small cranes, and almost no warehouses. In November there were nearly one hundred ships in the harbor at anchor, awaiting unloading. The port simply couldn't handle the traffic. The Army and Navy pitched in, got their cargoes out and transshipped, and by late December goods were flowing evenly and adequately to the front.

From Noumea the fuel, food, arms and medicines were moved by military transport, destroyer, or air. They went to the intermediate island of Espiritu Santo, a more primitive town about halfway to Guadalcanal. It operated as a forward base and staging area for troops and supplies moving from the rear to the Canal. The Japanese were not the only ones to rely on old destroyers to deliver food, medicines, arms, and reinforcements. The US made heavy use of this tactic in the Guadalcanal campaign, especially the early part. They also pressed old minesweepers, tugs, and other ships. They even tried to use a river patrol boat, the USS Lakatoi. This venerable old patrol boat had seen duty on the Yangtze River in the 1920's and 30's. She proved unequal to the open seas between New Caledonia and Guadalcanal. After she burned up the part of her diesel fuel which had been in ballast inside tanks below the water, she became top heavy, turned turtle, and sank.

The crew got into lifeboats where they were two weeks awaiting rescue. One crewman was lost.

Neither Guadalcanal nor Tulagi had docks, cranes, or unloading facilities. Troops were used to unload the ships as they arrived. The new Army commander of Guadalcanal was General Patch. In observing the shore work, he noted that combat troops were "apathetic toward labor." But the goods eventually got unloaded. From there, as in New Guinea, the supplies moved forward by jeep, mule, or porter. Some goods went up river on rafts pushed by people. Both natives and US troops served as porters.

Later in the war both the Army and the Navy developed sophisticated, purpose built transport depots, ships, barges, pipelines, roads, and other facilities. Both were able to supply the American citizen soldiers in a style considered lavish by other nation's Armies.

All the belligerents needed a large support structure to supply their fighting troops. For every 100 US uniformed troops, over 90 of them were working to supply and sustain the remaining 7 to 10 who were actually fighting at the front. Other nations also had a high proportion of total troops involved in support and supply roles and a low proportion in the combat arms.

The US and to a degree Britain were the two countries which needed a global network to project and sustain power. Both had outposts around the world. They had strategic and commercial interests to foster and protect as well. Germany and Russia were continental powers. They were chiefly concerned with their armies fighting on land in central Europe. Japan had taken and attempted to sustain a regional empire, with maritime and continental elements. Even at its largest, their empire was in east, south, and southeast Asian with western Pacific elements only. It had no global outlook or pretensions.

Logistics and politics were managed far from the fronts, from offices and warehouses in capital cities. The men at the front were not concerned with politics or commercial interests. They were concerned about their next meal and the next patrol. They cared about logistics only when they were hungry, wounded, or needed ammo.

One force was face to face with the stark reality of logistics. The German force near Cairo, the Afrika Korps was hungry with gas tanks nearly dry. Its advance there was in fact its high water mark. They would go no further. Several factors contributed to their stopping near but not on the Nile River. The Korps was at the end of a long predictable and vulnerable supply line. Fuel, food and ammunition had to come from Italy across the Mediterranean to Tunisia and Libya. Once it got there it had to be sent east along the shore for almost 1000 miles. Just moving goods along that consumed huge amounts of food and fuel. The Allies attacked this vulnerability wherever they could. Having broken into German communications, they were often able to pinpoint when a supply run was scheduled. Plus they could learn where it was leaving from and its planned route. Fuel tankers were targeted in particular, to keep Rommel's planes grounded and tanks stationary. British submarines were waiting to send torpedoes. Many supply ships did not get through. Also, the British Desert Air Force, based in Egypt, kept pressure on the supplies being trucked in. This too hurt the Afrika Korps' mobility and limited its options. And the food and fuel to supply the suppliers added to the overall logistical load. Ask the generals and admirals. They will tell you that this is always a problem.

Logistics aside, on a strategic level Rommel and his Afrika Korps were pretty much fighting with leftovers. In the last half of 1941 and all of 1942, Hitler had huge forces in Russia. On the German side alone there were over one hundred infantry and armor divisions and scores of fighter and bomber squadrons fighting there. And there were another twenty or more Nazi divisions and squadrons on occupation duty all over Europe. Rommel had only two panzer (tank) divisions and several German and Italian infantry divisions, some motorized. He had a few Luftwaffe squadrons attached. Even with such a small force he was master of North Africa and stood at the gates of Suez.

It is worth speculating, what if Rommel had been reinforced with two panzer divisions, two fighter squadrons, and more supplies? He may well have been able to take Cairo and the Suez

Canal. He, and Hitler, would have been positioned to end the European war from there: with a sweep north through Palestine and Lebanon he could take Iraq and its oil. The British had had to put down a German attempt to take Syria in 1940. No doubt there were still sympathizers who could have risen and helped Rommel. Had Rommel linked up with German forces in the Caucasus, Germany would have gained control of all of Europe and much of the Mideast and Africa. With oil from those places, the Nazis could have turned their attention to other goals. It was oil that Hitler needed to keep his blitzkrieg machine going. Sometimes he kept that in mind and attacked accordingly. Often he fell back into moving his divisions around like toy soldiers.

If Rommel had been assigned a few more divisions and planes, the war would surely have turned out differently. There may have been a negotiated settlement with Britain. The Allies may simply not have been able to continue. Or if they had continued the fight, had the Allies not come to terms, it would have changed the war's center of gravity. The fighting would have been not in northwest Europe, but in the Persian Gulf and Iran. Japanese warships freely roamed the Indian Ocean in mid 1942. Perhaps they could have returned to cross the Indian Ocean. They might have transited the Suez Canal, signaling a linkup of the Axis forces. Russia and especially India would have been squeezed, perhaps fatally. Or maybe England would have sent the Royal Navy to Canada and continued to fight from the Western Hemisphere.

But the Fuhrer would not send meaningful reinforcements Rommel's way. He considered Africa to be a sideshow. His main goal and effort had always been to defeat Stalin and Communism in Russia. In any case, by late 1942, Rommel had gone as far as he could with the men and equipment he had.

The Allies, having done all they could to hurt Rommel's supply buildup, were amassing their own stores. They had their own logistical challenges. With the Mediterranean and Suez Canal closed, everything for Egypt and the eastern Mediterranean had to come from North America or Britain around the Cape of Good Hope, clear around Africa. This added thousands of miles and used up tons of fuel. It tied up many ships for long voyages and exposed them to Uboat attack. American tanks and British and Commonwealth troops came this long way to build up reserves in Egypt.

General Montgomery was the newly appointed commander of the British Eighth Army in Cairo. In fact, he was Churchill's second choice for the job. The general who was first choice was killed in a plane crash on the way to assume command. Bernard Montgomery was a prim, blunt man with definite ideas. He had no doubts about how to live life, about how his soldiers should dress and act, or about running an army and battles. And he was generally right, at least about fighting battles. His plans entailed a buildup of forces and a battle on his terms to shatter or badly hurt the Germans. He faced a German force encamped about 100 miles west of Cairo at the small village of El Alamein. Even though it was close, this group was running on fumes. It was having real problems supplying itself. The British sponsored government in Cairo was on alert to evacuate, and some papers had been openly burned by civil servants. Britain had pushed Axis forces away several times over the previous two years. But the Germans and Italians had managed to rebound and come back, the last time under Rommel's leadership. The Allies wanted an offensive to push him and his Axis troops out of Africa all together. The plan Montgomery and staff devised to do this was called Operation Lightfoot. It took advantage of Allied buildups of material and men, and looked to destroy or nullify the Axis hold on the south shore of the Mediterranean Sea.

Operation Lightfoot started October 23 with an immense artillery barrage. It happened that Rommel was in Germany on leave, thus was not present. His assistants stepped in and managed the battle and subsequent retreat. It was a huge well planned assault on German lines at El Alamein. The British Eighth Army was made up of Commonwealth forces—British, New Zealanders, Australians, South Africans, and Indians. There were also Polish, French, Norwegian, and other Allied components. On the opening day of the offensive, Montgomery's guns and infantry started hitting German lines with the aim of drawing German armor out for destruction. This was a slugging match and went on for almost two weeks, with both sides taking and giving. By early November, Montgomery saw the Afrika Korps was wearing down. Allied efforts to disrupt and destroy them and their supplies were taking a toll. Montgomery had been pulling units out of Operation Lightfoot in anticipation of a breakthrough and pursuit. That pursuit was called Operation Supercharge. On November 4, it happened. British X Corps (Read, Tenth Corps; roman numerals are traditionally used to designate army corps) broke through. They were in the rear of the Axis forces. This started a retreat which ended up one thousand miles away in Tunisia. The Eighth Army and Desert Air Force chased the remnants of Afrika Korps all the way. By mid November the Korps had abandoned northeastern Egypt and was hustling all its units west along the coast.

At the western end of the Mediterranean Sea.... The North African invasion was going pretty much to the Allies' plan. That day, November 8, a British-American force came ashore at Oran and Algiers in Algeria and a purely American army invaded three places in Morocco: Safi, Port Lyautey and Rabat.

Operation Torch was an immense effort. It was the largest amphibious invasion ever, up to that time. Fleets carrying the invasion forces came from Britain and from the US. Those from the US came directly across the Atlantic from the American mainland, nonstop. The armada, Task Force 34, had 101 ships and carried thousands of troops. But secrecy was kept and not one ship of the TF 34 was lost. The fleet that sailed from Britain was almost as large as TF 34. It was not molested by Uboats along the way either, until it entered the Mediterranean.

German Admiral Doenitz knew something was brewing. From radio traffic and patrols they knew there would be an attack. Intelligence data led them to believe it would be in Africa but just where they could not say. Their best estimate was that the attack would come on Dakar, on the western bulge of the continent. There had been an abortive attempt to take this port in 1940. DeGaulle's Free French were planning to invade then with British support. Word leaked out and the operation was scuttled. Dakar was strategic and could be used as a Uboat surveillance base and a stopover for planes flying from the US. The German consensus in late 1942 was that Dakar was the target. So Doenitz ordered all of his Uboats pulled out of the north and central Atlantic. He sent them south, off of west Africa. He hoped to catch the invasion fleets as they approached Dakar. Some subs were also grouped around the Straits of Gibraltar. These dispositions proved useless to the Germans, but were good for the Allies.

Operation Torch is significant not only for its political and strategic aspects. It broke ground in its command arrangements as well. It was a textbook example of alliance warfare, of shared command and control. This was the first British-American effort with a multinational command team: The American general Eisenhower was supreme commander of the invasion. He waited out the invasion, literally, in the tunnels of Fortress Gibraltar. Once the invasion started, the supreme commander could do nothing to influence events. The forces had been trained, armed, and were started on the way to achieve their goals. He could not communicate with the forces at sea because radio silence was enforced. This was standard procedure as an invasion force was on the way. The invading fleets would not send messages so they couldn't be tracked. In any case, the supreme commander's job was oversight. The overall commander would not try to micro manage battles and actions on the ground. So Eisenhower had to sit in Gibraltar and await word of progress. His immediate subordinates, the commanders of the ground, sea and air components, were British. They and their subordinates would manage the individual battles, skirmishes, and operations. In the Army, the Navy, and the Air Forces, at sea and on the ground, rear echelons and at the front, British commanded Americans and Americans commanded British. This arrangement worked effectively and well.

The American Army hadn't seen combat for a generation. The British were skeptical of Yankee performance. Even so, the GIs performed ably and effectively. The Navy delivered the troops and provided gunfire support, the troops stormed the beaches and fought bravely and well. Air support was given by carrier based planes. Ashore, airfields were taken and put to quick use as well. The French navy fought back and several of their ships were damaged or sunk. By and large the fighting was over by the first day's afternoon. After a brief fight on the ground, the white flag came out and a truce called. A truce was soon agreed to and an armistice was negotiated.

The coming months would see Allied troops fight and eject the Axis from the continent. There would be ebb and flow, reverses and much fighting. Already Allied troops were advancing east and Axis forces were moving west. The American GIs and their leaders would learn the hard lessons the British had already absorbed. In the campaign, both would take some knocks from experienced Germans. By campaign's end, both the GI's and the British Tommys would turn the tables on the Nazis and the Italians.

CHAPTER III
November 8
Early Guadalcanal; The War, 1942

Around the world, in the South Pacific, November 8 saw no Allied forces storming ashore. These theaters of war were literally backwaters. This was a part of the world where few people went and not much happened, ever. It is located between northeast Australia and the islands of Polynesia and the Philippines. In peacetime New Guinea and the Solomon Islands were home to many tribes and groups of natives, most scarcely touched by modern life. There were a few gold mines and some coconut plantations. Missionary stations were scattered throughout the area, made up of orphanages, schools and hospitals.

New Guinea and the southern Solomon Islands were unlikely settings for any significant action. No one in power in 1939 had given a thought to their importance. But suppose someone had asked about their significance, their accessibility, their logistical infrastructure. To answer, generals and admirals from all countries would likely have had to consult an atlas just to see where they were. Then the brass would no doubt have blandly stated that they would play absolutely no part in any future war. The fates would have laughed. For these two unlikely arenas were to be the sites of many savage, prolonged and important battles, the first lengthy campaigns of the Pacific war. Troops of all nations struggled with the steep, boggy, and unmapped terrain, unknown and dreadful diseases, extreme weather, and thick jungle, alive with its own forms of hostile life.

Troops from Australia, America and Japan would fight each other as well as the terrain, the jungle, and the climate. In New Guinea Allied forces would fight to take three small northern coastal villages held and fortified by the Japanese Army. On the island of Guadalcanal, in the Solomon Islands, Allies fought to keep Japanese ground troops and Navy ships away from an airfield.

The first recorded westerner to see the island we know as Guadalcanal was the Spanish explorer Alvarao De Mendano de Neyra. In 1597 he was exploring the Spice Islands. He stumbled on the island and named it Guadalcanal in honor of his hometown in Spain. After his visit the isle faded into obscurity for several centuries. The British took possession in the 1800's. It is a mountainous, malarial, and primitive island near the south end of the Solomon Island chain. To find it on a map, look about 600 miles east of New Guinea, 600 miles north of the Pacific island of New Caledonia, and about 1000 miles east of northern Australia. It is not on the way to anywhere else of note. One has to want to go to Guadalcanal because it is not a convenient stopover. It is, in fact pretty much in the middle of nowhere.

The Canal, as it was called, came on to the world stage in the spring and summer of 1942. In May, the Japanese Navy had put a seaplane base at Tulagi. This small island is 22 miles north of the Canal, across Sealark Channel. It has a good harbor and is well suited for a seaplane base but is too small and craggy to hold an airfield. It held the British provincial capital when the Japanese came. In June crews of the Emperor's sailors and laborers were sent across Sealark Channel to the much larger Guadalcanal. This island had enough room to develop a base. They started to build a landing strip. This activity did not long remain unknown to the Allies. A patrol plane from MacArthur's command saw and reported it. When word of it got to Washington, it caused concern among the movers and shakers there. An active fort there would extend the reach of the Emperor's forces by hundreds of miles. With an operational air strip, the Japanese could cut or make difficult access from the US to Australia.

Why was access to Australia so important to the US? Why did the brass care if the Japanese could dominate the air around it?

Australia was a secure base. It had to be kept secure since it was to be the Allied base to start fighting and taking back Japanese conquests. Indeed MacArthur was already planning his campaigns to protect it and fight back towards Tokyo. Particularly concerned by the Guadalcanal airstrip was US Admiral King, Chief of Naval Operations and Commander in Chief of the Fleet. He viewed the Pacific war as the US Navy's show. He wanted to start fighting back and he wanted to forestall any further Japanese advances. At his prodding, George Marshall, Chief of Staff of the Army, and the President agreed to a preemptive invasion. Actually, it was the Allies' intention all along that Operation Torch, the invasion of North Africa, would be the first Allied offensive. But a patrol pilot's report of construction equipment working on Guadalcanal changed all that.

Operation Watchtower was ordered. This was sarcastically called Operation Shoestring by some on the scene. It was cobbled together in a month or so. That itself is a tremendous accomplishment. All the other Allied amphibious invasions were all planned, rehearsed and prepared for months or even years. Not Watchtower. It got a complement of ships, troops and commanders. Virtually none of them had worked together. It is helpful if the teammates know each others' strengths and weaknesses, know what to expect from their colleagues, and recognize each other's roles and responsibilities. The staff and troops of Watchtower could not call on common experience, but they had a common goal.

The commander of the landing force, US Marine General Archer Vandegrift, was a Virginian with experience in the Caribbean police actions of the 1920's and 30's. The Marines had been the defacto government of several Caribbean nations during unrest there. In June the General was at sea with his division heading to New Zealand. Vandegrift had every reason to believe the purpose was to obtain training. When he left the US, he had been led to expect he would have six months or more to train and prepare his men. But circumstances had changed. When he landed, orders awaited him to plan and mount an invasion of Guadalcanal in about a month. An amphibious invasion of its scope had never been successfully staged by the US. It would be the first American amphibious operation of any size since the Spanish American War in 1898. And that was going into Spanish Cuba, ninety miles from Florida. Guadalcanal was two thousand miles from New Zealand and seven or eight thousand miles from the US. General Vandegrift had a tall order to fill.

At first the Joint Chiefs ordered the invasion to go in the first day of August but the local commanders simply could not get it ready by then. They appealed and got one week's reprieve. This shows how seriously King and Marshall took the threat. They simply could not let Japanese planes operate from Guadalcanal. Cargo and troop ships were hurriedly loaded in New Zealand. Local labor unions refused to work overtime so the Marines had to stow guns, food, barbed wire, jeeps etc themselves. They were cramped for time and just got it done. This would come back to haunt them: normally ships headed to support an invasion were "combat loaded." That is, whatever would be needed first on the beach got loaded last, and what was needed last on the beach went on first. This was not a particularly efficient use of shipping space. But it sure was helpful to the poor Marines and GIs taking fire while trying to get a beach head established. At this time, it was early in the war and no one really recognized the importance of loading ships this way. The Marines just got things on board because they had no time to sort and prioritize.

When the ships were loaded, they left New Zealand. The task force of troop and cargo ships, with escorting warships, rendezvoused for a rehearsal near Samoa. The rehearsal did not go well. There were reefs which made it impossible to practice the coordinated landing of boats. Keeping boats on station and moving at the correct speed in the right direction was not achieved. That particular set of skills and tasks had to be figured out on the landing day.

Worse, the senior commanders did not see eye to eye on some pretty basic matters. They disagreed about how long the carriers would stay to provide air cover to the Marines ashore. The South Pacific Theater Commander (ComSoPac) was Admiral Ghormley.

He did not see fit to attend this rehearsal, to see that the first offensive of America's war got off on the right foot. He sent his Chief of Staff who offered no guidance on his boss' position. The amphibious invasion commander and the ground troop commander wanted planes and air cover to be kept around until the airstrip could be made operative. The Admiral commanding the operation overall wanted to pull his carriers back after just a few days, airstrip or no. In the absence of orders or guidance from ComSoPac, his orders prevailed. The carriers would leave after three days at the latest. It was early in the war and no one really recognized the absolute need to provide air cover until the invading forces could provide their own.

In the event, Vandegrift's invaders were about 19000 troops. Mostly it comprised elements of the 1st Marine Division with a Raider Battalion and some aviation and construction units. There were Coast Guard components driving some of the landing craft. Members of this Service served gallantly in most amphibious invasions with scant credit from the public. The Raiders went ashore on Tulagi and the 1st Marines on Guadalcanal on August 7 1942. Opposition was savage on Tulagi with the Raiders exterminating their Japanese Special Landing Force counterparts. Fighting was light on the Canal. The Korean labor troops wanted nothing to do with the 1st Marines. They scattered into the hills. The partially completed airstrip was overrun the first day.

As came out at the invasion rehearsal, there was basic disagreement at the senior officer level about how to run the show. There was also mismanagement, miscommunication, and inexperience. Add in a lack of war mindedness, of a wary, alert, "shoot first and ask questions later" attitude. This lethal mix of ignorance and naivete' had the makings of a defeat. This was precisely what happened.

The Japanese responded to the incursion. They did not think this was a major invasion, rather a nuisance raid. Admiral Mikawa headed out from Rabaul, their major base in the area. He led a fleet of cruisers and destroyers. It took them two days of steaming to get to the southern Solomon Islands. The second night after the invasion they came in to Sealark Channel and wrought havoc.

They were primed and ready for battle and had a fairly easy time of it. With virtually no damage to themselves, they sank three American and one Australian cruiser as well as some destroyers. The Americans and Australians were not ready and in fact were caught totally unaware. They fired almost no shots. The Allied ships had their guns trained in. They were not even ready to shoot if they had detected hostile intruders. By the time some ships got their guns out and shooting the damage was done.

There had been American miscommunication about air patrols. An Allied pilot saw the Japanese force approaching but his report was delayed until useless. He waited to report until after he landed, and in any case he misidentified the type and apparent direction of the ships. A few alert American sailors saw the intruders and raised the alarm. But those warnings of unknown prowling ships in the area were ignored or discounted.

The victory was great for Mikawa. It could have been a grand slam for him. After killing six or seven enemy warships, his way was clear to bombard the defenseless freighters and newly landed, unfortified Marines. For some reason, he did not go on to shell the invasion beaches or shoot up the freighters disgorging supplies for the Marines. Perhaps he thought he had taken care of a hit and run raid and shooting up the freighters was not worth the effort. In any case, he decided just to head for home. It was early in the war, and he apparently did not understand how vulnerable an amphibious invading force was at that point. This action was given the name of The Battle of Savo Island. It was the biggest single action defeat in the history of the US Navy. It was big enough that the Navy sat on the story. The American press was not informed of the battle or severity of loss for months.

As a result of the confusion and the Savo Island defeat, air cover was needed more than ever. The Japanese had come down from the north with impunity. If there was no American air support they surely would come again. But the US carrier force with their air cover was withdrawn the next day and the carriers retreated south. The admiral in charge was shortly transferred stateside and spent the war commanding the naval base in Seattle and its approaches.

The lack of air cover was bad enough, but worse was to come for the Marines. The partially unloaded freighters carrying food, supplies, barbed wire, artillery, ammo, and other necessities pulled up their gangplanks. Marines watched as they sailed away. The ships with their ability to run supplies were too valuable to risk in unprotected areas. A lot of the arms, goods and food supplies for the Americans never made it ashore. Rations were immediately cut. The Marines stretched their supplies with food and equipment left by the Koreans. Rice and fish heads became staple foods for a few weeks.

One can imagine that would be true loneliness: You are ten thousand miles from home with people trying to kill you, and half your supplies and all your air protection just sailed off. General Vandegrift was not the self pitying type. He wholeheartedly took on the job, made his troop dispositions, and got to work finishing the airstrip. His troops took the cue and energetically got on with their jobs too. The first task the General had the engineers undertake was to lengthen the runway by a thousand feet. They started up their bulldozers and graders. They also took and put to use every piece of construction equipment left by the fleeing Korean laborers.

This invasion, Operation Watchtower, set off a savage six month campaign. It was fought on and under the sea, in the air, and on the ground and swamps of the island. It would involve the efforts of all the armed forces of both combatants and would cost many men, ships, and planes their lives. About fifty ships, evenly split between the two sides, were lost in nearby waters. The roster of sunken ships started with what Mikawa did to the US and Australian Navies.

In the Japanese way of doing things in this part of the war, Guadalcanal was the responsibility of the Imperial Japanese Navy. They were surprised by the invasion and at first considered it merely a raid. The Japanese Army provided most of the ground troops for the campaign. The generals were not consulted about the operation nor did their air force participate. It was a Navy show.

New Guinea is a buzzard shaped island, one of the world's largest. At one point its southern coast is about a hundred miles from northern Australia. It too is a malarial, mountainous and primitive island. At the war's outset, the western half belonged to the Netherlands East Indies, and the eastern half was an Australian Protectorate. This changed in early 1942 when Japan took effective control of the region. The land is so rough that even in the 1960's and 1970's, tribes were discovered which had lived for centuries in their own isolated valleys. They spoke unknown languages, had never seen a white person and knew nothing of modern life. In 1942, the veneer of civilization over the island was even thinner. There were no roads to speak of, a few small towns on the coasts and several gold mining towns in the interior. Away from the coast, the only practical way to get around was by air. Headhunting and cannibalism were still widely practiced by the native population. Cannibalism would rear its head among the Japanese before too long.

Command arrangements in the Australian area had been set up in April shortly after US General Douglas MacArthur escaped the Philippines and reached Australia. The General had commanded all American forces in the Philippine Islands at war's start. By March, the Japanese had taken the main islands and left MacArthur marooned on a tiny fortress near Manila. FDR personally ordered him out to Australia in March. His trip with family and close staff was by PT boat, bomber, and train. It was an epic and unlikely trek. The group dodged Japanese warships and planes much of the way.

He was named commander of all forces, American and Australian, in the Southwest Pacific Theater. His title was Commander, South West Pacific Area, or in military jargon, ComSoWesPac. Like Eisenhower in Britain, he started with a multi-national staff. He had Australian subordinates who commanded land, air and sea forces. Technically he kept this structure for much of the war. In reality he wanted to rely on known and trusted Americans. Rather than fire anyone or get into a political struggle, he went to the organization chart. He reassigned forces and men and for all intents and purposes took the Australian commanders out of the picture. He gave them reduced forces and training jobs. They commanded only Australians, no Americans.

To justify this, he created a parallel structure called "Alamo Force." All American ground troops were part of this and they did not report to Australian officers in any way. He put trusted subordinates in charge of Alamo Force. These were all men who had worked for him in the Philippines and who had accompanied him when he escaped from there. This inner circle was called "The Bataan Gang," for the fact that they had all worked with MacArthur in the losing Bataan campaign in the Philippines. The General also created a separate Air Force, the Fifth Air Force. Its commander worked directly for MacArthur. This all worked well for the war effort; witness the outcome. But it did not sit particularly well with the Australians.

In any case, MacArthur's plan was to defend Australia by going on the attack. He did not intend to wait for the Japanese to come invade the continent. Rather he proposed to take the fight to them in New Guinea. He planned to send troops to the northern shore in July. Using those forces, he would build a base for future offensives.

The Japanese also had their eye on northern New Guinea. They intended to take and use it as a protective outpost for their newly conquered empire. They called this empire "The Greater East Asian Co-Prosperity Sphere." This was their name for what the Americans, Dutch and British knew as the Philippines, the Netherlands East Indies, Borneo, Malaya and Burma. Also they wanted a New Guinea base to project power to isolate Australia. There were even those in the Imperial Army who wanted to use it as a springboard to invade the continent.

Nippon had already made efforts to land on the south coast of New Guinea, at Port Moresby. An invasion force was at sea in early May. On the way to Moresby, it dropped a small force at Tulagi which set up the seaplane base the Marines took in August. In fact, American carrier planes attacked this new base on their way to find and attack the Japanese invasion force. The Nipponese convoy had troop laden transports escorted and covered by carriers. It was attacked by planes from nearby American carriers. The Yanks sank one small Japanese carrier and damaged several large fleet carriers. The Japanese convoy turned back. The Moresby invasion was postponed, permanently as things turned out. This was the Battle of the Coral Sea.

The fight at Coral Sea was notable for several reasons. It was the first ever battle where the two sides' ships and commanders never saw each other. It was strictly a carrier battle with only the planes making contact. No surface ships fired at each other. It could be considered a Japanese tactical victory in that America lost a fleet carrier while Japan merely lost a small carrier and had their fleet carriers damaged. But it was an Allied strategic victory in that the invasion of southern New Guinea was stopped. As important in the long run, a number of Japanese pilots were killed. And two Imperial fleet carriers were put out of commission. They were damaged enough that they could not participate in other battles for some time. Both missed the Battle of Midway where their weight might have averted the American victory. Two more expertly crewed flattops for Yamamoto there could easily have made a difference in the outcome.

The Emperor's men had not given up on New Guinea. In July, the Army landed a small invasion force at Buna on the north coast. This is precisely what MacArthur had intended to do, but he was beaten to the punch by days. It is interesting to speculate how things would have turned out had the Allies held the north shore, not the Japanese. Perhaps it and not Guadalcanal would have become the focus in Tokyo and Washington....

The Japanese invasion troops were led by General Horii and were designated the South Seas Detachment. His unit was at the end of a long supply line. His men were lacking food for a long campaign. They planned to capture Australian supplies along the way. This turned out to be a bad decision, and many starved because of it. In July, they confidently strode out on the Kokoda Trail, a simple footpath which goes coast to coast. It starts at sea level and climbs over the Owen Stanley Mountain Range which has 13,000 foot peaks. It crosses a 10,000 foot pass at Templeton Gap.

Australian troops were in the area guarding the settlements and the Track itself. These troops were militia units, not regular infantry. They were equivalent to the American National Guard.

They gallantly but unsuccessfully contested this Japanese incursion, falling back repeatedly. They fought and finally stopped Horii's Japanese on September 26. In part Horii's men were too weak to fight effectively due to lack of supplies. Also part of the situation was that Horii had been ordered to stop his advance. Indeed he was ordered to pull back which he reluctantly did. The stop was made only about 30 miles from Port Moresby, the capital on the south coast. At this same time, the US Army's 32nd Division sent a Battalion north over a trail that runs parallel to and east of the Kokoda. It is called the Kappa Kappa Trail. Even in the twenty first century it is a rugged and challenging trek over high passes and rain forest. The men of the 32nd met no enemy but nearly starved before they got through to the north coast.

In all of this campaign, New Guinea was totally the sphere of the Imperial Japanese Army. It was strictly an Army show. The Imperial Japanese Navy provided support but was not consulted about operations and was chiefly involved in bringing in troops and supplies. Their air arm did not participate at all.

By mid September, Guadalcanal had heated up enough to concern Imperial Headquarters in Tokyo. They ordered the Army to pull Horii's forces back and to go on the defensive in New Guinea. They wanted to concentrate on retaking Guadalcanal from the Marines. General Horii and his men started back up and over the Kokoda Track. The Australian Militia and then regular Australian infantry chased and harried them. It was not a pell mell Japanese retreat, rather a slow, fighting retrograde movement. The South Seas Detachment made the Aussies earn every foot they retook. Horii died on this retreat. He drowned while trying to ford a river.

The Track has a town, really a small settlement, called Kokoda. It is on the north side of Templeton's Crossing so the Aussies were pushing the Nipponese away from Moresby. It was retaken by Australian forces on the second of November. The previous day, November 1, the commander, Australian General Vasey saw the tide turning. He told his staff and commanders," The enemy is beaten. Give him no rest and we will annihilate him." This was premature but also prescient: There was a lot of blood yet to be shed by all before that part of the Island was secured by the Allies. After that, the Emperor's forces never again went on the offensive. Even so, they continued to fight savagely and bloodily with no regard for self. For the rest of the war, Japanese soldiers and sailors would not give up an inch without a determined fight.

In the first, successful months of the war, the Emperor's forces had pushed three prongs south towards Australia. One prong was through Thailand, Malaya, Singapore and Java, and came no closer than that. Of the two that came into strategic play, one prong ended at Guadalcanal in the southern Solomon Islands. The third prong was probing south over Papua New Guinea. The Sons of Nippon would have these prongs turned around and pushed right back at them. The Japanese would repeatedly experience having to fight on both prongs, shifting from one to the other. And they would have to curtail or alter one campaign because of an Allied threat or attack on the other prong. This occurred and recurred often from September 1942 through 1944 to the end in 1945. The Allies' prongs met when MacArthur's drive up through New Guinea and the Philippines met Nimitz' drive across the central Pacific. The prongs then joined as the Allies fought at Iwo Jima in February and Okinawa in the spring of 1945. On those two islands the Nipponese faced the combined might of the US Army, US Navy and US Marines in one combined front. They found it no better than fighting on multiple fronts.

But in 1942, early in the war, prongs were of little concern. Even if the Emperor's forces did not use these islands, New Guinea and the southern Solomon Islands, to invade Australia, they at least wanted to deny them to the Allies.

The two islands were interlinked, strategically speaking. From the Japanese point of view, both were well placed to protect their new colonies. And they could be used as springboards. If the time came, they could be jumping off points for further conquests to the south and southeast. Tentative plans had actually been drawn at Imperial Headquarters to take Samoa and Australia.

The Allies' point of view was the converse: Each island could be used to help shield their main base, Australia. Each isle was a waypoint on the road to Tokyo. Either could be used to protect, take or retake territory. In the event, each could be and was used by the Allies as a jumping off point to roll up the Japanese from south to north. This forced two lines of attack, two lines which needed defending, on Nippon. The Allies ultimately defeated each of these tentacles of the Emperor's forces in detail. Looking back, it is not hard to see that that is just what happened, but at the time, all both sides knew is that they were in a bloody brawl.

After the Marines took part of Guadalcanal in August, they improved and finished the airstrip. They named it Henderson Field for Major Lofton Henderson, a Marine flier killed at Midway. They were building up and trying to secure their foothold. The first combat planes landed at Henderson on August 20. It was a long twelve days for the groundpounders without their own air protection. Thirty one dive bombers and fighters were the first US planes to arrive on Guadalcanal. They were a welcome sight and tangible evidence to the Marines that they had not been forgotten. These planes enabled Vandegrift to extend his range of attack. Now incursions by enemy ships and planes could be contested.

The fighters and bombers stationed there were collectively known as the Cactus Air Force. Cactus was the code name for Guadalcanal. The US fed planes into Guadalcanal from many sources. The Army Air Corps sent pilots and planes. The Navy stripped carriers to provide pilots and planes, and both the Navy and Marine Corps sent land based planes and pilots. During the first months, the Cactus Air Force seldom had more than fifty operable planes at any one time, often less. Combat losses, night bombardments, and the primitive conditions all took their toll. But as fast as planes were lost ComSoPac found new ones to send in. There were always at least enough to keep the field going. Sometimes the search for planes and pilots went up the line. More than once, General Marshall or another very senior officer would find and divert a squadron to the South Pacific.

On the American side, more planes were lost than pilots. It was of benefit to the Yanks that the fight usually took place over and near Guadalcanal. Those plane drivers who survived the fall from the sky had a fair chance of landing in or making it back to friendly territory. Some pilots were able to bail out over American held ground. Many plane drivers went down to the sea. Some of them got out to be picked up by boat or plane. Some were rescued and sheltered by natives. A few landed behind Japanese lines but managed to survive and make it back to friendly territory.

The Japanese pilots found themselves hundreds of miles from friendly territory unless they happened to come down over their part of the Island. Probably there were a few Japanese pilots who became infantry when they landed on the Canal. Another reason for Japanese pilot loss was the relative lightness of their planes. Their airplanes did not have the armor and pilot protection that American planes did. As a consequence Nipponese planes, especially the Zero fighter, were lighter and more maneuverable than the Yankees'. But with pilot armor and self sealing gas tanks the American planes could take more punishment. The American's plane, and the pilot, was more likely to survive an encounter with bullets than was the typical Japanese.

In a way this is a snapshot of national motivation and philosophy: The Japanese fighting man was steeped in Bushido, a philosophy of ferocity and self denial. For him, fighting hard and well was almost the most important thing and dying for the Emperor was most glorious. For the American fighting man, fighting hard and well was important. Even more important was surviving to fight another day and some day, to go home.

The pilots of both sides fought bravely. Many did not survive. The campaign came down to a simple fact: as long as the US held the airfield they had control of the air. As long as they had that, Japan could not retake the island. This is precisely the lesson the Royal Air Force taught the Germans when they defeated the Luftwaffe in the Battle of Britain in 1940. Germany could not invade England as long as the RAF was up in the sky controlling who came and went over Britain.

As the Marines consolidated their hold on the Canal, the Japanese were striving to push the 1st Marine Division into the sea and retake the airfield they had started to build. The Japanese Navy was commanded by Admiral Yamomoto. He and his staff continued to underestimate the size and grit of the Guadalcanal Force. They stuffed troops and some supplies onto the island. Their Navy regularly bombarded Henderson, and planes bombed as well.

Yamamoto oversaw at least three concerted land based attempts to annihilate the Marines. These attacks took place in late August, mid September, and late October. The first was an ad hoc attempt to root out and destroy what the Japanese thought was merely a nuisance raid. The other two involved large naval forces, carriers, and fleets of transports in support of Army operations ashore. The planned attacks looked good on paper but were too complicated to work on the miserable terrain, in the jungle. Of course, the Marines and later the GIs had something to say about their failure, too.

The first attempt was simply inadequate—the 916 man 28th Brigade, hardened troops with China experience under Colonel Ichiki came ashore in August. This was an elite unit which had been slated to invade and occupy Midway Island in June. Of course there was no need for their services there so they were available for work in the Solomon Islands. Japanese intelligence had surmised that the Americans had only a large raiding party on the island. At that point of the war the Japanese regarded westerners as soft weaklings who were afraid to face the Nipponese fighting man. Ichiki's was a small force which made a frontal attack on prepared defenses. And it was wiped out almost to a man. One wonders what went through the Colonel's mind as he saw his unit torn to shreds. He did not charge the machine guns, rather he burned the regimental colors and committed suicide.

America had some elite, hardened troops as well. One such was a battalion of Marines called Edson's Raiders. This unit played an important role in the Guadalcanal campaign. In fact a case can be made they fought and won the pivotal land battle for the island.

The Marine Raiders were inspired by FDR's admiration of the British Commandoes. These elite troops were the precursors to today's US Navy Seals and similar units. The idea of the Raiders was not universally popular at the time The Marines considered that they were an elite group to start with, and saw little need for an elite unit within an elite unit. The purpose as FDR saw it was to have small units which could operate behind enemy lines, conduct raids, and perform nontraditional tasks. This is in fact how it worked out. Against some opposition, there were two Raider Battalions formed in early 1942. They both played a part in the opening offensive of the Pacific War.

There was the Second, under command of Lieutenant Colonel Lewis Carlson. This unit conducted a raid on Makin Atoll in the Marshall Islands. The Army would be back to take this real estate from the Japanese permanently in late 1943.("Makin taken," read the message announcing victory there.) The raid was staged in August, about the time citizens of Stalingrad were digging tank traps and Australians were desperately fighting Japanese along the Kokoda Track. The 2nd Raiders' incursion was intended to roughly coincide with and draw attention from the Guadalcanal and Tulagi landings. In fact the raid drew attention to Makin and the island was fortified perhaps more than it would have been, and the US Army had to take those fortifications later in the war.

The Second were delivered by submarine. They shot the place up but did little lasting damage. Aside from that there are two memorable facts associated with this action. First is that FDR's son James Roosevelt participated as an officer of the force. He did so creditably and with no special privileges. The other, sad, fact is that nine Marines were left stranded there. There was confusion about the exit rendezvous. The surf was rough and some Raiders drowned. It is unclear if no head count was taken or Carlson felt he was in danger of losing his entire force, or thought the nine were KIA. In any case, some Marines were left to fend for themselves. They were captured and executed, beheaded. In 2011 their mass grave was discovered on the island. The Second Raiders went on to serve elsewhere bravely and competently. They later performed a nearly flawless month long trek on the Canal. They went behind the lines on an extended raid, repeatedly hitting the Japanese and disappearing.

The First Raider Battalion was commanded by Lieutenant Colonel Merritt "Mike" Edson. He was known as "Red Mike."

He had red hair. His name also may have come from his politics. There is some speculation that he was sympathetic to the Communists he saw while on duty in 1930's China. Edson was a hard man and a fine leader. His Raider Battalion was formally set up in February 1942. The Colonel trained his men thoroughly and hard. He concentrated on small unit tactics, hit and run raids, and weapons proficiency. The Battalion was sent to the Pacific. It was attached to the 1st Marine Division and became part of the force sent to take Guadalcanal.

It was a major part of the invading force that took the isle of Tulagi on August 7. This island is 22 miles north of the Canal. It held the British colonial capital. One problem with any amphibious invasion is keeping the assault troops fit. There is little room to move and lots of time to kill when troops are being moved from port to the target. It was early in the war and no one really realized this might be a problem. The Marines were loaded on transports in July to go to the rehearsal then on to the big show. So on landing day, the 1st Marines and attached units had all been on transports at sea for about a month. They were unable to train or exercise much. Coming ashore even if unopposed after that much inactivity would have been physically difficult.

The 1st Marines were able to walk on and over Guadalcanal with very little opposition. Not so the Raiders on Tulagi. They had to fight their way onto the shore and inland. Being a little softened from the trip did not make things any easier. The Raiders and other Marine units were up to the challenge. They took Tulagi and several small nearby islands in about a day against determined but outnumbered opposition. After the first shooting, they had to dig the enemy out of underground shelters. They had to use dynamite charges and grenades to do so. Even at this stage of the war the Japanese troops held out in caves and bunkers which would easily withstand mere gunfire. The Marines learned one harsh lesson early on. This would be a war to the death, no quarter asked or given. They had to kill virtually every Japanese man there. The sons of Nippon did not surrender and could be captured only if wounded, unconscious, or somehow incapacitated.

After taking the island the Raiders went into bivouac and took garrison duty for a few weeks. During this short time they saw no combat, just rested and pulled guard duty. On August 30, they were moved over to Guadalcanal. Their skills and training for behind the line, hit and run operations were needed.

The Japanese had already sent one unit to destroy what they thought was just a reconnaissance force. They assumed the Americans would come ashore, explore the island, destroy the Japanese installations there, and then leave. The thinking was that the Americans just wanted to see what the Emperor's men were up to in the area. So Tokyo sent a unit to deal with the situation. They figured the unit sent had to be small enough to transport easily, but big enough to take care of itself and the Americans.

The unit chosen, made up of 916 men, landed August 17. It was the 28th Infantry Regiment under command of Colonel Ichiki. After brief scouting, he and his men rashly charged prepared defenses. They were wiped out. General Kawaguchi of the Imperial Japanese Army was then sent to the Canal. With him was a Brigade sized force (5000 men more or less) which Kawaguchi thought adequate to do the job. Vandegrift had a pretty good idea of what Kawaguchi intended to do. He had patrols out looking and listening, and native scouts fed him information too. He also received intelligence from a network of planters and other westerners who had stayed behind when the Japanese came. They were called the coastwatchers and used radios supplied by the Australians to warn of enemy movements. Vandegrift wanted to disrupt Kawaguchi's plans. To do so he tapped the 1st Raiders.

On September 8 the Raiders embarked on small coastal boats and headed west towards the settlement of Tasimboko. Edson wanted to find out where and how many the Japanese were. The Raiders met some opposition after coming ashore and found evidence of Kawaguchi's newly landed force. Life jackets and new gear was strewn around. The Japanese had apparently fled when the Raiders appeared. Apparently they feared a major assault and were not prepared to fight it. Edson led his men on in to the village of Tasimboko. They found and destroyed a radio station which Kawaguchi had intended to use to coordinate and control the units under his command. The raiders also destroyed a large stock of ammunition, estimated at half a million rounds. They found and took home food, medical supplies, and papers for intelligence analysis.

The destruction the Raiders wrought delayed and confused Kawaguchi in his planned offensive. What Edson's men saw on landing and the information they collected were valuable to analysts at Division headquarters. Vandegrift and his planning staff learned a lot from the raid about what specifically to expect from Kawaguchi. The Raiders returned to base that day having suffered only two killed and several wounded. The Japanese lost twenty seven lives and a number of wounded, and loss of ammunition and supplies.

Edson's Communications Officer was Captain William D. Stevenson. A recent graduate of Dartmouth, he had gone through the reserve officers training program there. He was commissioned and went on active duty after graduation. He was one of many Americans who in those days freely joined the military. Before embarking on life and career, a lot of men took it as an obligation to put in a stint in uniform. Men like Stevenson made the US Armed Forces a true citizens' Army even before the passage of the Selective Service Act, or the "draft." He may have been a civilian through and through, but he took the Raider training regimen to heart. As the Battalion Communications Officer, he insisted that every man in the commo platoon learn to operate every weapon and every communications system. He wanted his men to be able to step in and continue the job if someone fell or was wounded. Stevenson had a straightforward and understated view of things. For instance, writing home on August 25th, he was low key about the first battle. He wrote, "As you might have guessed from the recent activity and the news stories, I am on Tulagi Island in the Solomon Islands. It must have been a nice place before the war." The censor passed the name but Stevenson chose not to pass on any details of the fight.

Kawaguchi's scheme to dislodge the Marines from the airfield was a typical Japanese battle plan. It was slated for mid September.

The scheme had feints and a variety of units converging from several directions on the objective. He first planned to send in attacks along the coast on the east and west side of the American lodgment. These were essentially diversions. The main thrust would be put in by troops marching and pulling artillery through the jungle. The point of attack was below a ridge, south of the American lines. Japanese infantrymen would then attack uphill. The goal was to gain the ridge which runs more or less north and south like a javelin aimed at the airfield and the coast. Kawaguchi intended to take the ridge half a mile or so south of the airstrip. Once he had that high ground he could use it as a highway to feed troops in and take the field. He had several thousand men on the move to gather below the ridge, awaiting the time to attack. The plan was for the east and west beach and the ridge attacks all to go in simultaneously. The time was to be 2000 hours (8PM) on September 12.

Vandegrift saw the importance of that ridge as well. He already had units guarding the perimeter, including where the east and west beach attacks would come. He could not put up a solid fortified line all around the airfield because he didn't have enough men. What he did was to space the units so they were pretty much within supporting distance of each other. Then the General put Merritt Edson's 1st Raider Battalion on the ridge. They set up warning outposts ahead of their lines, laid barbed wire, sited their guns, had the artillery sight in on the terrain, got some rest as they could, and waited. The bare, jungle surrounded crest would become known as "Edson's Ridge." The pivotal battle that played out there is known as "The Battle for Edson's Ridge."

The action started September 12, after dark. The east and west attacks went in and were repulsed with little American loss. The attacks on the ridge got off to a ragged start around midnight. Kawaguchi had not allowed for the difficult geography. Men struggled with the terrain, with its steep volcanic ridges and gulleys. Arroyos, they would be called, in the American Southwest. They were steep sided, deep ravines across which men had to climb. All were in full combat gear and some were trying to pull mortars and small field artillery pieces. Going through a rain forest during the day it was not easy for them to determine just where they were. It was worse in the dark. Off and on rain, some of it heavy, did not help matters. Some men straggled, others fell out entirely. The result was that units were mixed up and arrived piecemeal at Kawaguchi's attack point. In the end he had less than half of his force available on site when he needed them. He had no reserve available.

The Raiders were the largest contingent of Americans on the ridge. There were also Marine Parachutists, Engineers, elements of the 2nd Battalion, 5th Marine Infantry Regiment, and artillery spotters from the 11th Marines (the artillery regiment). Kawaguchi had elements of the 4th, 24th, and 124th Infantry Regiments. They had to attack up the slope and the first surge was at 2130, 9:30, on the 12th. About this time the Japanese cruiser Sendai came into Ironbottom Sound and started lobbing shells at the ridge. It also used its powerful searchlights to illuminate it. The Raiders were hunkering in foxholes and many felt, well, naked up there. The author could find no accounts of how the Japanese infantryman felt about being illuminated. Lit up or not, the Japanese soldiers charged, not in one mass, but in seven or ten smaller attempts. The Raiders were not counting that closely nor were the Emperor's men. The attacks surged back and forth. Most of the action was between C Company of the Raiders and several companies of the 124th. Other than those two units, most of the Japanese and many Raiders didn't really shoot much that night.

Bravery and desperation were on display among American and Japanese alike. As dawn lit the sky on the 13th, Raiders held the high ground. But many Japanese had infiltrated and were sniping at any marine or flier they saw. A small contingent of Nipponese soldiers even got within bayonet distance of the division Command Post. They were killed before they got in. It took some time to find and eliminate all the snipers and infiltrators. The Raiders had been driven out of some prepared positions below the heights but still had the ridge. The men rested up, deepened foxholes, cleared lanes of fire. Edson sent out men to regain territory lost, and generally straightened and strengthened lines.

Kawaguchi's men were in the jungle below the ridge. Some units which had been late the night before were readying to renew the attack after dark. Larger, more coordinated attacks were planned and carried out. The Raiders, parachutists, engineers and marines were up there, shooting back. Some Japanese destroyers came into Ironbottom Sound and fired 5 inch shells up and down the ridge for half an hour or so. The infantry attacks up the hill started, in seemingly endless waves. Marines called in artillery, nearer and nearer to their lines as the Japanese surged up and sometimes onto the ridge. They were never able to take the heights. The fighting was desperate, confused, and bloody. Scores of marines and hundreds, maybe a few thousand, Japanese died.

Captain Stevenson was in the thick of it. Along with the Raiders and others, he and his men were fighting. Also, they were keeping the phone wires spliced, the radios working, the messages delivered by runner, making sure the word got out to the Marines. Edson moved men back and forth in the dark, called for more ammunition, pulled outlying men back, and managed the battle. But to do so, he had to communicate up and down the line and with Division Command Post. The fact is that Raider battalion's communications never failed. That was one key element to the Raider's success. Stevenson himself received the Navy Cross for leading a recon patrol, maintaining the communications net uninterrupted until infiltrating Japanese cut the phone wires behind him, and calling artillery fire down virtually on top of himself.

In a letter home, written in January, he tells of actually receiving the medal:

"Today was a red-letter day....Admiral Halsey, Commander of all the forces in the South Pacific, (COMSOPAC), came out to camp to pin 23 medals on us. He presented me with the Navy Cross 'for extraordinary heroism in action against the enemy,' the Navy's highest honor except the Congressional Medal of Honor, and I was very overawed and knock-kneed. Five of my men were decorated, one Navy Cross and four Silver Stars for gallantry in action against the enemy.

Admiral Halsey certainly impressed me. He is a real fightin' man who knows his ships and his men. He gave us a fine, short but fightin' talk. The glitter of his four stars rendered me temporarily blind, and I must have looked rather stupid when he pinned the medal on me. I probably will never see four stars again. While I feel greatly honored, it is sad to think that the real heros were not here to get their medals."

The citation read:

"For extraordinary heroism in action against the enemy during the defense of the Guadalcanal Airport on the night of September 13–14, 1942. Captain STEVENSON, battalion communications officer, daringly led a reconnaissance patrol to reconnoiter the left flank of the battalion reserve line and determine the location of hostile troops enveloping that flank. With utter disregard for his own personal safety and while exposed to severe enemy rifle and machine gun fire, he skillfully directed the scouting of enemy positions. He was then ordered to return to the battalion command post to supervise the maintenance of wire communication to the division command post. In carrying out this mission he remained at the battalion switchboard even after all other command post personnel had displaced to a position in the rear. In spite of the fact that his position was entirely surrounded by a group of infiltrating Japanese, he continued to maintain communication with the division command post and with the supporting artillery until the wires to the rear were cut by the enemy. His unflinching bravery and courageous conduct were in keeping with the highest traditions of the Naval Service."

Many other survivors also earned medals in this battle. Edson received the Congressional Medal of Honor.

After the Edson's Ridge Battle, the Raiders went to bivouac for a short time. The battalion stayed on the Canal and fought as regular infantry in some later forays along the Matanikau River.

They also fought in other efforts to enlarge and bolster the lines. The unit made no other behind the lines raids and undertook no further special missions. The surviving 1st Raiders were evacuated from Guadalcanal in December, leaving about the time Vandegrift handed the island over to Army general Patch.

They took a period of rest, refit and restaffing in New Caledonia, Australia and New Zealand. They were called to the front again in July. The 1st Raiders did some behind the lines work in the New Georgia campaign. This island is in the middle of the Solomons chain, perhaps two hundred and fifty miles north of the Canal. It boasted an airfield the Japanese had built the previous November that the Allies wanted for themselves. The Raiders attacked overland. Their objectives were the north coast towns of Enogai and Bairoko. This offensive was in support of the Army's attack to take the airfield on the south coast.

They found that the roles had switched. This time it was the Japanese who had the fortified interior lines. It was now the Raiders who were trying to muck through the jungle to get at them, doing so on near starvation food supplies. They found it difficult to gain the objective, indeed they failed to take the town of Enogai. It was not a particularly successful part of the campaign. The Army did take the airfield in August after prolonged fighting. The Raiders were sent back to Guadalcanal to rest and refit. Cactus was by then a rear area.

The Raider Battalions played an important part in the first phase of the Pacific War. That period was first defensive and retreating, then stopping the Japanese tide, finally reversing it. The Marines, Navy and Army bent, but held. They in time took the initiative in late 1942 into 1943. In that period, and fighting that type of warfare, the Raiders excelled. They slashed, hit and ran, and were ferocious fighters. The second part of the War, from late 1943 on, had little call for swashbuckling, behind the lines work. That later phase of the war saw squadrons of aircraft carriers, huge fleets, and whole divisions attacking small islands. When you have fifty ships and 25000 men overwhelming an islet of only eight or ten square miles size, there is simply no need for the likes of

Merritt Edson, Bill Stevenson, and other Raiders. Industrial warfare as opposed to entrepreneurial warfare, if you will….

In one of the most crucial and finest moments in the Pacific war, when the Raiders were needed on the Canal, they delivered.

In late October the Emperor's men tried again. A scenario similar to the run-up to Edson's Ridge played out in late October, from the 20th to 24^{th,}, in the Battle For Henderson Field. Again, the intention was to deliver a decisive Japanese hammer blow from several directions, all at once. But weather, terrain, mismanagement, and American interference caused the "hammer blow" to be delivered piecemeal over several days. The Nipponese troops were defeated in detail by Marines and newly arrived GIs. The GIs were green but they acquitted themselves well. They went into their first action, units broken up piecemeal. The GI's were fed into foxholes next to Marines two and three at a time, led in the dark in the rain to their posts. These GI's were from a National Guard unit from North Dakota and upper midwest states, and they gave better than they got in the Battle for Henderson Field. This is the first appearance of US Army ground forces in the Solomons, and it boded well for American aspirations and plans there.

The Nipponese plan was for this action, the Battle for Henderson Field, to be part of a coordinated operation. Army troops were to work with the benefit of a fleet of bombarding cruisers and battleships. It was all to be protected by carriers providing distant cover. The carriers were involved at the naval Battle of Santa Cruz Islands. It was fought by Japanese and American carriers on October 26. The Japanese Navy lost over 100 planes and pilots. The Americans lost the carrier Hornet. Even so, the Japanese did not retake the 'Canal.

Around the globe, far from the South Pacific, the war ground on. A significant but little known early November event is the clearing of Madagascar. This is a big island off the east coast of Africa. Having been a French colony, it had been in control of Vichy France. As such it was available to and was occasionally used as a base by German and Japanese submarines as they preyed on Allied shipping. The British had invaded in May but it was

November 5 before the remnants of the Vichy government surrendered. The securing of Madagascar made the sea lanes to Egypt and India safer. It also meant one less part of the sea which needed to be closely monitored and patrolled by the Royal Navy.

CHAPTER IV
November 9

Warriors and Administrators; Russia; Technology

On November 9 Operation Torch was progressing well.

The Allied invasion of northwest Africa was firmly established ashore. After sharp fights at the landing beaches, the shooting had subsided. There were three separate landing zones in Torch. General Dwight Eisenhower was in overall command. American General Patton commanded the troops that landed in Morocco. His GIs had come straight from ports in the mainland United States. The fleet had had an uneventful transit, with no Uboat losses or attacks. Patton oversaw three separate landings in Morocco. His troops came ashore at Safi, Rabat and Port Lyautey, all on the Atlantic coast. By the second day of the invasion, he was starting to consolidate his gains and was already preparing to drive towards Algeria. There had been some ground opposition inland but it had been overcome.

The second landing zone was under the Central Task Force commanded by American General Fredenhall. This fleet had sailed from Britain through the Straits of Gibraltar. It had landed at Oran, Algeria and met considerable opposition. The French had surrendered but only after gallant and stiff fighting.

Also in Algeria, the Eastern Task Force under British General Ryder came ashore at Algiers. This force too had to overcome considerable opposition. This Task Force lost two destroyers while bombarding and covering the invasion. After French opposition was silenced, the Allied troops started pushing east towards Tunisia.

North Africa was considered by the French as part of France. It was protected by the French Army and Navy answering to the Vichy government. American and British planners had hoped that French Forces might receive the Allies with open arms, at least with minimal opposition. America made diplomatic efforts before the landings to try to minimize bloodshed. Robert Murphy, a State Department official, was sent there under cover to open discussions. Give him credit for effort, but he was trying to box with one arm tied behind his back. He couldn't divulge when and where or even if the invasion would occur. Even so he tried to get agreement not to oppose any invasion. His efforts were only partially successful. French forces did in fact oppose the landings. In many cases after a show to satisfy honor the fighting subsided. In most of the landing sites a truce was shortly arranged.

Almost immediately, the German commander in the Mediterranean acted. Field Marshal Kesselring was the top German commander in the Mediterranean. He immediately started sending reinforcements. By every available means he sent Axis troops from Italy to northern Tunisia. Boatloads and planeloads landed in Tunis, Bizerta, and other Tunisian coastal towns. He managed to send in a total of some 112,000 troops, about 81,000 German and 31,000 Italians. Kesselring faced the commander's dilemma of having to feed and arm his men after he got them there. He needed some 24,000 tons overall of supplies per month in order to continue operations. The Luftwaffe flew in food and arms from Italy and Sicily. At the peak of their efficiency 585 tons were being delivered by air daily. This was below the ideal amount but with surface supply it sufficed. Allied air and surface efforts eventually cut into this and by spring less than 190 tons were coming in by air each day.

These additional troops secured the Tunis-Bizerta area of northern Tunisia and started moving west and south. Kessleing had two aims. First was to reinforce and secure the Axis foothold in Africa. Second was to protect Afrika Korps' rear and be sure it wouldn't be caught in a vise. Montgomery's 8th Army was headed west and Eisenhower's forces were heading east. The Allied commanders of course intended to close the vise which Kesselring wanted to keep open. It took only a few days before Allied and Axis forces met and clashed in northwest Tunisia and northeast Algeria. They would fight and contest ownership of northern Tunisia for months yet.

There was action towards the east end of the Mediterranean Sea as well. Montgomery with his Eighth Army and Desert Air Force were pursuing Rommel's Afrika Korps west from El Alamein. On the 9th, The British X and XXX Corps took Sidi Barrani in western Egypt. The 8th Army remained a multinational effort, with New Zealand, British, Australian, Polish, French, Indian, and others in on the pursuit. One of the biggest problems Montgomery had was supplying his lead troops. Getting adequate arms, food and gasoline to them was a task which took an increasing share of resources. They were moving fast and he wanted to keep them, and their prey, to keep moving fast.

The German plan for invading Russia was named Operation Barbarossa. Frederick I, head of the Holy Roman Empire in the 1100's, went by this name which translates as 'Red Beard'. He is considered among the greatest of Holy Roman Emperors. Hitler considered himself in the same league and insisted on the name for the operation.

As the invasion opened, dive bombers and armored spearheads followed by infantry were sent not only towards Leningrad and Kiev, but at first and especially, Moscow. The German effort to take the Soviet capitol almost succeeded. In it, the 9th Army covered the Nazi's left flank. Its job was to hold the shoulder and isolate the objective on the north. At first the Red Army retreated but later went on the attack.

From July 1941, Wehrmacht forces held Rzhev. This city of 50,000 is 140 miles west of Moscow and held a strategic crossroads. In German hands it was a spear pointed at Moscow; the Soviets wanted it as a protective shield. A number of battles were fought in and around the city. Over time the battles drew in more forces on both sides; Red Army Generals Zhukov and Koniev both oversaw some of the fighting. This went on until October 1942. It was only then that the Soviets were able to slowly move the Wehrmacht back.

Each side suffered immense casualties. Soviet troops came to call the area 'the Rzhev meat grinder'. The Russians lost over 300,000 men; the Germans some 60-75,000. In comparison, the Americans lost just over 400,000 men in all operations, all theaters, the whole of the war.

This series of battles was essentially a backwater to operations in Leningrad, Stalingrad and the Caucasus. Even so it was big enough to be the main show anywhere but in Russia. The Western Allies didn't field or face similar sized armies until Overlord and D-Day in 1944.

Rzhev is another showcase of the sheer size, complexity, and misery arising from the war in the east.

Another chapter in the worldwide struggle continued far away. It was a huge distance, some two thousand to the northeast. It was also taking place in its own unique and wildly different environment. In the Mediterranean theater armies were chasing each other over huge, sandy distances. They also put up with sun, heatstroke, scorpions, thirst, and radiators boiling dry. But on the steppes of Asia conditions were as different as they could be. Troops here endured mud, snow, ice, and frostbite. There was no running pursuit in this fight. Here, in an area about the size of the Island of Manhattan, a quarter of a million men were locked in close quarter fighting. In south Russia, the rains and mud of fall morphed quickly into the weapons of General Winter: cold, snow and ice. The battle for Stalingrad continued.

The Germans had for some time targeted this city. The 1941 invasion came to a halt in the winter. But the Nazi offensive had started again in the spring, as soon as the roads and airfields dried. Panzer tanks and infantry swept hundreds of miles east from their winter camps. In 1942, Hitler wanted this town. He had good strategic and tactical reasons. The Germans had long targeted the line of the Volga as a stopping point. Stalingrad was situated on the western shore of that immense river. Hitler wanted a defensible line to mark and hold Nazi conquests. And he wanted to dominate and strangle a major symbol of Soviet identity, transport and commerce. The Volga is important to Russia. It is as meaningful as the Yangtze is to China or the Mississippi is to the US. Standing astride the Volga would give the Nazi propaganda machine something to crow about. It would also give the Werhmacht a good place to make a defense against attack by the Red Army. Hitler may have had another, perhaps subliminal reason for wanting to take it. Hitler's men conquering Stalin's town would give a lift to the Axis, and dampen the spirits of the Russians.

Stalin had good, logical military and strategic reasons to resist. This city was an industrial center and an strategic crossing of the River Volga. In addition he may have had a similar subliminal reason for wanting to keep it. No matter. It likely would have been fought over if it had been called something else. Stalingrad, Tsaritsyn, Volgagrad, by any name it was important in its own right.

Hitler had not clearly thought through his plans for Russia. Yes, he clearly wanted to conquer it. But he was not so clear when it came to directing armies in where and how to do it. He had literally been sending troops back and forth, directing whole armies here and then there. In 1941, he had wavered between taking Leningrad, Moscow, and the Ukraine. He had moved forces around from front to front, often taking troops away just as they were about to take their objective. And reworking the logistical organization and arrangements took time and resources, which were limited for everyone. It is possible that he forever lost the chance to take Moscow in fall 1941. He had troops within sight of the city walls and they had momentum. But he then stripped troops and moved them south to take the Ukraine. Similarly, he had waffled in spring 1942, shuttling troops around and between Stalingrad, the Ukraine and the Caucasus. His generals tried to stop and discourage such meddling. No one dared disobey or come out and frankly question his thinking. The Fuhrer had absolute, life and death power. He used it freely. So, after early in the year directing troops elsewhere, in mid summer 1942 he decided his war machine should, after all, take Stalingrad.

This decision was executed in August. This was about the time the US Marines were getting acquainted with Guadalcanal, Tulagi, and the jungle. At the same time the Japanese Army was pushing the Australian militia south over the Kokoda Track in New Guinea, and General Patton was going over plans and orders for his upcoming assault on Morocco.

Long sweltering summer days saw things start to heat up even more for the citizens of Stalingrad. Luftwaffe bombers started hitting the city. Panzers and German infantry approached in September. The city was not the usual symmetrical shape built up around a cross roads or a river junction. Rather it was three to five miles deep but thirty five miles long. And, it was built up only on the west side of the Volga River. To the east stretched the steppes, treeless plains not unlike western Kansas.

By mid September the Germans had pushed forces clear to the banks of the Volga. They stood along it to the north and south of the main part of Stalingrad. The central part of the city was still in Russian hands. Pinching off the central Soviet held part was the plan. Nazi columns from north and south would fight towards each other. They would meet in the middle, crushing out opposition and destroying whatever Russian forces were there. Similar tactics had been used repeatedly with good results. The Germans expected to succeed again here. Around the world, many hoped they would not succeed but feared and half expected that they would.

Russians, both civilians and the red Army, fought hard, contesting every inch. Again, the logistical ogre appeared. German General Paulus and his Sixth Army were at the end of a very long supply line. This line was protected on its flanks by Romanian, Hungarian, and Italian troops. The Sixth Army and its Axis allies were kept supplied but with some difficulty. Trucks, horse drawn wagons, trains and planes all contributed. They kept ammunition, food, and gasoline coming and took out the wounded. By this time, the first half of November, winter was threatening. The Volga hadn't frozen and snowstorms were intermittent. Roads and fields were muddy rather than frozen solid. People were chilled but not frostbitten. It was just a matter of time before the season definitively changed.

The Red Army and many civilians had been fighting the Germans. Civilians had been digging tank obstacles as early as late summer. General Lopatin, commander of the 64th Army had been running the battle. He was relieved in September. Not unlike a developing problem in the South Pacific, Stalin and senior Generals saw that he simply lacked the fire, the imagination, the energy for the job.

A unique, aggressive and single minded general replaced him. General Chuikov was commander of the 62nd Army. In September, Stalin gave him command of the city and the battle. He had a plan in mind to defeat the Nazis. Chuikov had his soldiers and many civilians fight for every house, every rubble pile, every meter of ground. He was merciless. He did not hesitate to have deserters or stragglers shot. After the battle, he acknowledged having ordered the deaths of over ten thousand Soviet citizens who failed to measure up. But his style of urban close in fighting was to the Russians' advantage. Buildings and factories, hills, street corners, even sewers, would change hands. Some changed several times a day, some every few days. Chuikov insisted his army stay within fifty to one hundred meters of the enemy. He kept his headquarters that close to the action. He wanted to set an example and more importantly to keep a finger on the pulse of the battle. This worked to his army's strengths and to the German's weaknesses.

The German successes came from shock tactics, blitzkrieg was their name for it. This form of war had tanks running free behind enemy lines shooting things up and causing confusion. Dive bombers sowed terror with their explosives, their flamboyant attacks, the sirens which shrieked as they dove. Then the infantry came along and secured the area, mopping up any remaining opposition. It was a war of movement and it kept the initiative in German hands. These methods had been used repeatedly and with virtual impunity for a long time. Blitzkrieg was something the Germans were good at. However, the German Army was not trained nor equipped for urban, close quarter fighting.

Chuikov recognized this and came up with a counter to their operations. The Germans were made to fight in ways they hadn't had to before. Gone were the days of movement, of shooting up and surrounding whole armies. Now they had to fight things out street by street, man to man, building by building, scrabbling for every block, every rubble pile, every bombed out building. And they often had to go back and retake a street or building because the Russians would infiltrate at night and fire on their rear. Quite different from their conquests in France or Poland!

The Russians were able to feed fresh troops in across the Volga. They also scoured their jails for prisoners who they made fight in penal battalions. And some residents had stayed to fight for their homes. The point is, they took advantage of their interior lines. Their tactics worked, killing Germans and making them use up supplies. And they never did permit the Nazi pincers to join up. The two arms of the Wehrmacht looked to meet and crush the Russians between them. They did not even get within visual range of each other. They never did unite and push the Red Army from Stalingrad. The Russians held the Germans out, bleeding them almost white. Buildings became fortresses, sewers became lairs, every heap of debris was a sniper's hide or maybe a booby trap. The Red October Tractor Factory in the northern part of the city never did fall. It was not usable as a tank factory late in the battle. By then it was just walls with part of its roof shot away and pockmarked by artillery. That factory was to Stalingrad what Stalingrad was to Russia—a symbol of guts and determination not to give in.

The Germans and Russians were fighting in many other places across the miles. In the north, the town of Kirkenes is just inside the Norwegian side of the Russian border. The fighting there was severe and prolonged. In fact, Kirkenes suffered more bombing than most any other town in the war. When one considers what happened to Malta, London, Berlin, Dresden, or Tokyo, it is clear that the fighting in northern Norway between Nazi and Red Army was intense indeed. A ways south of there, near the southern Russian-Finnish border, the Germans held their siege, their near stranglehold on the city of Leningrad. This city was originally built by Czar Peter the Great and modestly named Saint Petersburg. Before the Russian Revolution it was the Imperial capital, built as Czar Peter's window on the west. He intended to modernize Russia and started with St Petersburg. It was an industrial and commercial powerhouse, a port on the Baltic. Wehrmacht forces had surrounded that city in 1941. They were on the verge of taking it when Hitler withdrew troops for some offensive to the south. Some Leningraders were evacuated but most stayed. The city was almost wholly besieged for several years and the citizenry suffered greatly. During winter months the city received some supplies by truck convoy over frozen lakes. Later there was limited rail service. Even so, many starved, thousands every month. All suffered. German artillery and the Luftwaffe added to the misery and death.

Russia is immense. The Germans had several Army Groups fighting there. That amounts to somewhere around a million or so men. In the far south, the Germans designated their forces Army Group A. That Group had pushed into southern Russia. They were in the Caucasus, near the borders of Turkey and Iran. And they had the Maikop oilfields. Petroleum was the grail, what Hitler wanted and needed to keep his war machine running. Taking the oilfields was why Hitler had diverted troops from Leningrad and Moscow early in the campaign. He overrode his generals' objections because he deemed the oil more important than any one city. Time would tell if that was a good call. In any case, the call was made. Germans had taken Maikop in August. However, the oil field and its machinery were thoroughly destroyed by retreating Russians. No significant amount of oil was ever taken out by the Germans.

Mount Elbrus is in the Russian Caucasus. It is Europe's highest point at 5633 meters. It was climbed by Germans. This happened on August 21, 1942, just about the time Marines were greeting the first American planes onto Henderson Field. On that date, a group of twenty three men from the German First and Fourth Mountain Divisons planted the Swastika flag on top. Expedition leaders were Hauptmanns Heinz Groth and Max Gammerler. This marked the furthest point to the south and east that the Wehrmacht ever got.

The high point, so to speak. Hitler was angry when he heard about this alpine trek. He went on an enraged shouting spree, yelling that troops who should have been fighting were wasting time hiking up a mountain. Perhaps. It seems unlikely that an additional twenty three men would have made a lot of difference in the big scheme of things.

Farther on around the globe, battles were being fought in yet another environment. It was neither sandy nor icy, but had islands, mud, jungle, and disease. The campaign in the Solomon Islands was reaching a boil. Since late August the Japanese had been able to regularly reinforce their troops on Guadalcanal. They did this not all at once, but by loading troops and supplies nightly onto destroyers and transports which then ran in under cover of dark. Night flight was not done in those days, at least not intentionally. It was too hazardous. Reliable instrument flying was a project in some aviation engineer's or crazy pilot's imagination. So ships could freely and safely come and go after dark.

If the Japanese supply fleet timed it right they would stay out of reach of the Cactus Air Force in the afternoon, and be gone back north out of range in the morning. This went on night after night, and Marines called it "The Tokyo Express." As a bonus several of the Emperor's warships would shoot up Henderson Field while the transports were unloading. This not only injured and killed men, it damaged planes, runways and maintenance facilities, and morale. This was an ongoing issue for the Americans. They could not stop the Japanese from reinforcing and bombarding. Far away, in Honolulu and Washington DC, people were starting to see this problem. Senior admirals were beginning to think a change of some sort was needed.

At a very basic level, nations win wars by wise management of their people and resources. When it comes to people, there are two basic types: warriors and administrators. Every viable organization has them, call them what you will—doers and minders, entrepreneurs and managers, outside sales and inside sales. Both types are needed. There is a time for each to come to the fore. During normal times with business as usual, administrators come into their own as they manage processes and people. They embody the old saying, "a place for everything and everything in its place." But when things are in crisis, when matters are literally life or death, the warriors come to the fore. This is so for a business struggling for economic life or a sports team down by a point near the final buzzer. Someone, some fighter, always steps up and gives a valiant effort to make the sale, hit the run, manufacture a new model, whatever is needed to seize a victory.

This is especially true in the military. By its structured and seniority based nature, those who rise in peacetime are good rule followers. They are good organization administrators. By definition, they are not chance takers or opportunity makers. Officers who show the skill and patience to rise to seniority and fill responsible peacetime positions are not necessarily the fighters needed in wartime. But the talented warrior by nature shakes things up. He (in the twenty first century, he or she) tries things, takes risks, asks "Why not?," believes it better to ask forgiveness than permission. These traits limit advancement most of the time in the peacetime military. But they are needed when the bullets start flying.

Senior officers recognized these facts and generally tried to match the person with the job's demands. General Marshall, Chief of Staff of the Army, had to clear a lot of deadwood when he took office in 1939. One instance of this is how he reached down in the seniority lists to promote Eisenhower. When he made Eisenhower a general in late 1941, he reached way down the seniority lists. There were more than one hundred eligible men more senior than Eisenhower whom he bypassed. This is because he recognized that while able, those men were by and large good peacetime soldiers, not warriors. Another example of this is General Douglas MacArthur calling his air force chief, General George Kenney, "a pirate." This was not criticism. It was a compliment. Kenney had the right combination of aggressiveness, innovation, leadership, strategic vision, and organizational savvy. He made his fliers a skilled and integral part of MacArthur's Command and its successes.

America's South Pacific Command was the hot seat of the war in the autumn of 1942. It was the highest profile theater of war in the American press and public consciousness. It was where the Americans and Japanese were facing off on more or less equal terms. Of course it wasn't the only battleground but it was the most visible one. The military acronym for the area commander was ComSoPac, short for Commander South Pacific. The man who held it would raise or lower the bar, set the standard, for US Theater commanders everywhere in the world. His actions, decisions, and results would set precedents and steer the future. He would influence not only the tone and direction of the Pacific War, but also influence events, tactics and strategy in other theaters.

But not every wartime personnel choice was the appropriate one for the job. The first ComSoPac was Admiral Robert L Ghormley. He had had a respectable career. After graduating from the Naval Academy he spent time as a line officer and also did aide and observer duty. In 1940 he was the US Naval observer in Britain. He saw and reported on the Battle of Britain and the Blitz, when London was bombed every night for weeks straight. This was a critical time for Britain and he served ably and well as eyes and ears of the US Navy. He returned home in 1941.

On May 17 1942 he was named commander of the newly formed South Pacific Area. It was a new position and he had to staff it, set it up, determine priorities, set the tone, and fight for resources, all while holding off the encroaching Japanese. At the time no one knew that in a few months the job would become the focal point of the US war effort. Ghormley was an intelligent, able, knowledgeable officer. He drew on his experience in administrative and aide positions as well as line commands. On paper he was a good fit for the ComSoPac slot. But the demands of the job soon revealed that he lacked the skills and vigor to fill what was probably the most demanding, active and public role of the war up to that time. The man appeared to be overwhelmed. He rarely left his office. Visitors remarked that he seemed harried and fatigued. Ghormley never visited Guadalcanal nor any of the forward bases. He never left New Caledonia. In fact he never so much as sent his chief of staff or some other aide to observe and report. He was practically a detached observer during the planning and preparation for the Guadalcanal invasion, providing scant guidance or leadership. He openly talked to his boss Admiral Nimitz about his fears and doubts of holding the island. Overall he showed defeatism, exhaustion, and lack of support for the front line. These traits alone made Admiral Nimitz think a change was called for. The demonstrated ability of the Japanese to send reinforcements and bombard Henderson Field added to that opinion. He consulted with his boss, Admiral King, and got the okay to name a replacement. In October he was seriously considering Admiral Bill Halsey to be the replacement.

Background on Halsey is interesting in itself even had he not played a major role in the War. The admiral was a colorful character and an able and experienced officer. He graduated from the Naval Academy and served well in destroyers during World War I. When he was older than fifty he somehow got himself admitted to the Naval Pilot program. He took the course and passed it, becoming a certified Naval Pilot. He never served as a pilot but he did serve as Captain of some of the early US Navy aircraft carriers.

The week before the Pearl Harbor attack he was leading a carrier force at sea delivering planes to Wake Island. The US was not at war but he saw the (Japanese) handwriting on the wall. He put his crews on war orders, shoot to kill. Even though no formal war had been declared he thought the safety of his men and ships important enough to go out on a limb. He wanted his fleet to be alert. Needless to say, among the sailors of the fleet he had a fighter's reputation. That status was polished when he went on to head up the first American carrier raids of the war.

These were raids on the enemy held islands of the Gilbert and Marshall Groups of islands. Taking place about seven weeks after Pearl Harbor, they were a mere swipe at the Emperor's nose. Places like Roi, Kwajalein, Wotje, and Makin were then little known island dots in the middle of the Pacific. But they would become better known two years later. These islands were among the first stops for the Army, Navy and Marines in November 1943. That is when the US stormed through on the way to the Marianas, Iwo Jima, and Tokyo.

In April, Halsey led the fleet which delivered the Doolittle Raid on Tokyo. It was so called after its commander, Lieutenant Colonel James Doolittle of the Army Air Corps. In terms of damage done, the heavy bombers he led to bomb Japan did not do a whole lot. From that point of view, this raid was nothing to write home about. It cast a long shadow, however. It proved that America was coming back and would hit back. It lifted American public morale. American innovation showed through in that carriers delivered land based bombers to the Emperor's doorstep, something generally thought impossible.

This incursion humiliated the admirals and generals at Imperial Headquarters. They were so shamed they looked for ways to hit back themselves. They tried to maneuver the US Navy into battle near the Midway Island where it could be destroyed. That is a story in itself; suffice it to say that most of the destroying was done by, not to, the US Navy. Halsey led several more carrier raids in the South Pacific later in the spring. About that time the stress and fatigue from multiple combat patrols combat caused him a case of shingles and he was put on medical leave. Even with mild health issues, it is clear that Admiral Halsey was a fighter. He was not averse to taking risks, indeed he sought and relished them. He was willing to experiment and innovate.

After several months' convalescence he was put back on active status in the fall. In October, Nimitz had seen and heard enough, and was ready to make a change in the South Pacific. Halsey was on Nimitz' short list of candidates to take the ComSoPac job over. In late October Halsey was sent to the area, ostensibly to inspect progress in the area. At that time, the powers that be had seen enough. The Chief of the Army Air Corps, the US Secretary of War, and the Commandant of the Marine Corps had all visited the area. The Secretary and the Commandant in fact visited Guadalcanal. On the way there they had gone through Noumea and met Ghormley. Each of those senior government officers was of the opinion that the job was too much for him. The consensus among those senior officers was that he had to go. Accordingly, orders were awaiting Halsey on his "inspection trip." On his arrival in Noumea he received written instructions to take over as ComSoPac immediately. The story, perhaps apocryphal, is that Halsey said "Jesus Christ and General Jackson! This is the hottest potato they ever handed me!" Ghormley was an old friend of Halsey's and it had to be awkward for both, but the change was made immediately.

The Frenchman in charge (New Caledonia was a French colony) had been a reluctant host to the US Navy. He had refused to make a building available to Ghormley for offices. One of the first things Halsey did was to seize what had been the Japanese Consulate for use as his headquarters ashore. This aggressiveness and focus was a foretaste of what would come under the new commander.

His taking over was a breath of fresh air. He was well known to the Marines, GIs and sailors who had to do the fighting and dying. Sailors throughout SoPac cheered, literally cheered, when his appointment was announced. Halsey was not one to just sit in an office and read reports and fill out forms. One of the first things he did was to get Vandegrift and other senior officers together in Noumea. He wanted to meet them and take stock, and get everyone on the same page. The admiral asked Vandegrift if he could hold the island. The Marine answered yes, he could. Halsey then promised the Marines and GIs there everything he had in support of the mission. And he went out to see Guadalcanal for himself.

On November 7 Halsey flew in to Cactus. This is just about the time the US and British fleets were getting ready to open fire on Morocco and Algeria. Around the world, the new ComSoPac toured Guadalcanal, the air base, and the beach defenses. He intended to spend the night. It was a good opportunity to look things over. It was also a time ask questions of officers and men, and to listen to their answers. He also awarded some medals.

Probably the most memorable and impressive part of the trip for him occurred after dark. Like most nights, Nipponese cruisers and destroyers came calling. They had escorted some supply ships down on their nightly run. The troop transports unloaded their cargo of troops and supplies at the Japanese beaches. While they were doing that, the warships gave the American area a good working over. It was not a shelling specifically aimed at the new

ComSoPac or some other special mission. It was just a routine plastering of Henderson Field. This was the Admiral's first time on the receiving end of a naval bombardment. He talked later of being scared even though as the senior officer present, he ordered himself not to be. He was not alone. Many men felt fear that night, not just William Halsey.

This trip is vintage Halsey: there was no substitute, no other way to learn the conditions. And if he wanted men to fight, it was important to get a taste of what the Marines, sailors, flyers and GIs in the field routinely underwent. Before he flew out to Noumea the next day, he again promised Vandegrift his support. This visit was a boost to morale throughout the Canal and Tulagi.

As part of the promised support, Halsey and staff decided the main task was to disrupt and end the nightly Japanese reinforcement convoy and bombardment run. He had personally tasted their bombardment. He wanted to put an end to it because it was terrifying for his men, and it made their job much more difficult. The SoPac theater was receiving men and planes, and had available a number of ships. It was early in the war. The gigantic armies, air forces, and navies the US fielded in 1944 and 1945 were still being built and trained. There weren't the resources nor the time to organize every fleet and every battalion. Units were sent into the fire of battle as they came into the theater. Ships were thrown into the fight with little or no chance to work together. Time was short and no fleet or task force had the chance to rehearse. Sometimes there wasn't time to have more than a quick review of a commander's battle plans and ideas. More than a few ships went to battle in the early part of the Pacific War with a plan from the commander that was almost this simple: "Follow me and conform to my movements."

Be that as it may, Halsey had promised support. He was determined to do his best to stop the nightly reinforce and bombard routine the Japanese put on. On November 9, the day after Halsey returned to Noumea, ComSoPac ordered Rear Admiral Norman Scott forward with a force of four cruisers and five destroyers. His orders were to escort a reinforcement and supply convoy there.

Then he was to report to senior authority and take steps to disrupt or stop the bombardments.

Now it turns out that Admiral Scott had local battle experience, a rare commodity for US admirals in the Solomons. He had commanded the US side in an Ironbottom Sound fracas, the Naval Battle of Cape Esperance on October 11 into the 12th. In this clash Scott had led his nine ship fleet against Admiral Goto whose fleet had three cruisers and two destroyers. Goto was covering (what else?) a separate bombardment and reinforcement group. Scott, learning from the Japanese, had arranged his fleet to maximize effectiveness. He used his radar and trusted what it told him. He saw Goto before Goto saw him so Scott was able to get in the first punch. His men sunk a cruiser and a destroyer at cost of one US destroyer. Even though Goto was killed and his ship was put out of action, the convoy he was covering did its job. The troop reinforcements landed and the shore bombardment was made. Cactus Air Force made them pay the next day by sinking two of the bombarding destroyers as they retreated.

The point is, in this battle Scott used his radar and surprise to his advantage. Had the US Navy built on Scott's action and experience, perhaps more Japanese ships would have been sunk, sooner. The night's events showed that Americans could fight the Japanese on even terms. He was the first US admiral to trust and use the radar. His victory proved that the night did not belong to the Imperial Japanese Navy. Now, a month later, Scott was coming north with a small fleet to again contest the Japanese reinforcement convoys.

The Japanese military had worked for years to develop night fighting skills and tactics. Both branches of the Emperors forces excelled at this art. The Imperial Japanese Army had practiced and innovated night infiltration and movement since the Generals in charge of World War II had been junior officers. They used these techniques to great advantage in their early campaigns of conquest. The Imperial Navy too had long practiced night maneuvering and formation keeping. They also stressed the skills of ship sighting and identification. The practice sessions were realistic and more than one sailor was lost overboard during exercises. The purpose was to excel at spotting the enemy at great distances. In ship to ship battles, getting the salvos and torpedoes ranged and aimed is important. Getting the first shot off is critical. Making the first punch often makes the difference between victory and loss, between a watery grave and a homecoming. The Imperial Japanese Navy used and improved these fighting in the dark skills during early campaigns. They certainly put them into practice to damage and sink US warships in and around Guadalcanal. Japanese sailors gave better than they got in ship to ship actions during the first months of this campaign.

The Americans, by contrast, had done little of this type of war training and preparation. In the first part of the Pacific war, Allied sailors and soldiers had a very steep learning curve. Americans and Australians had to learn in weeks or months the lessons the Japanese had taken years to teach their forces. It is only fair to say that the Allied troops were reacting with minimal nighttime training to a well planned offensive. Add to that, Japanese soldiers and sailors were thoroughly trained and gallant and were focused on their goals. Looking back, it is clear that the amount of training each side did for night operations had a direct impact on results for the first part of the Pacific war.

As Admiral Scott proved, the Allies had one big advantage. It was particularly useful to the airmen and sailors: radar. Radio Detection and Ranging is the full name for a technology we take for granted decades later. In the early 1940s it was new, secret, and revolutionary. It was so new and different that many old line officers and NCOs did not believe or trust it. Charles Fields was a scientist for Westinghouse Corporation who was involved in the development and practical application of radar. He had faith in it, and said "We knew it worked and that it could let us see ships or planes far away. Men in the army and navy, especially senior officers just couldn't believe it."

This device sends out pulses of radio waves; they bounce off whatever is out there. By timing their return the originating radar sets could see the distance to the item, be it ship, plane, island, or heavy rain storm. As the technology improved, it could discern not only location, but speed and direction as well. One can imagine that being able to "see" in the dark would change how you approach a naval battle. Or being able to "see" planes coming ten, twenty, one hundred miles away would make fighting air battles dramatically different. If you can see the enemy before he sees you, or if you can see from where and how fast he is coming, things change. It will make you adjust how battle is sought and how it is fought. This technology revolutionized the military art. As is so often the case, technology moved faster than human ability to use it.

It took time and a lot of trial and error for line officers to figure out how to trust and use this technology. Ignoring its benefits cost many lives. An early example of its being misunderstood and misbelieved is Pearl Harbor. Early Sunday morning, on December 7 1941, a radar station on Oahu was ready to be shut down for the day (?). Some men got permission to keep it up and operating to learn more about how it worked. They saw, on the scope, a mass of planes. It was the incoming Japanese air fleet, looking to sink the US Navy. They called it to the attention of the officer in charge. He dismissed the reading as either a flock of birds or a group of B17s expected in from the mainland. That misunderstanding and distrust lived on. It would raise its head in the Solomon Islands in November almost a year later.

The new technologies which came out of this war make a long list. One was the Norden bombsight. This was a revolutionary scope which allowed for much improved accuracy in placing bombs where they could do maximum damage. It was top secret, an optical-mechanical computer a little smaller than an army issue duffel bag. The sights were not left in planes on the runway but were taken out each day and locked away. An armed guard would bring a sight out to the plane before a mission. It was so secret that pilots had instructions to destroy it if they went down behind the lines.

America's industrial and knowledge base for making this innovative item, one of many to come out of the war, is impressive. One example. Al Brookes graduated from the Colorado School of Mines as a metallurgist in 1938. He had participated in the reserve officer training corps there and held an Army commission. He was working at a stainless steel plant in Maryland in late 1941. The day after Pearl Harbor he got a telegram to report for active duty. Duty assignments were passed out, and his put his experience and training to good use. His duty station was at an artillery spotting device factory in Connecticut. He supervised the production of this top secret device for most of a year. From there in mid 1942, he went to the Washington DC and ended up doing equipment loss analysis and control all over the world. Noumea, New Caledonia was one place he worked. One interesting experience he had there was not a war fighting one. Officers could sign out and use Halsey's yacht if the Admiral had no need for it, so Brookes signed it out once and went fishing. That day he caught a big tuna. The mess officer got it—Brookes didn't want to deal with it. The fish fed everyone at the Officers Club that night. Major Brookes was transferred to the Mediterranean and served on the staff of Allied Force Headquarters in Caserta. He helped to equip numerous American and Allied divisions in that theater. His expertise helped the war effort in the production of high tech equipment. He also used his industrial experience to help equip and supply fighting formations.

Making weapons and defenses better and armed forces more efficient happens in war. There is also a spillover effect. As manufacturing becomes more efficient, even civilian goods improve. And some of the developments and inventions made for the military are later adapted to civilian use as well. The GPS is a twenty first century example. Each side trying to gain an edge on the enemy is a real spur to innovation and invention.

Here is a list of some of the advances, improvements and discoveries that came out of or were made practical during WWII: atomic energy and the atom bomb, jet aircraft, pressurized aircraft, advanced aeronautics (airframe and power plant), rockets and guidance systems, radar and sonar improvements, acoustic torpedoes, the proximity fuse, medical advances in battlefield and hospital treatments, burn treatment, radio and telecommunications, computers, public health and diet, tropical disease management, cold weather gear, weather forecasting, mathematical modeling and management (search for and targeting of Uboats), new submarine technology, mass production techniques, synthetic rubber, coal gasification, understanding of the jet stream, knowledge of ocean currents, organizational management, navigation....

Japan, Germany, Britain, and the US all had projects aimed at making an atom bomb. In the end only the US had the brainpower, space, time, and resources to succeed. The Manhattan Project was an immense, expensive, and complicated effort. Many books have been written about it. The peaceful use of atomic energy is a direct offshoot of this effort. Allied efforts sabotaged Germany's efforts when they seemed to be making progress. One example is the sinking of water. A cargo of heavy water, a type of water useful in uranium processing, was being sent from Norway to Germany. The ferry carrying the tank car full of it was sunk. British guerillas planted a bomb to explode when the ferry was over the deepest part of the bay. It was important to minimize any knowledge Hitler's scientists may have developed. The Allies wanted to eliminate any advantage the Germans may have had in the race for the atom bomb. In this case it was unfortunate that a number of civilians were killed along with the Germans moving the heavy water.

The B29 being pressurized allowed crews to fly long missions at high altitudes. Fleets of this plane took the war to the Japanese homeland in 1944 and 1945. This technology was the forerunner to the pressurization of passenger airliners. Flying high enough to need a pressurized cabin is more efficient in fuel use, and is more comfortable for the passengers.

The US in particular was constantly developing new, more powerful and capable planes, ships and tanks. Powerful fighter escorts, unavailable at war's start, later allowed US and British bombers to penetrate and damage parts of the Axis which otherwise would have been too dangerous to attack.

Hitler's V1 and V2 rockets certainly did much damage to Britain. At war's end longer range rockets were in development with New York and Moscow the likely targets.

The list goes on. Every one of these innovations had an effect on the course of the war. As Admiral Scott demonstrated, by adapting to and adopting the advantages of ship borne radar, he was able to fight the Japanese Navy on more or less equal terms. This can be generalized, and those who learned to adapt and use new developments gained advantage. Those who did not, lost advantage. The warrior versus administrator divide comes into play again and often even as a war is being fought....

Another example is technical improvements in radar. The Allies developed 10cm, or short wave radar. This allowed planes or escort ships to see Uboats on the surface at night and in fog. They gained the upper hand, being able to bomb or shoot the boat before it knew an enemy was near. But soon German scientists developed a way to detect radar searching for its boats. Then they reduced or eliminated the Allied advantage by being able to dive before being bombed.

CHAPTER V

November 10

Submarines; Battle of the Atlantic; Intelligence

The German navy, the Kriegsmarine, never had a huge part in Hitler's master plan. Der Fuhrer was a soldier at heart, and he did not understand naval strategy and warfare. He had scant use for ships and seas. By his thinking, the steel to build one battleship could be used to make a thousand tanks. Tanks, he understood and liked. His notions of war involved armor and infantry taking and holding land. Land taken from other countries would be settled and used by Aryan Germans. Ships of the Kriegsmarine would have a small role in all of that. However the navy did have a role in the overall strategy. It was responsible to make it hard for Britain to supply itself. The plan was for surface warships and especially Uboats to sink ships carrying trade into or away from England.

The part of the plan with surface ships sinking British trade lasted less than a year. German cruisers, battleships, and armed freighters prowled the oceans at the start of the war. Some freighters were sunk by them. The Royal Navy sank or neutralized these Nazi hunters. Cruiser Graf Spee was caught in the south Atlantic and forced to scuttle itself in the River Plate between Argentina and Uruguay. Battleship Bismarck was sunk in the north Atlantic after an extensive hunt and chase. Both were dispatched by the Royal Navy before summer of 1940. Other surface ships were soon sunk or driven to seek shelter. One German armed freighter was interned up in Goa, a Portuguese enclave in India. Interned ships were not supposed to take warlike actions, but the captain of this ship was radoing shipping schedules and data. The resulting intelligence enabled Uboats to sink freighters. The German ship was boarded and taken by a raiding party. Calcutta Light Horse was a militia type of cavalry unit and its members saw no further action in the war. In northern Europe, several German heavy warships were bottled up in Norwegian fjords. A ship unable to reach the open sea may as well be sunk for all the harm it can cause. British air and naval forces kept those warships immobilized and of no use to the German war effort.

There was a more successful side to the naval war for Germany. It can be said that the submarine campaign was the only part of the German naval scheme that had some triumphs. November 1942 was its pinnacle in terms of ship tonnage sunk. That month, Uboats sunk more Allied freight hauling ships than could be built in a month. This was a long sought goal of the submariners. If they could keep it up the Allies would have to respond. Americans, Canadians and British would then have to use more resources to protect shipping. That would mean less planes and ships available to attack the enemy. If the Uboat campaign remained at that successful level, perhaps it would have other results. If it got bad enough, so bad that England couldn't feed herself, there might be a negotiated settlement to the war. Either would be to the Nazi's advantage.

Submarines were really just armed ship killers which happened to be submersible. The boats were not designed to be true underwater fighting boats, living and staying underwater indefinitely. As a rule, Uboats fought on the surface. Rarely did they fight submerged. They used their ability to submerge chiefly to approach undetected, or to hide from enemy escorts or planes.

Admiral Doenitz' pre war plan had been to have hundreds of Uboats ready when war broke out. In fact there were only a total of fifty or so. That meant a much smaller patrol force, only twenty at any one time. Why twenty, not fifty? Ogrus Logisticus, the supply monster, raised its head here: Doenitz simply could not keep all fifty boats out on patrol at one time. One third of the fleet, eighteen or nineteen boats, were always refitting and going out to patrol. One third of the fleet was coming back from patrol for rest, repair, and refitting. That meant that only one third of the force, eighteen to twenty boats, could be on active, aggressive patrol at any one time. The size of the Uboat fleet grew but the one third–one third–one third rule still applied. (The Allies had the same problem.)

Admiral Doenitz and his fleet of Uboats (short for Underseeboot) were doing well in their campaign to sink enemy ships. Even with a smaller than desired active fleet, the strategy remained. Uboaters wanted to put so many ships under that the Allies could not supply themselves. This effort took place on many fronts and took a number of forms.

One approach was to lay mines, passive explosive devices. On about November 10 a German Uboat laid a minefield in the harbor of New York City. This boat was sent out not with torpedoes to sink ships on the seas. Its cargo was still of explosive death, but mines don't run towards a target. They are passive, lurking below the surface, floating or tethered to a cable. A mine must be hit or nearly hit by a passing ship before it explodes. They are dangerous, often fatal to a ship, but they are easily seen and avoided.

Just when the Uboat made this minefield in New York harbor was not clear. On seeing the devices that day, the authorities closed the port to traffic. They found and swept or detonated the mines. One of the busiest ports in North America was out of action for two days. This was the only time during World War II that the port of New York was closed for business. Eight other US port closures were declared in 1942 from Uboat laid mines. These closures were for short periods, from three to eight days. In all eleven harbors were discovered to have had mines planted in them. Only one tugboat was sunk by all the mines in these eleven minefields. Some of the fields that were put out by Uboats were discovered only some time after the fact. They were laid so poorly or so far out of place that they came to light only after German records were examined after the war. The success of laying mines to sink ships or choke off ports was very poor. Sending Uboats into shallow waters where they couldn't hide negated their best advantages and strengths. Tying them up for weeks while they transited and deposited mines did not really pay off. Doenitz scrapped this tactic and put his Uboats to more effective use. He concentrated on the open seas. He preferred his captains be putting torpedoes into merchantmen, also called freighters, in the open seas.

Admiral Karl Doenitz had long been the commander of the German Uboat force, since well before the war started. A submariner himself during World War I, he had studied the art, the tactics and uses of submarines. After Imperial Germany collapsed in 1918, he stayed in the Navy. He devoted his life to planning for a rematch with Great Britain. He was confident that if he had enough Uboats he could win the war. The war started before he had his fleet complete, in fact far from it. He wanted hundreds but had only about fifty in 1939. He sent his boats out anyway. The sooner they started sinking freighters, the better.

With all of the world's oceans open to him, he started quickly. His Captains used the Uboat's stealth. Doenitz showed a ruthless disregard for survivors or generally agreed rules of war. His Uboats struck without warning. Passenger liners were attacked and put under as were merchantmen and tankers. Warships were sunk as well. Using these tactics, Doenitz' boats were able to send a number of enemy ships under.

His strategy evolved. At the start, it was a matter of single Uboats finding and attacking single ships. He soon changed his approach to a team effort he called wolfpacks. Picket subs were boats stationed in outlying positions to observe and report. As they found convoys they would radio their location and heading in to Uboat Headquarters. Then Doenitz' staff would radio instructions. Uboats in the area would be assigned to take the convoy. Generally they attacked at night on the surface, using their submersibility only to approach or hide from escorts. This tactic was quite effective at first.

Doenitz and his Uboaters frightened the British but never came close to strangling their trade and supplies. Winston Churchill said the Uboat threat was the one aspect of the war which truly scared him. He focused on the threat and the Allies concentrated on fighting Doenitz' forces. It was a campaign that went on during the entire war. It was fought on and under the Atlantic, the Gulf of Mexico, the Caribbean, even in the Indian Ocean and Saint Lawrence River. It saw surface battles between Uboats and warships. It saw sinking of merchantmen, passenger liners, other subs, and warships. This was a continual and never ending dance of death. The ongoing game of cat and mouse between and among subs, escorts, planes, and prey claimed many lives and used up immense resources. Actions took place virtually every day somewhere on the seas from late 1939 to mid 1945.

In September 1939, when Hitler crossed the Polish border and started the war, there were not a lot of usable German Uboats. Undersea warfare was supposedly governed by international agreement. The rules said that subs were supposed to stop targets and let the passengers and crew get into lifeboats before the ship was sunk. Purely civilian targets such as passenger liners were to be left alone. The aim was to give the crew a fighting chance at survival. This humane practice couldn't have gone by the wayside any quicker than it did. A Uboat sank a British liner on the first day of British-German hostilities, September 3. Without warning, the liner SS Athenia was torpedoed and sunk off of Ireland. Of about eleven hundred people on board, one hundred and eighteen drowned. Britons as well as Americans and other neutrals went down. There was an outcry and Germany denied involvement. After the war records showed it was indeed a Uboat, the U-30, that fired the torpedoes. In any case, this set the tone for the war.

At that point the gloves came off. The contest between Uboat and surface ship was merciless. It didn't matter if the target ship was civilian or naval, freighter or liner. Uboaters considered as fair game anything afloat not flying a Swastika or a flag from a Nazi friendly country. The only exception which all sides tried to observe was hospital ships. Clearly marked hospital ships were off limits to combatants. There were a few mistaken attacks on such ships of mercy but they were rare. Some clearly flagged and marked merchant ships of neutral countries were spared. Whether such a ship was attacked or let go kind of depended on the whims of the Uboat's captain. Generally, no quarter was given or asked. No mercy was given by either side and none was expected. Ruthless and ferocious well describe the struggle. No warning was given by Uboats of an impending attack. No effort was made by escorts or planes to force subs to the surface so the crews could surrender. They simply tried to sink the sub. Many seafaring and Uboat crew members underwent a watery death in this campaign.

At the outset of the war, the Royal Navy started convoying. It had learned from experience. At the start of World War One in 1914 it did not form convoys, thinking it better for ships to take their chances. But there were substantial and ongoing losses of ships sunk by Uboats. The Royal Navy then started organizing convoys for the ships coming and going to Britain. In 1939 they had already gone through the drill and immediately put convoys and escorts into use.

The practice was to have civilian ships held in harbor to gather and sail in groups. Each group was escorted by at least one and often several protective warships. The practice was effective in protecting commerce. But it took tremendous resources and many hours of management. A huge number of people and ships were needed for the escorts. Any warships used to protect convoys of course couldn't be used elsewhere. Those escorts could not take the war to the enemy. And ashore, it took a small army (navy?) to gather, schedule, monitor, and direct the convoys and escorts. And then there was the need to get the ships to the right dock for unloading when a convoy of thirty or forty ships came into port all at once.

The Royal Canadian Navy played a huge part in the effort to convoy ships from North America to England. In fact the RCN escorted, scheduled, and managed much of the traffic along the North American seaboard. They usually escorted convoys out to a point in the mid Atlantic before turning them over to the Royal Navy. By war's end the Canadians had the third largest navy on the globe. Their contribution was essential to winning the Battle of the Atlantic. For the war as a whole, Canadian troops and fliers and Canada itself contributed out of proportion to size of its population and economy.

The US did not formally enter the war until late 1941. The US Navy had been patrolling the western Atlantic for months. By mid 1941, it was alert, locked and loaded as if in a declared war even though it was technically neutral. The US Navy had at least one warship sunk by Uboats in the fall months. The USS Reuben James, a destroyer on Atlantic patrol south of Iceland, was torpedoed and sunk on October 31, 1941 with a loss of 115 men. Of course any merchantman regardless of flag headed to or from Britain was at risk. They were all considered fair game by Uboat crews. Soon the US Navy would find itself in a shooting war, no holds barred.

The first half of December 1941 was chaotic. It was an intense and trying time for the military. The Navy had their hands full with assessing and reacting to the Pearl Harbor attack. On top of that they had war with Japan, and, a few days later, war with Germany and Italy. No one really expected that Germany would declare war on the US after Pearl Harbor. After all, what happened in the Pacific was between the US and Japan. But Germany jumped right in. Hitler considered the US a nation of "mongrels" who, he thought, would not fight well if at all. The German government, that is Hitler, invoked the mutual aid treaty with Japan and declared war on the US on December 11.

With everything else happening, the US was slow to recognize the Uboat threat to its shipping. The Navy knew how the Uboat war was being fought out on the open oceans. American civilians and their local and city governments were not aware of how Uboats might affect them. The military took no steps whatsoever to protect seagoing commerce. There was no effort to organize convoys. In fact the Navy specifically decided that convoys were not a good idea, a waste of energy and time. Education of ship captains about the hazards was nonexistent. The Army and Navy squabbled over who should provide air cover over water. In fact neither did at first. No proactive steps were taken to help or protect merchant ships in US coastal waters.

It wasn't just the military which was squabbling and slow to react. American cities and citizens continued to act as if there were no change, no war, no reason to be inconvenienced. People acted as if things were just going along as they had been. No one wanted to face the fact that war conditions are harsh. It is true that the closer to the front, the harsher the conditions. But even minimal safeguards and common sense steps close to home were ignored or rejected. Denial is a wondrous thing. From Houston around the Gulf of Mexico to Miami, up the Atlantic to Maine, cities refused to dim or black out their lights. Chambers of Commerce feared loss of business. Civic leaders did not want to create panic. Citizens saw no reason to be inconvenienced. No one wanted to get out of their routines. At that point many refused to face up to the country being at war. No one wanted to tighten their belts or be put out.

The Uboats went to work quickly after Germany declared war on the US. Doenitz sent subs to the eastern US seaboard. They found easy pickings. Ship captains there were still in peacetime operating mode. Cities were lit up like Christmas trees. Escorts or air cover for freighters and tankers were non existent. It was a setup for the easy sinking of many ships at minimal risk to the sub. Early 1942 off the east coast of the US was later recalled by German Uboat commanders as "The Happy Time."

Those eastern coastal waters were for all intents and purposes a target range for Uboats. Ships sailing along the coast were not alert and were running straight, not zigzagging. And at night as they cruised the coast they were backlighted by the city lights. They stood out like a fawn walking through a clearing at noon. The ships were running singly, usually with their running lights aglow. There were no escorts in sight. No airplanes patrolled the area. The ships were visible and vulnerable. The Uboat commanders were used to trying to find darkened ships alert to danger. For quite some time they had been dodging and matching wits with the Royal Navy. They had been seasoned by two years of constant combat with a hard enemy. To them, this setting was a dream come true.

Doenitz organized Operation Paukenschlag, variously translated as "Drumbeat" or "Roll of the Kettledrum." This was a campaign to take advantage of the US lack of protection and war mindedness. He scraped up all the Uboats he could. They were sent to the US east coast to sink as many ships as possible. And it was successful. Scores of ships were sunk all along the eastern seaboard. Full backdrop lighting was provided by people driving along coastal roads with headlights on full and streetlights glaring. And those very people watched helplessly as ships were sunk a mile or two offshore.

This lack of protection went on for months. In fairness, citizens everywhere took some time to adjust to the new reality of war. It was mid 1942 before the US Army and Navy got cities to go on a war footing. They agreed to darken their shore lights and partially cover auto headlights. The military started patrolling the seas with planes and blimps. Even private yachts were pressed into service. A yachtsman could at least report the location of a Uboat even if he dared not try to harm it. There was still disagreement between Army and Navy about who would fly over water. That got ironed out. The US Navy formed a fleet, the 10th, for the express purpose of antisubmarine warfare. It had no ships itself but provided training, convoy management, sonar training, and other related services. By May a limited and rudimentary convoy system was devised and installed.

After the US military got some control of the coastal situation, sinkings slowed. The "Happy Time" was over for Uboats. But they still lurked in American and Caribbean waters. And they preyed, not as successfully as early in the year, but many ships still got sunk. Worldwide, sinking losses trended up. By November 1942, Uboats sank 721,000 tons of Allied shipping. This was more tonnage than could be built in a month. If the trend continued the Allies would have tremendous problems getting troops and supplies to Great Britain. And if the total stock of shipping shrank there would be real challenges in supplying other active fronts around the world. Invading a Nazi occupied France, or storming a Japanese occupied Manila, or sending supplies to the USSR might prove impossible.

German Uboats took the fight to Allied ships the world over. They hunted the British and Russian Lend Lease traffic in the

North Atlantic. Ore carriers and oil tankers were targeted in the Caribbean and Gulf of Mexico. British bound raw materials were sought and sunk around Africa, in the Gulf of Guinea and off the Cape of Good Hope. Some Nazi subs lurked in the Saint Lawrence River and others plied the Indian Ocean.

A few of Doenitz' Uboats even went to Singapore. Staging out of there, they patrolled in the Southwest Pacific. They operated with the knowledge of, but independently from, the Imperial Japanese Navy. As in all phases of the war, the Germans and Japanese did not truly cooperate. They really never even coordinated plans with their Axis allies. In fact Uboats in Singapore did little more than use docking space, top off the diesel tanks, and get resupplied. There was at least one incident. A Uboater was lounging on a Singapore dock, enjoying the tropical warmth and sun. A passing Japanese soldier mistook him for a British or Australian POW and kicked him. The Uboater was enraged and tossed him into the drink, to Nipponese's surprise. It could have developed into a brawl but officers intervened. The incident was smoothed over. No doubt steps were taken to prevent a recurrence.

The Uboat war is called Battle of the Atlantic. As an ongoing campaign it was the longest of the war. Arguably it was the most costly in terms of lives lost, wealth destroyed, number of people involved ashore and afloat. It had ebbs and flows. Thousands of ships and planes and tens of thousands of men and women fought in it. Overall hundreds of ships and many thousands of sailors, civilians and Navy, went to their deaths. Everything needed to sustain society and a war was carried on the freighters targeted by Doenitz. The cargoes alone that the ships carried had to have been valued in the billions. The ships themselves run that much more. Add up the time to mine the ore, manufacture or grow the goods, haul them to port, load them on the ship. Give that time and effort a value and add it to the value of the cargo. And this is the just the value of things, stuff, property. Valuable as property is, it is replaceable. Lives are not. Add in all the people lost and survivors' lives destroyed, and the costliness of this battle starts to come clear.

The casualty rate for the German Uboat service was around 70%. That is, seven of every ten Uboaters rest forever on the ocean floor. Only about three out of every ten Uboaters who went to sea returned. Doenitz himself lost a son whose sub was sent under in the North Sea.

This struggle took place in an immense arena and involved myriad people. But in the final analysis, there were really only two spears in this battle: One, the Uboat shooting torpedoes or guns, trying to sink freighters. The other, escort ships and planes dropping bombs and depth charges, trying to sink Uboats. But how did they find each other, their prey? Intelligence played a big part in this giant lethal chess game.

The Allies' ability to capture and decipher German radio traffic was instrumental in their victory. This is true of the overall victory and the winning of the Battle of the Atlantic. The Allies probably could have beaten Nazi Germany even without the knowledge of enemy intentions and plans. It was achievable but it would have taken more time, been costlier, and more difficult than it was.

The code story stems from the German defeat in 1918 and their treatment by the victors. The German armed forces were severely limited after World War I. The Versailles Treaty strictly defined the size and scope of the army and navy, and prohibited an air force. It also required the Germans to pay huge, cripplingly huge, financial reparations. The treaty assigned all blame for starting World War I on Germany and Germany alone. Naturally the Germans disagreed and worked to develop and protect their own interests.

Sometime in the 1920's, the German armed forces started to redevelop, at first clandestinely. The German Army even worked with Communist Russia, using facilities there, to help this redevelopment along. Part of the effort to rearm was to work on secure communications. German technicians had developed a sophisticated enciphering machine (later called by the Allies "Enigma"). It had hundreds of separate circuits with three, later four, rotors, and a keyboard. With the use of multiple rotors and circuits an operator could encrypt a message in one of millions of possible combinations of code. He could type in a message and have it printed out and ready to send, uniquely enciphered. If the receiver did not have the sender's rotor and circuit settings he faced trying to figure which of the millions of possible combinations were used. The Germans considered it an unbreakable encipherment system for their military and diplomatic communications.

Polish operatives too were hard at work protecting their interests, one of which was keeping track of their counterparts in Berlin. Polish intelligence agents tracked German code and cipher efforts. They were able to learn enough to reconstruct a working model of that encipherment machine, the Enigma. Late in the 1930's they saw the writing on the wall and realized that Hitler was readying to attack them. In August 1939 they took steps to share their knowledge. Polish agents, with consent of their Prime Minister, gave a working model of an Enigma to British intelligence agents. The device was passed to them in Poland on August 16. It reached London on August 25, six days before the Nazis crossed the border and invaded Poland. The French intelligence office was aware of this handoff for they too were concerned with German intentions and plans.

Having a nearly perfect copy of this machine gave the British a leg up on reading German communications. Theoretically, if they had the machine, they could read any messages run through it. But it took thousands of cryptographers tens of thousands of hours to be able to do so. Even so, they were never able to read all the messages. The decoding efforts were based at Bletchley, an old manor house northeast of London. This coup, this ability to read much of the enemy's message traffic, helped the British in a number of areas. Among other things, it enabled them to know what boats Doenitz was sending against a given convoy. They couldn't read every message but often deciphered enough to reroute convoys away from wolfpacks. Of course, they were interested in more than just Admiral Doenitz and his efforts. Intelligence was gleaned on other Nazi activities and was put to use as well.

The Germans too were busy examining what the enemy was saying. By war's start, the Germans had broken the British naval code and were reading much of the Royal Navy's mail. The

Kriegsmarine had hundreds of people deciphering messages and analyzing their content. The organization was called BDienst and was located in Hamburg. So, in the Battle of the Atlantic, they were able to send boats where they knew convoys were scheduled to be. In an interesting twist, Doenitz used Enigma to send out interception directions and plans to his Uboats.

So the code making and breaking went along with all sides working diligently. It was almost a chess game. But this match had deadly consequences: Allies were routing their convoys to avoid known concentrations of Uboats and the Germans were maneuvering wolfpacks to get at convoys. Ironically, both sides operated in the "sure knowledge" that their coded communications were secure but the enemy's were not.

There were also other types of intelligence being devised and put to use. The Allies developed several technologies for use out at sea, on a more personal and local level. These used tactical intelligence, or information on the spot derived from a particular Uboat. One was high frequency direction finding, abbreviated as HF/DF, popularly known as "huffduff." This was high tech, secret gear. Using it, one could pinpoint the location of a radio transmitter. Even if it was on a boat or ship, the exact latitude and longitude was discoverable. It worked by intercepting a radio message—not decoding it, simply getting a bearing on the sender. When two or more stations got a bearing, it was simple geometry to see where the bearings intersected. That told where the boat was when it radioed the message. From that point, the action depended on the situation. The boat could be avoided if you were a convoy master. Or if you were an aggressive escort, you could find the boat. Early in the war Uboats were simply driven under or avoided. Later in the war there were more planes and escorts available. Then the boats were found, driven under, and attacked.

Another new and secret technology was 10cm radar. This upgrade of detection technology used a shorter wavelength of radio energy. It enabled escort ships and planes to detect Uboats on the surface whatever the visibility. So the night and fog were no longer the friend of the Uboat captain. When used, the same procedures applied. The radar operator could avoid the boat altogether. Usually it was used to locate and attack. The Germans developed a detector so Uboats could dive if they detected a foe searching with the 10cm radar. The chess game continued....

These are practical, on the water examples of tactical and actionable intelligence gathering. They greatly helped the Allies' efforts. At first the HF/DF equipment was large and temperamental. It had to be land based. Later, units small and durable enough to go on ships were developed. These practical devices were used and their information sent to the antisub airplane flying off of small carriers. So the planes could locate and drive down or attack the subs far from the convoys. The 10cm radar was also miniaturized and put out on front line escorts and planes. The resulting escort knowledge and air cover over convoys made it very difficult for Uboats to approach and easy for escorts to deal with them.

The longer the battle went on the more Nazi subs were sunk. Allied training and gear got better and more plentiful as the war went on. Also, the training and experience of Uboat crews diminished. The experienced crews were being sunk and new crews rarely survived long enough to become experienced. Early on the Uboaters were all volunteers. But later in the war the Kriegsmarine had to draft people into the Uboat service. Enthusiasm to serve diminished. The quality of personnel and their performance suffered. Survival rates dropped.

The Battle of the Atlantic was a gigantic sponge, using vast resources and involving hundreds of thousands of people. As noted, Uboat losses were very high. The losses on the Allied side of the ledger show a dramatically different picture. It is true that thousands of people and hundreds of Allied ships rest on the bottom because of Uboats. But overall Allied freighter casualties were approximately 1%. That is to say, only about one in one hundred of all ships carrying freight for the Allies was sunk by Uboat. This includes all convoyed ships as well as stragglers and those steaming alone, without convoy or escort. The vast majority of cargo ships made their runs and delivered their goods with no fatalities, injuries, or damage at all. Throughout the war, most cargo and troop ships went their way totally unmolested. This speaks well to the protective activities and efforts of the convoy escorts and anti submarine patrols around them.

Submarines were present in all theaters of the war and were active in some of them.

In the Mediterranean, British subs sank many a transport headed from Italy to North Africa. They played a big part in Rommel's supply problems. Dutch, Norwegian and other nations' submarines contributed as well. These submarines knew the where and when of the convoys because they were told by the breakers of the Enigma messages.

Some Soviet subs operated in the Baltic Sea. One sunk a ship taking German refugees from the advancing Red Army in December 1944. Loss of life was great. Overall, there was little German naval activity in the Baltic and little Soviet submarine combat.

The Pacific submarine war was chiefly carried out by Americans. No American submarines offered combat in the Atlantic or Mediterranean. They were in the Atlantic only long enough to leave eastern US ports and get to the Panama Canal for transit to the Pacific. Actually at least one American sub on (under?) that transit route was sunk by friendly fire. A patrolling plane spotted it and the sub either didn't or couldn't give the right recognition code. The plane dropped depth charges and sent it to the bottom. Submarine warfare is a merciless business.

An important phase of the Pacific war was the American submarine campaign against Japan. Like the Royal Navy and Uboats, the gloves came off early in this effort. Mere hours after the December 1941 Pearl Harbor attack by the Japanese, the gloves were off and the dukes were up. At that point the US carriers were still at sea and the US battleships were sunk in the harbor, and submarines were the only known to be intact part of the Navy. The orders went out: US submarine commanders were told to "immediately execute unrestricted warfare against Japan." The US sub forces were soon prowling in contested waters. They attacked warships as well as freighters in the Indies and Philippines early in 1942. They also evacuated some people from the Philippines after they brought in supplies. American submarines played a part in the Battle of Midway in June. They also had a part in the Solomons Campaign later in the year.

American submariners suffered from defective torpedoes the first two years of the war. One American sub commander found a lone freighter out in the Pacific. He surfaced and disabled the ship by gunfire. Then, he fired almost all of his torpedoes at it. The effort was to no avail. They missed deep if set to run at what seemed the proper depth. When they were set to run shallow, they bounced off, not arming themselves. He kept one and returned to port to have it examined. There was finger pointing, bureaucratic and political wrangling, and a rear echelon attempt to blame the problem on the sub drivers. But the problem—a faulty arming device—was finally identified and corrected. Results and morale then improved for the US submariners.

Like in the Battle of the Atlantic, Intelligence played a part in this campaign. The US had broken the Japanese Naval Code in early 1942. They were able to read a portion of naval messages. This was a highly guarded secret. Great care was taken to act only when the intelligence could have been obtained some other way. This was so that the Japanese would not suspect their code had been compromised. There was one instance where this rule was blatantly violated. In early 1943 the US intercepted information on Admiral Yamamoto, Commander of the Japanese Fleet. His itinerary for an April inspection trip to the central Solomon Islands was read and decoded. This was passed up the line and President Roosevelt approved an attempt to intercept and shoot down his plane. He was deemed to be worth several carriers to the Imperial war effort. Six P38 fighters from Guadalcanal were fitted with extra gas tanks and sent out. The target was so far out that the pilots had only a few minutes to seek, find, and destroy the Admiral's plane. They did so successfully. Mission was accomplished. The Japanese Navy's faith in their codes was so staunch that even this ambush left it unshaken. They never seriously considered that their communications might have been breached.

In any event, using broken codes, American subs could often be stationed for attack when a carrier or convoy came by. The

American commanders put this practice to good use and sank many warships and tankers. By late 1944 wolfpacks were used by the US Submarine command. Unlike the German approach, they were not tied to headquarters but were independent flotillas. A US wolfpack consisted of groups of three subs with a pack commander on board. He would coordinate an attack with his boats. By war's end, American subs were able to go pretty much wherever they wanted around the Japanese Islands. They even penetrated the Sea of Japan. By early 1944, subs were also used for lifeguard duty. One or several boats would be ordered to be near islands being attacked by carrier planes. If a pilot went down they would do their best to rescue him. George HW Bush, the 41st US President, was the youngest pilot in the Navy at one time. While flying a mission in September 1944, he was shot down and rescued by a lifeguard sub. Numerous fliers were rescued during many raids, some in dramatic fashion. The lifeguard sub program greatly improved flier morale.

Ultimately, US submarines sunk more Japanese tonnage, both warships and freighters, than did Allied air and surface forces combined. The US undersea campaign did to Japan what Doenitz could not do to Britain. American subs in fact imposed near starvation on the Emperor's Island and people. By mid 1945 virtually no seaborne commerce came to or went from Nippon. American submarine casualty rates were about 30%. Although this is less than half of that suffered by Uboaters, it is still the highest casualty rate of any American service.

In 1941 the Imperial Japanese Navy had a strong submarine force. Their size ranged from two man miniature subs to large oceangoing seaplane tenders. The Japanese submariners were gallant and did their jobs well. They were never turned loose on American or Allied freighters or transports. Imperial naval doctrine called for subs to be used as adjuncts to the fleet. They were not generally allowed to attack independently, but were used chiefly for scouting and other military purposes. Miniature subs attacks were part of the Pearl Harbor operation. These two man submarines traveled to the action on the back of a full sized sub.

At the target the smaller sub detached and went to do its duty. Such mini-subs were also used in raids against Sydney Harbor, Australia and in Madagascar off east Africa. Full sized Japanese subs sunk or damaged many US warships. This was especially true early in the war. They singlehandedly sank two carriers (Yorktown at Midway, Wasp in the South Pacific), and damaged battleship North Carolina and carrier Saratoga in the first eight months. A Japanese sub surfaced off Long Beach California in early 1942 and shelled the city. The gunfire caused slight damage but big concern and even panic.

As the war went on Japanese subs continued to stalk warships. They also ran some special projects, delivering mini subs for commando type raids and so forth. An Iboat sank the cruiser Indianapolis in 1945, after it delivered components of the atom bomb to Tinian Island. By miscommunication and incompetence, no one knew where or when the ship was due in port. It sank quickly with no time for an SOS to be sent out. The American survivors had to spend days in the sea and relatively few survived. By about 1944, Japanese subs were used chiefly as freighters. The Americans had cut many island bases off entirely. Normal freighters or other surface ships would have been destroyed had they tried to resupply many of these outposts. For lack of a better alternative, IJN submarines became the prime means to run supplies to some of the far flung island outposts in the vast Pacific.

Submarine warfare was not easy. It was difficult whether in the North Atlantic, the Mediterranean, the Baltic, or the Pacific. First of all there is the sheer immensity of the sea. Simply finding and knowing your location was a feat. These were the days of taking a star sight and making pencil and paper calculations. GPS wouldn't be invented for at least fifty years. Satellites for navigation were something out of a science fiction novel. Before facing the enemy, submariners of all nations fought to survive waves and weather. Ice, typhoons, mechanical breakdown, battery explosion, torpedo malfunction, friendly fire, all were real hazards. The US lost at least one sub, the USS Tang, to a malfunctioning torpedo which it fired at a target. The tin fish did not run straight but circled around and took the Tang out. Only a handful of the crew survived and they spent the remainder of the war slaving for the Japanese. It was difficult and rare that a submersible would even find a convoy or a target.

The men serving in German Uboats, British subs, Russian, American and other Allied subs, and Japanese I-boats all fought gallantly in deep and lonely wars.

CHAPTER VI
November 11, Armistice Day
Pact of Steel; Civilians in the War

This day was originally a holiday to celebrate the day the 1914–1918 Great War was called off. After it ended, with literally millions of men killed and maimed by machine guns and gas, the world hopefully called it The War To End All Wars. Sadly, it wasn't the last war. And it certainly did not end future wars. After about 1940 or so, that struggle was renamed World War I. In 1942, of course, there was no celebration. The world was busy making more veterans, widows, orphans, cripples, and battle anniversaries. World War II was a European war in its origins. But it was fought out all across the globe. Most citizens of South America and sub-Saharan Africa were spared. Citizens of just about every other country and region were drawn in. Whether they wanted to or not, they participated and suffered in one way or another.

In 1942 Stalingrad, the Russians fought as would anyone defending their homeland. The city saw more door to door, close in fighting. The fight for the Red October Factory and the Tractor Factory continued even as workers in some remaining buildings repaired and made tanks and guns for local, immediate use. Germans were pressing, pressing, the Russian forces back against the Volga. Yet they never quite finished the job. They never shoved the Red Army to the other side of the river. The Russians fought with anything at hand, tanks, machine guns, sniper rifles, grenades, even with fists. They sought and took every advantage they could.

They were able to hold on to a minute but important part of Russia. It was an irregular sliver of land in the very heart of the city. It was a piece of land about 6 miles long and from 1 mile to mere yards wide along the west side of the Volga. The Red Army and Wehrmacht were in a deadly serious embrace. Both were giving it all they could and neither could yet gain the upper hand. The seesaw was balanced for the time being.

Hitler had been aiming at the USSR since he wrote his book *Mein Kampf* while in jail in the 1920s. His desire for years had been to destroy Communist Russia. It was his life's work. He was so eager to do it he turned his back on an undefeated and aroused England in 1941. He did not finish the job he started in 1939. He could have done so by invading the island, catching and hanging Churchill. The failure to do that before taking on Russia all but guaranteed him a two front war. Be that as it may, the attack on the Soviet Union went in on June 22 1941. The invasion was called Operation Barbarossa. It was an unprovoked and surprise act of aggression. Invading troops came across the border in to the north, central, and south central parts of the Soviet Union. At that time the Soviets were scrupulously adhering up to their agreements with Nazi Germany. The 1939 Nonaggression Pact between the two nations had trade provisions which the Communists were fulfilling to the letter.

That said, with the opening of Soviet archives in the 1990s, new facts and records came to public view. There is some reason to think that Stalin may have been planning an attack of his own on Germany. The Red Army and Red Air Force were massed on the border line between the German and Russian zones of Poland. That is one reason at the start of the invasion that the Luftwaffe was able to shoot up so many planes on the ground. It also explains why so many Soviet armies were just by the border, inadvertently waiting to be surrounded and forced to surrender. There was no reason for the Soviets to mass forces if they were peacefully living by the 1939 Nonaggression Pact. Not much is known of this possibility and the archives have since become difficult to access. The truth may not come out for some time.

In any case, Hitler struck first. The invasion has been called a surprise attack. But British Intelligence operatives had read the signs. More to the point, they were reading many of the Nazi messages directing various divisions to their jumping off points. British Intelligence analysts could see it coming. The British Ambassador and even Churchill himself warned Stalin specifically and repeatedly. The men at the border, on the Russian side, saw the massing of almost a million Germans across the line. And they had with them hundreds of tanks, planes and vehicles. It would be pretty hard to hide an army that size. The attack was really a surprise to no one but Stalin. For several days after June 22, he did not really respond. The records are not clear if it was due to battle shock, denial, sensory overload, or something else. Having gathered all the reins of power to himself, he seemed for a few days unable to give directions of any sort. His generals came to see him in late June. They were seeking direction and to buck him up. He joked when they came in that he thought they had come to execute him. In any case, the war went on, orders from Moscow or no. In the several days that Stalin sat dazed, German Panzers led by dive bombers and followed by infantry had penetrated. They got into Russia a long way, in places hundreds of miles. The Red Air Force had been shot up on the ground. Whole Russian Divisions and even armies were being surrounded. They surrendered and disappeared into the Nazi slave labor establishment. Cities fell one after another.

When Stalin finally came to grips with the new reality, he acted decisively. He ordered troops to stand and fight, to sell themselves dearly. And he shrewdly appealed to the Russian people. In a well orchestrated radio broadcast he urged fellow citizens to "defend our Holy Mother Russia." He cast the fight not as a war of ideologies, of Nazi versus Communist. Rather he defined it as a fight against an invader bent on the destruction of Russia. He tapped a deep patriotic strain in Russian citizens, and called them to resist, kill, and throw out the invaders.

The Germans, acting under orders from their Nazi leaders, did in fact intend to destroy the USSR. The Nazi plan was to annihilate the Communist government. Then the new owners would enslave the Russian people and make the land available for German settlers. Ironically, the invading Nazis were at first joyfully greeted as liberators by many people in the Ukraine and western Russia. Stalin's regime was brutal and arbitrary. In the 1930s literally millions of Russians, Ukrainians, and others had been executed or caused to starve. Millions more were exiled to Siberia or uprooted and moved from traditional homelands to somewhere else within the USSR.

As bad as that was, the Germans soon proved worse. They imposed a harsher, more savage and racially motivated rule. The Teutonic invaders went out of their way to antagonize and alienate the populace. After the front moved on past towns and cities the killing of civilians started. First thing done was to line up and execute all the Communist Party members and many others. The Wehrmacht was not part of this although they knew it was happening. The Nazis made a serious effort to decapitate Russian society. They tried to eliminate leaders of all kinds, whether Communist or not. Among those in their sights were teachers, intellectuals, most anyone who might think for themselves or cause the occupiers trouble. Then the Death Squads came. These were SS Troops. They were designated, specially trained Schutzstaffel units whose job it was to find and kill Jews, Gypsies, homosexuals, Priests, the disabled, and other "social misfits." The SS originated in the 1930's. Originally used as a bodyguard for high Nazis, it soon developed into a private army answerable to the Nazi party hierarchy. Specifically, Heinrich Himmler controlled it. He also took to himself over time the Gestapo, the state police, other police agencies, and even the German Post Office. Later in the war the SS owned and ran a number of factories. It never did answer to the government, just to Hitler through Himmler. The OKW, Oberkommando Der Wehrmacht, the German High Command, had no authority over the SS. It was a law unto itself.

On a wider scale the general Russian population was abused and mistreated. Food and resources were taken and sent to Germany. The Nazis didn't care, in fact they felt it their right and duty to impose starvation and destruction on the Soviet people. Before long it was apparent to the citizens of the USSR that they were not better off under the Germans. It was clear that they were worse off. So, as Stalin had implored, they fought for Holy Mother Russia. The Red Army fought. Civilians fought. Women fought. Men too old to be drafted fought. Partisan groups coalesced and fought on their own. They were also formed by soldiers infiltrated in to German held territory. Irregular fighting bands hid out in the swamps and the forests. Bridges were blown up. Roads were mined. German troops were ambushed. Even rear echelon Germans were sniped at, captured, harassed. Guerilla warfare and sabotage could and did plague German forces anywhere they trespassed on Russian ground. German reprisals became increasingly savage. It was not uncommon after some kind of a guerilla raid or sabotage for a random fifty or more nearby people to be seized. They were killed, many Russians for each German killed. And their bodies were publicly displayed as a warning. This barbarity did not stop the resistance. Reprisals simply fanned the flames of Russian patriotism and hatred of the invader. With any and every tool available, Russians everywhere struggled and scrapped and killed the invaders just like the defenders of Stalingrad fought. Many of these civilians died in battle or starved, and others became refugees.

On this eleventh day of the eleventh month, the last Axis forces were driven out of Egypt. The last of the Afrika Korps with their Italian allies crossed the border into Libya. It was in a way just a line on the map. The Axis had come to Egypt and gone back to Libya and Tunisia several times since 1940. But this time they would not recross that line on the map. Fliers of the Desert Air Force and soldiers of the British Eighth Army were prodding and chasing them along at every opportunity.

This closed a chapter which opened in 1940. Italy had not joined Germany at war in September 1939. Mussolini's government declared war on France and Britain on the following June 10. Not until Hitler had conquered most of Europe did the Italians jump in to get some spoils. Franklin Roosevelt's take on their declaration was, "…the hand that held the dagger has struck it into the back of its neighbor." France lay prostrate under Hitler's heel, signing surrender terms on June 19. (This was about the same time when, halfway around the world, Japanese troops invaded French Indochina. They too took advantage of French inability to fight back.) When Mussolini declared war, he intended to add to his North African empire. At the same time he invaded France, his latter day Romans (as Mussolini styled his army) also started making trouble for the British in their east African Colonies. The Italians had invaded and occupied Ethiopia in 1935. From Ethiopia he sent troops into British Somaliland.

Britain of course responded. They made use of their Indian Army. That army was officered by British but manned chiefly by Indians. The Indians fought back in Somaliland and Ethiopia. Ultimately the Italian aggression ran out of steam. Mussolini's "New Roman Empire" in Africa came to naught. The Duce's men suffered defeat after defeat. The Italian Army gave up big hauls of prisoners. Scores of thousands of Italian soldiers spent the rest of the war in British POW camps in Africa and the mideast.

Hitler felt a certain loyalty to Mussolini as his oldest Ally. And he wanted to keep his partners actively fighting somewhere. So in response to these Italian reverses the Fuhrer sent a token force to Africa. He wanted his German general to work with and lead the Italians in North Africa. And he intended that adding some German troops to the mix would stiffen the Italian forces and make them more formidable. The force sent was headed up by a little known General named Erwin Rommel. It consisted of just several motorized units, both Panzer and infantry. For its size, it had a grandiose name: the Afrika Korps. Its task was to bail Mussolini and the Italians out (again!). As important, another task was to keep the British stretched, distracted, and their armed forces occupied. In the Fuhrer's scheme of things, Africa was an unimportant theater peopled by inferior races. It and the Italian efforts there were really a source of bother. Hitler viewed Africa as a distraction and a drain of resources. It is intriguing that the British and their Allies were kept busy in that part of the world by the Axis. Africa was far from traditional centers of power like

London, Berlin, and Moscow. In effect Hitler used or was able to gain benefit from the African theater. He managed to keep both his Ally and British foes fighting. He was able to do that and keep his army and its efforts insulated and following its own goals. He wanted to concentrate while he took on the Russian Bear.

The association between Germany and Italy was formalized in a treaty called The "Pact of Steel." The "Pact" has an interesting history. The alliance between Nazi Germany and Fascist Italy was originally a pact of two outcasts from the western European democracies. The two countries had centralized governments and economies. Both had strongmen at the helm rather than elected parliaments and leadership. The two dictators were on the path of aggression. Hitler was looking East and Mussolini looking to Africa. The two countries were not traditional allies. Their histories and cultures didn't particularly mesh. One stemmed from the damp moors and marshes of northern Europe, the other tried to live up to the echoes of a Mediterranean based world Empire in its past. One big problem they had in common was their diplomatic isolation. Neither was interested in nor particularly friendly with the democracies of western Europe. In terms of a "Pact" or treaty, the two powers did little conferring or agreeing on strategy. There was virtually no exchange of technology or skills. At first, in the mid 1930's, Italy seemed the stronger. But by 1939 it was much the junior partner. Germany was richer, more populous and was highly industrialized. It had a more martial culture which had been encouraged and fostered by the Nazis. Of the two it was much the more organized for modern war.

In fact, Hitler repeatedly had to bail Mussolini out. This didn't happen only in North Africa. It had happened before when Italy got bogged down while invading Greece and the Balkans in 1941. Italy had had its hands full trying to conquer Ethiopia, a medieval country, in 1935. So it is not a surprise they had problems trying to take over Greece, a fairly modern nation. When Hitler sent troops to aid Mussolini, he had to push back the date to invade Russia.

There is a school of thought that the Allies encouraged Axis involvement in the Balkans in the spring of 1941. If Italy got bogged down it would need help. Germany would go to the aid of its oldest Ally. The time it would take to help would distract the Germans from other plans. It might slow or even stop the Nazi buildup for the invasion of Russia. We do not know for sure what drew Hitler into the Balkans in spring 1941. We do know that he took time to secure Belgrade and other areas. Because he did so, he pushed back the invasion date by six or eight weeks. And that delay may well have made a big difference: the weather in the fall of 1941 stopped the Germans before they had a definitive victory. Winter did what the Red Army had not been able to do. It stopped the Wehrmacht's Blitzkrieg. It is interesting to speculate what might have happened had Hitler let Mussolini stew in Greece, and gone into the USSR two months earlier than he did. He may have taken Moscow and brought Russia down....

The Duce's ultimate personal fate probably steeled Hitler's will. Hitler fought to the end and died a warrior. That was not how Mussolini's life ended. What happened to him started when the Allies invaded the Italian mainland in 1943. The Fascist regime Mussolini led collapsed and Italy came over to the Allied side. The Duce fled but was caught. He was imprisoned by the government set up after he was ejected from office. They had him in a secure mountaintop hotel with access by just one road. Hitler sent in a commando raid to rescue him. The raiders got in crashing their plane onto the mountain top. Mussolini was rescued and allowed to set up a new Italian government. It was a weak and ineffective organization and purported to govern only northern Italy. This was a "government" in name only. It had no power or authority of its own. It was under Nazi protection and used Nazi power to enforce its needs. It lasted only as long as the Germans were around. Mussolini and his mistress were caught and killed the last days of the war in Europe. Their bodies were displayed in public, hanging upside down. The Pact of Steel did little to benefit and nothing to protect Signore Mussolini.

The French authorities in Algeria and Morocco formally deserted the French government at Vichy when they signed an armistice with the Allies. This formalized the truce agreed to earlier. The Americans had taken the lead in the negotiations since there was some bad blood between France and Britain over events in 1940. The two Allies had hoped to get the French in their corner. Failing that, they at least wanted them neutralized. That, the Armistice accomplished. The agreement recognized Admiral Darlan as de facto ruler of French North Africa. He was a known Nazi collaborator if not a sympathizer. The American public was in an uproar when the Armistice terms came out. Many Americans asked why we were negotiating with people we should be fighting. This died down as the local French forces did not interfere, in fact helped, as the Allies fought Germans. Darlan was assassinated in Africa shortly after the armistice was signed.

The Armistice agreement took the French out of the war for the time being. They had much to work out, specifically who was in charge and who spoke for the nation and its people. The French had to sort out their domestic politics. There was maneuvering between those who stayed in France when Germany took over and those who left and continued the fight. The leadership of France came from those who left and spent the war years in exile. France was technically neutral in late 1942, but it would later come in as a full member of the Grand Alliance with the United States, United Kingdom, and Soviet Union.

The Axis reaction to the Torch invasion and Armistice was swift. German and Italian troops started moving into unoccupied France. The interior, southeast half of France had been left free of German troops after their 1940 victory. The French set up a rump government over that area at the sufferance of Hitler. Its capitol was located in the town of Vichy. This charade was ended as the occupiers rolled and marched in that November. France itself was henceforth fully occupied by Axis troops. These Germans and Italians were not front line fighters. Most were reserve units or made up of older militia members. But they were occupiers. As such they took all rights, property, and privileges of same.

Around the world, in the tropics: The contest for New Guinea wore on through the rain, heat, and mud. The land the Armies were fighting over is unbelievable, almost beyond imagining. The

Australians and Japanese had to fight the environment almost as much as they fought each other. And it was lethal in more ways than a bullet: tropical diseases known and unknown, jungle terrain, hungry jungle and river animals, torrential rains, hip deep mud, steep valleys and peaks, sea level plains and ten thousand foot elevations, same day temperatures near freezing or near broiling, rotting clothes....

The Aussies continued their drive up and over the spine of the island. They forced the Japanese Army out of Gorari. Gorari may have been considered a town in this part of New Guinea, but anywhere else it was just a settlement, several houses grouped together. It was notable only in that it was a clearing with buildings and wasn't jungle. If you split the distance between coasts into thirds, Gorari is two thirds of the way from the south coast to the north. The Australians were on the move. They now had adequate supplies, some reinforcements, and momentum.

The Sons of Nippon had been ordered to pull back, withdraw from their drive south. The retreat back north was miserable. They had little to eat. And they were closely pursued. Imperial Headquarters in Tokyo had decided that Guadalcanal had to be secured before New Guinea. They put the New Guinea operation on the back burner in order to concentrate on the Solomon Islands. The so-called South Seas Detachment which had come close to Moresby was called back. It was now retreating north, fighting jungle and Aussies along the Kokoda Track. Australian infantrymen are generally considered among the best fighters in the world. The Japanese in New Guinea, like those in Guadalcanal, were finding that westerners could indeed fight and fight well. The Americans were trying to outflank them, sending a Battalion of the 32nd Infantry Division over the Kappa-Kappa Track to the east of the Kokoda.

The South Sea Detachment, the Japanese invaders of New Guinea, was withdrawing to three fortified spots on the north coast. They were either small towns or missionary stations called Buna and Gona. There were also fortifications on nearby Sanananda Point. They were strong defensive positions. There were coconut log bunkers overgrown with vines, hard to see and virtually immune to artillery fire. Interlocking lanes for machine gun fire were set up. And the terrain was used to take advantage of swamps and inlets. The only way to approach many of the bunkers was along the few dry paths. These of course were covered by machine guns and rifle fire. Buna, Gona, and Sanananda were obscure names in late 1942. Even if someone could find New Guinea on a map, hardly anyone would find these settlements. They would soon be seared in the collective memories of the US, Australia and Japan. The Allies would pay dearly to take them and in the process would have to kill virtually every Japanese man there.

Imperial Headquarters had reluctantly and belatedly realized the relative importance of the Solomon Islands. Henderson Field on the Canal was a base being actively used. Not only could the Americans control the area with air power, they used it to sink Japanese ships and kill soldiers. And it was a long way from other Japanese bases. It was far enough that it used much time and fuel just to get there. In fact it took so much fuel to get there that the Japanese pilot couldn't stay long enough to finish a fight. He had to conserve enough fuel to get back home. Not to mention how many resources were needed to deliver supplies. Henderson Field had to be taken out. Guadalcanal had the potential, Tokyo recognized, to be a knife slashing at its underbelly. If it fell to American control, trouble. Rabaul, the Emperor's main base in the region could then be at risk. Then Japan's south sea islands of Truk and Yap would be endangered. Other strongholds were at risk from there. Ultimately the Emperor's conquest of all of Southeast Asia could start to unravel. Thus New Guinea was put on hold while the Imperial planners concentrated on the southern Solomon Islands of Guadalcanal and Tulagi.

Battles continued in jungle, desert and steppe, armies and navies slugging it out. But normal people everywhere also had their lives turned upside down. How the war was going for their country, what types of goods were needed to fight it, what it cost, all affected millions of regular people's day to day lives.

This war saw many millions in military uniform, fighting for patriotism or even for national survival. Campaigns and battles saw forces sweep over immense distances. On a purely personal level, in this stretch of time many more civilians than soldiers or sailors were enslaved, displaced, or killed. Armies came and went repeatedly over huge swaths of the earth. But they also came, stayed, and took control. And the civilians there had to cope and somehow survive.

What the Germans under Nazi control did to people in countries they occupied is fairly well known. A generation of European children grew up with privation and terror, at best. And they were the lucky ones who were able to stay in their homes. The unlucky ones, adults and children, got sent to death camps or became slaves. A short but nowhere near exhaustive list of Nazi brutality: Dachau (work and death camp), the Warsaw Ghetto (part of a city turned into a starvation camp), Treblinka (work and death camp), Babi Yar (massacre and mass grave), Lidice (town chosen at random, people killed, buildings razed in reprisal for assassination of the Nazi governor), etc ad nauseum.

But Nazi Germany also imported 7.6 million men and women as slaves. To give a little perspective to how many lives were taken over and destroyed, that is about the population of the five Boroughs of New York City. "Imported" is a clinical term which sounds as if people had a choice in the matter. They did not. Nazis rounded people up off the streets or emptied neighborhoods at gunpoint. They took Poles, Russians, French, Ukrainians, Greeks, Lithuanians, Dutch, Norwegians, and people from just about any other place they had troops. These slaves were fed poorly and were sometimes chained to the machine they had to operate in a factory. None were well treated. This unprecedented sweeping up and using of people is surely one of the largest mass enslavements in history. To add to this bleak snapshot, these millions of slaves are just part of the picture. Their numbers are over and above the millions of Jews, socialists, communists, gays, Gypsys, disabled, and plain unlucky people who were killed outright in the Nazi death camps.

What about those people in Nazi occupied areas who were left in their homes? They were robbed. The Nazis systematically stripped their conquests of valuables. Paintings, jewelry, machinery, wines, antiques, you name it. If an occupier wanted it he took it. It either went for his personal use and gain or ended up in Berlin. To this day it is difficult to trace what happened to the many items which disappeared into the Nazi looting whirlwind. Some of the riches never have reappeared.

What about civilians in other parts of the world? The Japanese had a consistent uniform record of barbarity and cruelty. But it was not directed at a specific religion or ethnic type. Everyone suffered. Even Japanese civilians and soldiers were subject to physical punishment and arbitrary treatment. In their way of thinking, reverence and obeisance to the Emperor was all important. Life was cheap and the needs or wants of the individual mattered less than the morning mist. The Japanese too looted their conquests. They rounded people up and forced them to surrender jewels, gold, art, and other valuables. Some of those riches reached Tokyo but much disappeared somewhere along the way.

There were a few isolated cases of humanity shown by Japanese officials. If a European Jew or other refugee could get a visa to enter another country, the Nazis allowed them to leave. Some of those fortunate enough to obtain a visa chose to go to Japanese controlled areas. A lot of people gave up their belongings and homes in Berlin, Warsaw or Vienna to at least have life even if in an alien and distant place. Many gravitated to Shanghai in China. There was a large Jewish population there during the 1940s. Fleeing refugees were aided at one point by a Japanese consular worker in a Baltic city. He bent the rules to issue visas. He gave papers to many people so they could escape Nazi rule. In Shanghai they lived, suffering and coping much as did others under the Japanese. Daily life was a struggle but they were treated no better or worse than the typical Chinese. At least they were not in a concentration camp.

In Indochina, the Japanese left day to day administration to the Vichy French. The Emperor's men were definitely in charge. Colonials were at the mercy of Imperial forces. Even so, they enjoyed limited autonomy. There is little record of enslavement or imprisonment of French colonial settlers or officials.

But such benign neglect was the exception. The early Western reversals and subsequent collapse of colonial Southeast Asia turned that part of the world upside down. Native civilians were not especially bothered nor were they treated well. Western soldiers were captured and imprisoned. Enslavement, death, disease, torture, starvation, humiliation were their lot. Japan did not accept the Geneva Conventions which set standards for treatment of prisoners of war. The Emperor's men did not recognize that a surrendered prisoner was anything but slime. They considered their men who surrendered as disgraced and dead and treated most anyone they caught the same way.

Many western civilians were rounded up by the Japanese. Wherever they were in the region, in their businesses, teaching, nursing, running mines, they were found, arrested, and imprisoned. Western nationals were interned in camps throughout Southeast Asia and the Philippines. Americans, British, Dutch, Australians were not left free. Some were killed outright. Some were treated reasonably well, having to work but not starving. Others were put to work as slave labor. They worked on railroads, in mines, as longshoremen, and at other sites where Nippon needed work done. Some western, along with many Korean and Chinese women, were forced into prostitution. They were made to be "comfort women," whores for the benefit of Japanese troops. Burmese, Indian, Malayan, Filipino, Vietnamese, Thai, Cambodian, Chinese, Manchurian, Indonesian, Melanesian and Polynesian peoples all suffered enslavement, brutality, mass executions, starvation, and abuse. Life was cheap, and anyone they conquered was at the disposal of the Emperor and his troops. They did not single out Jews, Gypsies, Priests, or queers like the Nazis. Nipponese occupying troops simply killed, looted, and raped as they went.

Prisoners of war of Britain and America were treated according to the Geneva Conventions: housed, fed, not required to work in war related jobs. Many Germans and Italians picked sugar beets, felled trees, or did landscaping work in the US.

POWs in Russia were treated much as the Japanese treated their prisoners. They were worked to death, beaten, and starved.

Civilians under British or American occupation were not starved or enslaved. Early in the war, Americans and Canadians citizens of Japanese descent who lived on the west coasts were imprisoned. Their property was essentially stolen from them, "bought" for pennies on the dollar, before they were put on trains to camps in the interior. That said, their camps, while not resorts, were not concentration camps. They were fed and got medical attention, and were generally free to work in surrounding communities. Many camps were closed by late 1943 or 1944 and the occupants returned to civilian life. This is certainly not a proud moment in America's and Canada's history. But the treatment these citizens of Japanese extraction is in no way comparable to the way dissidents or potential enemies of the state were treated in Axis countries.

Despite this treatment, Americans of Japanese descent volunteered for uniformed duty. Many served as interpreters and intelligence analysts in the Pacific. Others served in the European theater. The 442nd Infantry Regiment was made up of Nisei, people of Japanese descent born outside Japan. The unit fought in Italy. It was the US Army's most decorated unit for gallantry and bravery in the entire war.

When Allied troops invaded a country and had to administer it, the population had to be dealt with and a government set up. There were few collaborators and sympathizers on islands taken across the Pacific. The few found were dealt with, imprisoned, executed, or rehabilitated.

There were more sympathizers to be identified and dealt with in Europe. It was an emotional time when delivered from Nazi occupation. It had to be difficult for the survivors to draw the line between those who just tried to get along and those who actively collaborated and helped the occupiers. Many old scores were settled among the civilians of the occupied country. No doubt some collaborators got off without punishment and some who just went along got punished. In any case, the Allies routinely installed a civil government subject to military oversight and military needs as soon as the front moved on.

Much the same can be said of Russian occupation and reoccupation as they rolled west through central Europe. They routinely set up a government according to their way of doing things, then identified and dealt with collaborators and sympathizers. When Russians got to Germany they gave as good as the Nazis had given them several years earlier. Vengeance was wrought. In eastern Germany, as things settled down and the front moved west they established civilian government.

Russian engineers in combat in Stalingrad. Engineer troops made nightly reconaissance forays. The destruction here is typical of what the city of Stalingrad became in late 1942. Photo courtesy of Geert Ropier, www.stalingrad.net

General Vasili Chuikov, commander of the 62nd Army at Stalingrad. His house to house, fight for every meter of ground tactics bled the Nazi invaders white. The 62nd's headquarters was usually in a wrecked building. He moved his "office" often in order to stay within about one hundred meters of the fighting. The General is buried at Stalingrad. Photo courtesy of Geert Ropier, www.stalingrad.net

This is a Japanese reconnaissance photo of Guadalcanal taken in July, before work crews started building the airfield. The caption says "Bu Kadanadu Kanadu", or "Guadalcanal" (Translation courtesy of the Japan American Society of Colorado). The photo is from the collection of Martin Clemens. A British colonial official who went into hiding and stayed in the area after Japan took it, he was instrumental in bringing native Melanesians over to help the Americans. Their intelligence input gave new and trusted sources of information to General Vandegrift. Natives' information and help was crucial in helping the Americans fight off counterattacks in the first days of the campaign. Photo courtesy Peter Flahavin, www.guadalcanal.homestead.net

B17 reconnaissance photo taken August 18. American overflights took photos daily for intelligence analysis. This photo is of the Matanikau Village area, upper right, just outside of the American perimeter. About a week before this was taken, a patrol led by Marine Lt Col Goettge was lured to the village by a bogus Japanese offer to surrender. The patrol was boated in and was ambushed soon after it landed. Two men escaped into the surf and swam to safety. All the rest were killed. The Marines attacked and destroyed the village the next day. Photo is courtesy of Peter Flahavin, www.guadalcanal.homestead.net

This is Henderson Field. Probably taken late August or early September. At first planes were simply dispersed when not in use. No storage revetments or hardstands were built the first weeks of the campaign. Note the dark mounds between the bottom of the photo and the near end of the landing strip. They are burnt slash piles. The land is being cleared in order to lengthen the runway. Photo is courtesy of Peter Flahavin, www.guadalcanal.homestead.net

Yamazuki Maru, beached and burned. One of four Japanese transports ordered beached by Admiral "Tenacious" Tanaka on the night of 14-15 November. They were beached near American lines, between Cape Esperance and Tassafaronga. She and the other three ships were shelled, strafed, and bombarded the morning of November 15. Few of the soldiers she carried and virtually none of her cargo made it to safety. Photo courtesy US Marine Raiders Association.

Merritt A. Edson at the peak of his career as a Major General. He led the First Raider Battalion and attached units in the Battle of Edson's Ridge on Guadalcanal. They held the hill during this fray which took place September 12-14, 1942. His leadership there and in other battles earned him the Congressional Medal of Honor. Holding Edson's Ridge enabled the US to keep the airfield. That started to tip the seesaw and led directly and ultimately to the American victory at the Naval Battle of Guadalcanal. Photo courtesy of the Stevenson family.

Australia, January 1943. Admiral Halsey awarding the Navy Cross to Raider Captain Bill Stevenson for his bravery, clear headedness, and devotion to duty during the the Battle of Edson's Ridge. After awarding this and other medals, the Admiral gave a "fightin' talk" to the assembled Marines. Photo courtesy of the Stevenson family.

Captain Stevenson with his new Navy Cross Medal. Note the "passed by Naval Censor" stamp on the photo. Photo courtesy of the Stevenson family.

Lieutenant Fred Henderson, Lendlease administrator in the Aleutian Islands. Also served as training officer to Russian sailors learning to operate Sonar. Photo courtesy of the Henderson family.

CHAPTER VII

November 12

Throwing Lightning Bolts; Training Pilots; India

On the Solomon Islands front, by November 12, the campaign for Guadalcanal and its airfield was approaching a decision point.

Since August each side had been reinforcing and resupplying themselves while trying to kick the other off the island. For three months Yamamoto Isoroku, Japanese Fleet Commander and Pacific Commander Chester Nimitz had been going at it. Figuratively speaking, they had been throwing lightning bolts at each other. But neither could point to a big result. In mid November, things were still pretty much as they had been in late August: The Yanks had the airfield and could hit at the Japanese. The Japanese could sail around the island with impunity at night but got in trouble if they showed up in daylight. Matters were at a standoff; the seesaw was still about level.

In Greek mythology, Zeus sat on a mountaintop to throw his bolts. But not Admiral Yamamoto. He worked from his flagship in Truk, a fine lagoon and island group located some thousand miles northeast of the action. He lived and worked on the battleship Yamato. (Yamato is a variant of the word for Japan in that language.) This very specialized vessel had guns larger than any battleship anywhere on the globe, except her identical sister ship Musashi. Those 18" guns could shoot a shell larger than a brahma bull for twenty or more miles, and deliver them with pinpoint accuracy. These ships and their weapons were the pride of the Japanese Navy. Using such a ship as an office seems expensive and inefficient. It certainly did not put those huge guns to their intended use. Yamamoto apparently decided the good ship Yamato didn't need to be out bombarding Guadalcanal. He had long professed to have a high opinion of American martial skills and ability. His actions here seem to speak otherwise. If he really thought highly of the fighting ability of the Americans wouldn't he have thrown everything he could into the fray? Was it beneath a senior Admiral to office in a small ship or ashore? We will never know why he chose to use Yamato as a workplace not to send it out to fight.

About one sixth of the globe away, Nimitz was in Pearl Harbor near Honolulu, Hawaii. He directed his efforts from the base there. He worked out of an office building and lived in a traditional house a short walk away. The US Navy did not have the luxury of using a major combatant ship as a hotel. At this stage of the war, the Admiral was scrambling to find every ship and body of troops he could. He scraped every shipyard, harbor, and base in the American fleet looking for warships, planes, and men. He sent what he could scrounge and cajole to the fight in the South Pacific.

America was fighting and placing bases in many places. This generated huge almost un-meetable demands from all points of the globe. The old story of limited resources and unlimited desires certainly was the case in 1942. Now, in November, Operation Torch was demanding men and resources too. Not only were ships going into the maw at Guadalcanal, but the Navy needed hundreds of ships for its amphibious invasion of North Africa. Not to mention the ships needed to escort and protect convoys from the Caribbean, Gulf of Mexico, the Eastern Seaboard, and the North Atlantic. The worldwide need for ships, the men to operate and supply them, and planes to protect them far outran the amount of them available.

Yamamoto and Nimitz had each expended men, airplanes, ships and supplies with lots of fighting but little net result. The battle was at a stalemate. To use the playground analogy, the seesaw was balanced. Try as they might, neither side was able to get their side down to the ground. Yamamoto had not been able to recapture or even neutralize Henderson Field. The Emperor's men owned the night while Americans owned the day. They could, often did, bombard the Americans while landing troops and supplies. In fact, on October 14 the Yanks on Cactus suffered an hour and a half while two battleships pounded the field. Battleships Kongo and Haruna and supporting smaller ships put almost one thousand shells onto the airfield, destroying 48 planes and killing 41 Americans. That was an unusually terrifying and intense bombardment which Canal veterans forever remembered.

Nimitz' forces could not stop the shelling nor enemy reinforcements from landing after dark. But they could and did keep the airfield open. The technology of the day prohibited active night flight operations. Daylight hours, Americans ruled. The Japanese ground forces suffered from the bombing and strafing of Cactus Air Force. Any Nipponese ship found in the area was surely damaged and often sunk.

By early November, each side was readying another try to force the issue. Each was determined to have its way. Both were furiously working to get their end of the seesaw moving down, to get their feet on the ground.

The Imperial Headquarters had yet another attack brewing. They still needed to retake Guadalcanal, or at least gain control of Henderson Field. Preparations were numerous. From November 2 to 8, over sixty five destroyer loads of the Emperor's troops were sent down. Thousands of fresh soldiers and their supplies were successfully landed.

This was how the Japanese garrison was built and supplied. Destroyers and transports would gather in the northern Solomons. Usually they staged from the Shortland Islands. This base is on a small island located about three hundred and fifty miles north of Guadalcanal. The transports and freighters were escorted along in convoy by destroyers. Destroyers are small agile warships and are the workhorses of the fleet in every navy. In these operations they sometimes carried troops as well. Usually there was a cruiser, a heavier ship, along. They offered protection to the transports enroute. Once there they usually peeled off to shell the Americans while the men and supplies unloaded. Timing was the key to success.

A reinforcement group had to start out early but not too early. They left their anchorage and started their run so as to remain out of range of American air attack until dark. Sometimes they would have to make a u-turn to burn some daylight, then come back around and head in. They ran in fast once dusk slid to dark. The troop carriers would disgorge their cargoes of men and supplies. Some of the warships would stand guard and others go to fulfill their gunnery duties, bombarding the Americans. Escorts and transports would start home sometime around midnight. If the timing was judged right and all went according to plan they would be out of air range by dawn. Usually it worked out that way but sometimes not. In any event, this routine went on for months. There were some variations and different commanders ran the show at different times. But the process worked well for the Nipponese until the Americans finally got twenty four hour control of the sea around the island.

This time the Nipponese attack was scheduled for mid November. Yamamoto's grand scheme was for the new arrivals to join the men already on the island. Of course the goal was, as usual, to take the airstrip. The plan was a typical product of Japanese doctrine and thinking. Imperial Headquarters preferred not to simply go for the jugular. Their thinking was to take a less direct, more subtle approach.

They often started by spreading multiple small groups all over the area in question. Then these separated units were to attack the target coming from each of their various starting points. A problem was that sometimes they were able to communicate only poorly. Often once they started off to get set, they were not able to communicate with the others at all. It is virtually impossible, as Yamamoto found, to coordinate a complicated attack if you can't even talk with each other! The terrain varied as well. For some troopers it was almost a walk in the park. For other units it was an epic, difficult trek up and over horrendous obstacles. It was difficult to allow for such variations if you even knew they were there. This island was poorly mapped and not well explored. In many cases, the terrain was accurately mapped only as the Marines and soldiers patrolled or fought over it. That geographic variable added another layer of complexity to planning and coordinating attacking forces.

The goal was for each of them to hit the objective in quick succession or all at once, overwhelming the hapless and passive Americans. It was an elegant, sophisticated plan and on the drawing board it worked well. It was thoroughly drafted and planned. There were arrangements and details to the nth degree. It even specified where the senior surviving US officer should stand as the Rising Sun flag was raised over the field.

Yamamoto's staff designated that Henderson Field's capture date would be called "Z Day." November 13 was given that honor. The entire battle scenario was built around the sure knowledge that the timing of the attacks would fall into place and be successful. They were confident that Z Day would take place per the plan. Naval forces were gathered. Task forces of battleships, cruisers and destroyers were assembled and named. Transports, escorts, and bombardment units were collected.

There were three surface Groups with specific tasks and roles. The Attack Group was commanded by Vice Admiral Abe. He and his Group were to go in the first night of the operation. Their main job was to bombard the American enclave and put the airfield out of commission. Secondly, they were to meet and neutralize any surface opposition. The overall aim was to disrupt and destroy the Americans' installation, to make it difficult or impossible for the Marines to put up meaningful resistance. Under Admiral Mikawa, the Support Group was to come in the next night to bombard the field and provide gunfire support to the ground forces. They would also take on any American surface opposition. Admiral Kondo was to screen Admiral Tanaka's Reinforcement Group which was to deliver more troops and supplies. Kondo would deal with any surviving American ships. There was land based air support mixed in, from air bases in Rabaul and the Shortlands. The problem of distance would not ease or go away. Those planes continued to face the problem Japan had been facing since August: Yes, the Emperor had conquered a vast empire, but that very vastness had its costs and problems. Both bases were far away from Guadalcanal. It took the better part of a tankful of gas for planes to get from home base to the Canal and return. So the time a plane could stay on station was limited. At the time, there was no closer airfield for the Emperor's Navy fliers.

The Japanese carriers were absent. At this point in the war, the Emperor had suffered some carrier losses. Four were put under at Midway, and one light carrier was sunk at Coral Sea. Many ships remained although some were some seriously damaged. Others were intact but their air crews were decimated. The dearth of experienced pilots was a more serious long term problem for the Emperor than was number of carriers. It takes a long time just to train a pilot to fly. Learning to fly to and from carriers is another time consuming step. Then learning to fight well enough to survive actual combat takes time as well. In 1941, Japan had a very good corps of naval pilots. They were, man for man, probably the most experienced and combat wise group of carrier pilots in the world. Although they were deep in experience the group was shallow in numbers. By late 1942, war had taken its toll. A year of combat operations had taken a scythe to the corps of experienced pilots. Four or five carrier battles had reduced the number of experienced plane drivers. Unremitting combat with raids from Pearl Harbor to the Indian Ocean had further drained their numbers. And the debacle at Midway with the sinking of Japan's four main carriers forced many pilots to ditch their planes into the Pacific. Many of them drowned there, in water five miles deep. With no carrier to return to a pilot's options are grim and few. Some combat losses were anticipated. In spite of all this, the Emperor's Navy apparently did not enter the war with a formal, ramped up program to train replacement pilots. For lack of pilots as much as any other reason, Japanese aircraft carriers would not figure into the Pacific War again until mid 1944.

There was an American effort to keep the pipeline full of trained aviators. Senior officers recognized that it was critical to train and educate pilots, and to keep them coming. Army Air and Naval Bases were established all over the country to teach basic flying. There were training bases along the Arkansas River in southeast Colorado, and in scores of other places all over the country. Tens of thousands of pilots were produced to fill the demands of combat carriers, shore based antisub patrol, bombing, fighter escort, hunter killer antisub groups, transport, and other needs. Specialized skills such as overwater flying, carrier operations, night flying, low level operations, and others were taught at other bases. For instance, one place pilots were trained in carrier takeoffs and landings was on Lake Michigan. A small carrier was stationed offshore and pilots practiced flying on and off of it. This was one of many creative and efficient approaches to the problem.

One man's experiences will give us a look into how the naval training regimen worked. Wilmer Rawie came from North Dakota, a long way from the sea. He was appointed to Annapolis in 1934 and graduated from the Naval Academy in 1938. After duty with the fleet, he qualified for flight training. Basic flight training was rigorous and thorough, and was conducted from a naval air base near Pensacola, Florida. To this day Pensacola is the primary US naval flight training center. Rawie went on to become a fighter pilot and qualified for carrier operations. He served on the USS Enterprise early in the war, at first under Admiral Halsey.

The Americans made a two carrier raid on the Marshall and Gilbert Islands in early February 1942. Several notable facts about this: First, The Japanese in raiding Pearl Harbor thought it would buy them at least six months and maybe longer before the Americans could mount any offensive operations. That would give them, they hoped, time to conquer what they wanted in Southeast Asia. The rationale behind Pearl Harbor was simply to buy that six or eight months' time. They badly misjudged the effect of their undeclared war, not to mention US capability and fighting spirit. The Americans were able and willing to mount this raid a mere seven weeks after the Pearl attack, not six or eight months. Second, Nimitz and the Washington brass were reading much of Japanese naval radio traffic. They could not read it all, not even close, but enough to help the effort. They were able to deduce parts of Japan's plan to secure their conquests. Part of their thinking was to attack to the southeast of the Marshalls. If they could hurt or take Canton or Samoa they could dominate and make it difficult to access Australia. The Americans needed to keep those lanes clear and safe. Thus they made a disrupting attack of their own on the Gilberts and Marshalls. Later in the year they would take Guadalcanal and go on the offensive in New Guinea for the same reasons—to safeguard Australia.

These two raids were early in the war, and they did not in fact cause a lot of damage. The gunnery was not particularly accurate and not too many enemy planes were destroyed. But seeing America hit back gave homefront morale a big boost. People didn't care if it wasn't a major attack causing big damage. They were happy to see America taking the fight to the enemy. The raid gave the men and officers practice in real operations. Wil Rawie set a record in this raid. He became the first American carrier pilot to shoot down an enemy plane. Visual confirmation and postwar Japanese records confirm this.

Rawie went on to fly in later carrier raids that spring, raids the Japanese had not anticipated being possible. He flew over Marcus and Wake Islands. He also flew from the Enterprise when Halsey delivered Doolittle's B24s to raid Tokyo, and in the Midway battle in early June. By that point, he was one of the most experienced carrier pilots in the fleet. He had combat experience and at least one shootdown to his credit.

Lieutenant Rawie was sent Stateside in July 1942. As an experienced combat pilot with a kill to his credit, he was a real asset. He and others like him were not used up like their Japanese counterparts. Rather he was pulled out of active operations, and his experience was mined and taught to new pilots. He became an instructor. Rawie was posted to Green Cove Springs Naval Air Station in Florida. As an Instructor Pilot, he used his experience and hard won wisdom to teach fighter tactics and skills to upcoming pilots. He later became Superintendent of Air Training at Green Cove Springs and remained there till mid 1944.

NOVEMBER 12: THROWING LIGHTNING BOLTS; TRAINING PILOTS; INDIA | 149

Then he rotated out to the Pacific. He commanded and trained a night fighting squadron. This was an innovative development, and Rawie was the man to run it. It operated off of the USS Saratoga. Rawie led this squadron in the Okinawa campaign. He was in on the kill of the battleship Yamato late in the war. This is the same fine battleship which was Admiral Yamamoto's floating hotel in the fall of 1942. She may have fired her guns in bombardment at some time but she never fired a shot in anger at another ship. In the spring of 1945 Yamato was sent from the home islands towards Okinawa. Her orders were to steam in and shoot up the American invasion fleet there. If the ship survived that, then she was to beach herself and support Japanese troops with their guns. Wil Rawie and several hundred other carrier pilots found her. She was spotted between Japan and Okinawa, and she was sunk.

The vast majority of the several hundred pilots who put Yamato under were not professional Naval pilots. They were civilians when Pearl Harbor was attacked. They had come through the Naval pilot training network Rawie had been part of. Green Cove Springs Naval Air Station where Rawie taught was but one of scores of Naval air training sites. And the Army Air Corps had hundreds of airfields all around the country. There were Air Corps Training Bases in almost every state of the Union. The Air Corps utilized experienced pilots as teachers just like Wil Rawie taught for the Navy. As pilots gained experience some would be brought back to pass that learning and experience on. By the end of the war, the US military had tens of thousands of qualified pilots.

Even a well trained pilot with no combat time needs to be brought along. The US provided a steady supply of pilots with adequate flying time to step into combat with minimal problems. The Japanese military never did master this process. Lieutenant Wil Rawie was one of thousands of fliers whose experience was used to teach new pilots and expand the pilot corps of the US military.

Another man's experience will give a different perspective to the US aviation training program. Mike Negri was born in southern Colorado and grew up in Louisville, a coal mining town north of Denver. He worked at a mine right out of high school. His job was on the surface working with the processing machinery. Not satisfied with a mining career, he gravitated to southern California and went to work for Consolidated Aircraft, manufacturing bombers. He got drafted in the fall of 1942.

About the time big questions were being answered in Stalingrad, North Africa, and the south and southwest Pacific, the US Army's expansion was hitting full stride. Negri was one of millions of youth who got a letter or telegram ordering him to active duty. This draft program and its the influx of Americans brought the weight of the US population to bear in fighting the war. But that is another story. Negri was drafted into the Army Air Corps and spent two months in basic training in Miami. Then because he had a mechanical and aviation background, he volunteered to become an armorer. Those are the people who put bombs in the planes and make sure the guns are loaded and that the plane is tuned to be the weapon it is meant to be. He spent six months in Denver learning those skills. Then he went to gunnery school for two months in Florida, learning to aim and fire guns to maximum effect. From there he went to Oklahoma and was assigned to a plane. He spent the war with the 9th Air Force in the Mediterranean theater. He was a gunner on an A20 plane which provided support to ground troops. If a soldier needed support, an A20 would come and strafe the area and hopefully clear it for the GI.

Negri's experience is typical. Not only did it take a lot of time to train pilots, it took a lot of time and resources to train the crews and support staff. Negri was one of hundreds of thousands of men who went through thorough training and who made the American air war work. He ended the war a Staff Sergeant.

Canada too participated in a huge and sophisticated pilot training scheme. The country provided space and facilities for pilot training. Pilots from all over the British Empire trained at bases throughout the country. Their curriculum and training was similar to the Americans'.

Admiral Yamamoto may have known of the oncoming rush of trained American pilots. But he had to work with what he had. So, whether he had enough pilots to use his carriers or no, he was determined to fight it out in the Solomon Islands. His efforts to take the island and get it done on Z day were in full swing. Code breaking, traffic analysis, aerial patrols, and prisoner interrogation all told the Allies that something was up. They knew the Emperor's forces were assembling and a big push was coming.

In the South Pacific, Halsey had several task forces. One was hovering under the horizon to the south. It comprised two new American battleships and four destroyers under command of Rear Admiral Willis Lee. For the time being, it was part of the escort force of the USS Enterprise, the only American carrier operative in the Pacific. There were two more forces. Rear Admiral Norman Scott with a cruiser and destroyer force reported on the 11th to Cactus. There was another admiral already in those waters with a task force of his own. That man, Rear Admiral Callaghan, was senior to Scott in rank. Callaghan did not have a lot of seniority on Scott. But he had held the rank a little longer, thus was in command. The Navy always considered that the Senior Officer Present Afloat, or SOPA, was in charge, no exceptions. That way there was never a question about what to do or whom to obey. SOPA called the shots, literally and figuratively. On November 12 1942, Callaghan was SOPA in Cactus waters. He had his own cruiser–destroyer force.

Both Callaghan's and Scott's task forces had escorted in transports. Those ships had brought up supplies. There was also a contingent of Army reinforcement troops. GIs, Marine ground and aviation reinforcements, and navy forces were coming to Guadalcanal in greater numbers than early in the campaign. The US was able to bring in supplies and reinforcements without loss.

Halsey was sitting down in Noumea worriedly watching developments. He took seriously his promise to support Vandegrift and the troops on Guadalcanal and Tulagi. He took what warships and men he had available and sent them up to Guadalcanal. At this point of the campaign he did not have the luxury of sorting out exactly what should happen and who was best suited to direct the battle. His orders were essentially that they should go out and stop the Japanese. He could not mix and match his men and ships for the best combinations. He had to react to events and Japanese moves with whatever ships and task forces he could assemble and send in.

Scott had actual local night combat experience with a recent victory against Japan under his belt. Callaghan had no combat time. He had been an aide and friend to Roosevelt in the White House. Most recently, he had been chief of staff to the fired SoPac Commander Admiral Ghormley. For better or worse, he was now afloat and leading combat forces. Here again the warrior/administrator divide raised its head. Whatever the situation might have been, the actual situation was that Callaghan was senior and Callaghan was in charge. He and Scott had each recently sortied from Espiritu Santo for Cactus. They were now joined in one task force and on the prowl around the Canal. They were ready to do their best to stop the Japanese invasion. Their time in the crosshairs would come soon. Late on that night, they restlessly and warily patrolled the waters of Ironbottom Sound.

The middle of November saw a number of battles on waters around Guadalcanal. These battles stemmed from Z Day and Halsey's sending in task forces and reinforcements. That is, they stemmed from both sides trying to keep what they had and evict the other from the island. These struggles involved forces led by Scott, Callaghan, Lee, Abe, Kondo, Tanaka, and Mikawa. Or more precisely, it involved them all and killed some of them. Also fighting and killed were thousands of sailors and soldiers. This set of battles came to be known as The Naval Battle of Guadalcanal.

Fairly described as a turning point, in ways it was the fulcrum on which the seesaw of the Pacific War which had been balanced finally started to tilt down. It was a three day melee starting on the 12th of November, 1942. Air, naval, and ground elements all contributed. The primary action was naval with scenes straight out of Dante's seventh level of hell. This was experienced by American and Japanese sailors just offshore and further out around the island. It was also endured by Japanese troops being shipped south as reinforcements. The Battle cost each side men, ships and planes. Some Admirals' reputations were built and others got trashed. As the smoke cleared on November 16, the seesaw was definitely moving.

The war continued to gnaw away almost everywhere around the globe. Almost everywhere there were ruined economies, shattered bodies and lives, gutted buildings. Every populated continent but South America saw at least some bullets and bombs fly. North America saw a little action, but it was virtually free of war damage. The war was so pervasive that even on that continent, some countries felt its effects. For example, in Argentina and other southern nations the conflict was carried on by proxies. Bullets did not fly, but the sides vied and competed in most every other way. Spies and diplomats maneuvered as they sought political, informational, and economic advantage.

Another part of the world also experienced the war in its own way. In south Asia, life went on in India much as it had for centuries. Most of the Indian population paid little heed to the White Man's War going on in and around their country. Those who paid attention saw there were several types of warfare going on around them. In one aspect, it was a regular theater of war. It was a clear-cut, traditional war: the task was to find the enemy and kill him or make him retreat. In either case the goal was straightforward. But there was a subtler front to the war going on as well. This was an ideological and political war for an independent state, free of British colonialists. In it, sides were chosen, battles were fought, and some deaths occurred, but it was not a conflict between two uniformed forces.

India was a hotbed of colonial and domestic politics. This was manifested by espionage, riots, factions seeking independence, caste rigidities and hatred, religious rivalries and animosities, and incipient revolution. The British had in fact ruled India for over a century. Its government there was known as the Raj. What we know today as Pakistan was under the Raj as part of India then. India was an important part of the Empire and of the British economy, indeed it was called the "Crown Jewel of Empire." With relatively few Europeans, never more than several hundred thousand, the Raj ruled a nation of hundreds of millions. They did this several ways. They adroitly played off war lords, rajahs, and opposing political parties. They relied on superior technology and communications. Even more important in maintaining rule was prestige. Westerners, those of European descent, had an aura of invincibility. This impression had developed around the European, the westerner, the Anglo over centuries. It got stronger over time as the Europeans consolidated their holdings and power. India and the Raj started with merchants who were allowed to set up a trading post on the shore. In decades, using every means they could devise, they became rulers of the continent. Their methods, common language, and arms helped them to take charge. But it was this quality perceived by Asians that the westerners were smarter, quicker, and just better than anyone else that really carried the day. It was routinely exploited by the Raj and other westerners throughout the region. It was used to help keep social order. It was occasionally used to overawe and intimidate the native population. This phenomenon was not unique to India. All the western countries enjoyed this prestige throughout east and Southeast Asia, China, the Philippines, and much of Africa as well.

By the 1930's the Japanese were intent on creating and making secure their own empire. They felt entitled and divinely led to this. With their own belief in divinely inspired invincibility, they did not hesitate to ignore other countries which were in their way. They used their aura, their self belief, to intimidate westerners in the process. This was unheard of in that part of the world, an Asian standing up to a westerner. Japan had run roughshod over Russian interests and the Korea Peninsula around the turn of the century. Then in the 1930's they went into and annexed part Manchuria and made inroads in China. They were not hesitant to marginalize Westerners and their national interests. In 1935 Japanese planes even sank the American gunboat, the USS Panay on the Yangtze River in China. They claimed it was a mistake and paid an indemnity. But they were clearly willing to use force to advance what they saw as their interests in China.

The western mystique, the aura of invincibility Americans and Europeans had enjoyed for so long, was tarnished. The western inability to overawe Japan, an Asian nation, was seen by other Asians as weakness. In 1940 Japan occupied French Indochina (now the countries of Vietnam, Laos, and Cambodia). The

Emperor's troops simply came in and took the area over. This conquest gave them bases within striking distance of British and Dutch possessions. France was in no position to oppose this invasion since they were under Hitler's heel. While they let the local French colonialists stay in office, Japan ruled. The French there were puppets of the Emperor. They were just as subservient to the new masters as were the Hungarian or Norwegian governments installed and tolerated by Hitler. This subjugation of French Indochina further eroded the idea of western invincibility.

Then in late 1941 the Japanese unleashed a mighty war. Striking US, British, and Dutch strongholds on islands and the Asian mainland, they conquered quickly and easily. These conquests were a severe shock to Westerners. In late 1941, the general western belief was Japanese were bucktoothed weaklings who couldn't fight their way out of a closet. How wrong that stereotype! By mid 1942 the western colonial masters of most Asian possessions had been killed, enslaved, or run out. Japanese men, that is, ethnic Asians, had overrun the once invincible westerners. Within six months, all the western empires had disappeared. Gone were western preferential areas in China. Gone were colonies in the American Philippines, British Malaya along with Hong Kong and Singapore, the Netherlands East Indies, Dutch and Australian New Guinea, British Solomon Islands, a number of British and American owned central Pacific islands, British Burma. There was a new colonial overseer and he lived in Tokyo. Japanese might and power lapped up even to the edges of India itself.

These conquests, and the ease with they were made, drove a stake through the heart of any idea or aura of natural western superiority. People who had been colonial subjects, those at the bottom of the heap, suddenly saw a whole new and unexpected world. Their former masters, white men!, were humiliated, run off, or enslaved. The Asians who had lived in western colonies quickly found that they had just exchanged colonial masters. Their new overseers weren't Anglo or European, but Japanese. The story of how the Emperor's men treated their subjects and tried to exploit their resources is a tale for another time.

In India.... No Japanese boots trod on Indian soil in 1942. Even the remote eastern provinces near Burma remained in the Raj. Nipponese men would try to invade in 1944, but not yet. Many Indian eyes watched as their Japanese fellow Asians pushed the westerners in other countries around. The Emperor's men were pummeling and demoralizing every western Army and Navy they took on. In India, a long building patriotism took encouragement from this. It was nourishment for the very soul of the independence movement. The desire to eject the British, to have an independent India, was widespread. The many who had this desire were scattered with no voice. But with every day bringing down another old colonial power, with white men humiliated and defeated, the wish for national independence and statehood started to coalesce, take hold, and grow. Muslims and Hindus wanted their own countries but both sides could agree that they wanted the British out.

One longstanding Indian political faction was the Congress Party. It spoke for many, if not most, Hindus. It was led by Mohan Das Gandhi. This man was born a Hindu into the Bania merchant caste, a caste with an outlook roughly equivalent to the American Quakers. He went to London as a young man and studied law. London is where young men from around the Empire went to make contacts and improve themselves. Many, like Gandhi, became barristers. A barrister is a lawyer who is qualified to plea cases in court. Gandhi was not one to sit in an office and file corporation papers and wills. Debating, thrusting and parrying in making far reaching decisions and precedents was what he trained for. From London, he detoured to South Africa. It too was part of the British Empire. In Africa, he gained experience and a name by agitating for the rights of expatriate Indians who had settled there. In 1914 he returned home to India. His travels and the experience he gained served him well in his political career. While in London and South Africa, not only did he hone his debating and legal skills, he developed a feel for the British. He gained knowledge of and a sort of empathy for British motivations, strengths and weaknesses. The man recognized that the Raj was distracted and indebted by the war effort of World War One. He quickly became involved in the agitation for independence that racked the subcontinent from 1914 to 1918. His aim was to make the Congress Party dominant in domestic politics, and he largely succeeded.

One of the benefits of Empire is to use colonies' riches for the benefit of the home country. One way this took place in India is the Indian Army. Early in their imperial adventures the British had established an army based on India. At first they were troops in commercial employ. By the twentieth century those troops were part of a national, or properly colonial, army. It was funded and directed by the Raj. It was used freely over time. Often it was used in India proper to keep peace and order. It was also used as an adjunct to the British Army in its various wars and campaigns around the globe.

This force, The Indian Army, was paid for by taxes and duties raised from the Indian people. It was staffed by Indian nationals with a "stiffening" of British battalions attached. The low and mid level officers were chiefly British, Irish or Scotch. The senior officers were all British. A few of the enlisted men were British but most were Indian. The Indian Army fought in every theater in World War I. It even contributed troops to the maw of the trenches in Flanders. In the runup to World War II, the Army was used again. Indian Army troops fought Rommel in North Africa and were stationed in Burma and Malaya in 1940 and 1941.

Use of the Indian Army on foreign soil was not controversial, but use of it as an internal police force was decidedly unpopular. It was just another act of the Raj which stirred domestic Indian politics. Now after World War II started, independence issues came out and to the fore. The Congress Party led by Gandhi saw opportunities for political leverage or even perhaps independence. They wanted a "national government," presumably made up of Indians not British. The Congress Party's position was that they would encourage the populations' help in fighting the war only if they got participation in the government, a seat at the table. Gandhi worked to extract concessions to help the British with their war aims. But Gandhi was a Hindu. The Muslim population of British India wanted no part of him or his party. They, even in the early

1940s, stated a desire for a separate nation. They wanted the British out, the Raj gone, and the Hindus in another country. They talked about their new Muslim country and even had a name picked out for it. They got their country in 1947 when the colonialists left after WWII. The Crown Jewel of the British Empire was split with much bloodshed into Hindu India and Muslim Pakistan in 1947.

The war broke out in 1939. Up until 1942 the maneuvering and dissension around Indian independence stayed in the background. The Raj was aware of Indian desires and there was consultation with London on the matter. Things came to a head about the time Germans were nearing Stalingrad and Americans were invading Guadalcanal. In August, Gandhi and the Congress Party called for a widespread movement of non-cooperation and civil disobedience. Further, they called for the British to "Quit India." They publicly called for the British to get out. First response, the Raj rounded up and jailed many Congress Party leaders. There was much unrest and some outright rioting and destruction. This forced the tying up of railways to move troops around to keep peace. Even at this stage of the war the Indian Army had to be used for peacekeeping at home, not fighting at the front. From that point, August 1942, things were dramatically different. The British faced what their own General Lockhart called "An occupied and hostile country." These distractions weakened Allied war effort in the Far East. Having a huge, restive population at their rear was different from the united, motivated population the British had at home. The consequent diversion of men and resources which were needed elsewhere did not endear Mr. Gandhi to the Raj nor the Home Government.

Earlier that year, one of the Congress Party's main leaders upped the ante. Subhas Chandra Bose was a leader of the party. He was not as well known as Gandhi but still was a major part of its leadership. He had left, some say escaped from, India. He worked his way to Berlin and solicited support from Hitler. The Fuhrer was at best lukewarm to the idea of entangling his government in Indian domestic politics. There were several reasons. Mr. Bose not meet Nazi standards of Aryanism. Bose's being short, swarthy, and not of northern European ancestry did not endear him to the German leadership. Also Hitler deemed Bose's country, indeed the entire region as a sideshow. Center stage for the chief Nazi was his struggle with Stalin's Communist Soviet Union.

German foreign policy was officially supportive of the "Quit India" movement and Congress Party's efforts. The Foreign Ministry maintained some contact with the Indian independence movement. There were a number of German intelligence estimates about India. One estimate alleged that the Quit India movement had come close to toppling the Raj. This was wildly, even recklessly, optimistic. The movement certainly did cause problems and disruptions. The Raj was never near being overthrown and the British remained firmly in control.

After a face to face meeting, Hitler had Bose shunted off to the Japanese. The German Foreign Ministry arranged for him to be sent to Singapore by Uboat. The Japanese embraced him and brought him to Tokyo for consultations. The Imperial Government was looking for ways to take advantage of their immense new empire and its resources. They were interested in people who could help run friendly, subservient governments in the recently conquered territories. Imperial Headquarters later set him up as a general. He was made head of the newly formed Indian National Army. This was quisling force. It was manned by deserters and left behinds of the Indian Army defeated in Singapore, Burma, and Malaya. The Japanese supplied it and took it to India when they tried to invade in 1944. The INA pretty much melted away during that campaign. It never was a force to be reckoned with. Bose faded from the Indian scene and was reported killed in an airplane crash in 1945. There is a school of thought that he survived and lived anonymously into the 1980's.

The effort to oust the Raj did not enjoy universal support. Most Indians were not discontent with their government. For many it made no difference. Most Indians were focused on day to day life. Their main concern was this season's crop and when the monsoon would arrive. The British run Indian Army had no trouble filling enlistment rolls. There was never a draft or forced service. The number of volunteers was adequate if not overwhelming.

Late 1942 saw military forces in use in a number of ways in India. The Raj used the Indian Army to tamp down the widespread but localized rebellion. Of the total troops in the field, only a small percentage was so occupied. The Indian Army fielded many more troops against the Japanese than for peacekeeping. The focus of the Army was an active campaign to retake Burma. In autumn 1942 the Arakan Peninsula saw fighting. This was located on the extreme west of Burma, right next to India. It was monsoon season and rains came predictably and relentlessly. Even so, the 4th Indian Division attacked south down this peninsula on the northwest Burmese coast. The 55th Japanese Division and 213th Regiment stood athwart their approach. There was thrust and parry, with the opponents coming to a halt facing each other near the town of Maungdaw. This part of Burma saw fighting throughout the war. Its location and climate made it a difficult arena. The main reason it saw action was that it was fairly accessible to India. If it had been taken it would have given a base for attacking Rangoon. The Arakan really never was a major objective.

India served as a base for sending supplies and supporting China against Japan. Until very late in the war it was a secondary theater. By late 1944 and early 1945 major operations were undertaken to clear Burma and open road access to China.

CHAPTER VIII
November 13–15
Naval Battle of Guadalcanal

Emperor Hirohito and Uncle Sam had been fighting for months on, over, and around Guadalcanal. Things were coming to a head in mid November. The clash which would settle the ownership of southern Solomon Islands waters was building. It is known as the Naval Battle of Guadalcanal.

This struggle was not a single firefight, a single encounter of ships. It is actually a set of battles occurring over about three days.

The time from about midnight November 12 through the early hours of November 15 was when the seesaw started to tip. As the sun rose over the southern Solomon Islands on November 15 it was not apparent that a major change had occurred. All everyone knew was there had been a whole lot of shooting and ships damaged or sunk. And that a lot of people had been drowned, shot from the sky, or otherwise had their life ended. Those deaths had been put on the cosmic scales. Numbers, the manner of death, and the place of each had dictated that one side was losing the struggle, one starting to win it. We can see now that the outcome would be the start of the entire war going Allies' way. But at the start, on the afternoon of November 12 the men on the scene knew not the future. They nervously and seriously prepared themselves and their machines for a fight. The previous chapter listed all the various forces that were gathering, planning and organizing to do battle.

To recap, the Emperor's forces were aiming to use their

nighttime sea control to send ships to neutralize and then take back Henderson Field. If they gained domination of the local sea and air they could project power. Power projected south over the approaches to Australia and New Zealand would isolate those areas used as bases by the American enemy. The Allies were determined to use their daylight control of the air to stop that invasion and establish their own control of the local seas. Likewise, they then could project power. Their aim would be northward towards Japanese bases in Rabaul, Truk, and ultimately, on to Tokyo.

Each side had mastered part of the formula for regional domination and victory. Neither had been able to solve the entire formula but they knew what was needed. Both recognized the other had the part missing for solving the formula. The task was to wrest that part away from the other.

Like any battle, the Naval Battle of Guadalcanal really doesn't lend itself to exact, linear description. When the enemy was sighted, it was usually by many people on multiple ships. As soon as the enemy was sighted, things started to happen fast. Ships were trying to evade each other. They were firing torpedoes and shooting at others. Captains tried to keep formation which meant recognizing friend or foe, and communicating with team mates. In the dark, ships were illuminated as targets. And every ship was trying to do the same things. Much occurred simultaneously in the skies over and on the sea, in an area of several hundred square miles.

For these reasons, laying out a neatly segmented account is difficult. To start with, this drama had three acts.

- Act I 12–13 November. This was the Battle of Cape Esperance, a melee on the sea around Savo Island. It was a very confused battle with the two navies' ships intermingled and clawing at each other. American Admirals Scott and Callaghan were killed as were many sailors of both Navies. Numerous ships were sunk. Japanese Admiral Abe lost less ships than Callaghan but failed to get in to bombard Henderson. Retreating Japanese and American ships were sunk the next day.

- Act II. Cactus Air Force sank Japanese troop transports the 13th during the day. Japanese Admiral Nishimura got into the area to bombard Henderson the night of the 13th and early on the 14th. During daylight hours of the 14th, more troop transports were sunk by the CAF. Thousands of Japanese troops were drowned and hundreds of tons of supplies were lost.

- Act III Night of 14th–15th. The big boys collided at the meeting of the Battleships. Admiral Lee's big gun force met Admiral Kondo's cruisers and battleships. Both leaders had ships sunk but Kondo lost a battleship. He did not get through to bombard Henderson.

To summarize, here is the background as this Battle opened: Admiral Yamamoto expected that his complicated battle plan would culminate on Friday November 13. The plan called it Z Day. As mentioned, that was the day Henderson Field was to be taken by the Army. To aid the effort, the Navy would land an additional 60,000 troops to finish annihilating the few remaining Americans. Included in this battle plan were a number of fleets and task forces. These various flotillas were to bombard the airfield, sweep the area clean of American ships, and protect the troop landings. Land based planes would come down from the north to provide more air cover to the various ships.

The Americans did not know anything about Z Day. Had they known, they would not have been impressed. They did know another attempt to dislodge them was coming, and soon. Admiral Halsey continued to honor his promise of support to the Marines and everyone else on the Canal. He sent what he could as ships became available. ComSoPac had already sent Rear Admiral Scott to escort troop and supply ships with a mixed cruiser and destroyer. Scott headed north from Noumea to the front. On November 12, Scott arrived and reported to Admiral Callaghan. This officer himself had just escorted in a group of transports with his own warships. Callaghan's group, Task Force 67.4 was made up of cruisers and destroyers.

This scenario shows Halsey's plight: Scott had combat experience. In fact, he was the only American Admiral afloat in the South Pacific who had a fairly clear cut win to his credit. Callaghan was senior by several weeks. Therefore by US Naval tradition and regulation, he took overall command of his and Scott's ships. This grouping of combatants was a hastily assembled naval force. The ships of the two Admiral's combined force had not previously worked or maneuvered together. Most of them had not seen close quarter night combat. There was scant time, only hours, to form a battle plan. Time to practice or train for the battle simply did not exist. Dan Callaghan had not had his ticket punched as a fighting leader: he had been chief of staff to Admiral Ghormley. That slot gave him no combat experience. He had not really even driven a ship or managed a task force of ships at night in combat. No matter, as the senior officer, he was in command. But perhaps, and we have heard this verse before, Callaghan's fatal flaw was that he did not grasp the advantages radar could give him. All that is not said to criticize. The admiral fought the battle bravely, with determination, and ultimately his forces prevailed.

The curtain was raised on the night of 12–13 November. Admiral Abe formed up his Raiding Group in the northern Solomon Islands. He raised steam and headed his ships south to the Guadalcanal area. This flotilla was the first group of the grand Nipponese battle plan whose task was to bombard Henderson Field. Abe led a naval war party. He had no reinforcements or transports to guard. He had no carriers to escort. Job one was simply to put as many shells as possible on the airstrip. The Raiding Group's ships were loaded with high explosive ammunition, HE for short. This type of shell, the HE, is very effective against land targets. It explodes on impact and can destroy planes and buildings and kill people. However HE ammunition is not very effective if used against ships. For that the sailor needs armor piercing shells, AP for short. AP ammo is designed to penetrate through armor before exploding. Abe was loaded with HE ammunition, not AP. If he had to brush aside some Americans in order to get the gunnery done, so be it. Japanese intelligence told him he needn't expect significant opposition, maybe a few PT boats or a destroyer. Admiral Abe was focused on shelling the airstrip. For this assignment, he commanded two battleships, a light cruiser, and six destroyers. A thorough bombardment of the American holdings was the thing. The aim was to crater the runways, put holes in planes, set gasoline stocks afire and kill pilots. If well done, that would stop Cactus planes from jumping the approaching troop transports. Those soldier laden ships with their escorts were already at sea. They were scheduled to start landing troops the next day.

The timing of Abe's approach was delicate. The thing was to be there as soon as he could to pump lead at the enemy. But he had to avoid being seen or attacked by air patrols from Cactus. So he made sure he was out of range and out of sight until the proper hour of the night. On the way down the fleet had turned back once. By doing a u-turn he killed time. It was necessary to stall to keep under cover of a rain squall. The Japanese, remember, did not have or really know much about radar at this point. As far as Abe was concerned, if he was hidden in a rain squall no one on earth could know he was there. And it was important to use up some time to avoid detection.

As any fleet commander knows, keeping ships on station and in place is not easy even in good weather and daylight. In the dark keeping formation becomes much more difficult even for experienced sailors. Numerous turns with a fleet of nine ships on a dark rainy night makes it nearly impossible to keep station. And Abe's fleet experienced this. In all the maneuvering to kill time his formation became scrambled. Some of the destroyers became separated. This spoiled his tactical plan. The intent, the battle plan, was for his destroyers to be out front running interference for the heavies. They would be on the lookout for any enemy ships. Since they were out front, they would act as sponge if the enemy got the first shots off. The lead ships would, ideally, absorb the opening shots. If the destroyers took one for the team the heavies would have time to aim and fire undisturbed. The destroyers were also expected to launch torpedoes as soon as the enemy was detected. Even though Abe's destroyers were not in optimal position, he proceeded. He did not anticipate surface opposition. The admiral was willing to take on any enemies he came across but did not expect to see any Americans. A fairly easy night was anticipated. The hope, the plan, was to be able to run in, lob a number of shells, and leave.

As the Japanese force under Abe approached, Admiral Callaghan and his force were prowling the waters north of the Canal. This body of water was called Sealark Channel on maps. It would be known by another name later, for all the ships lying on the bottom there. But that night it was Sealark. American sailors of the task force were alert and on edge. They knew their force was an ad hoc creation. Everyone knew that they had not practiced together. Even so, they knew they would be relying on each other for better or worse. Callaghan had had little time to devise a battle plan and less to coach his ship captains on it. Every man there was ready to give all they had to stop the Japanese. Callaghan with his augmented task force led five cruisers and eight destroyers.

Due to a number of factors, his force, too, became scrambled. Keeping thirteen ships organized and coordinated in the dark while seeking to kill or be killed can't be easy. Perhaps those of us who haven't tried to do so ought not judge too harshly. There were many possible reasons the force got mixed up. Among those reasons are an imprecise battle plan, crew fatigue, less than crisp ship handling, lack of appreciation for radar, miscommunication or lack of communication.... This was early in the war and many of the ships and men had never fought at all, so sheer lack of practice and experience played into the scramble as well.

The two forces, Abe's and Callaghan's, were approaching each other in the inky night at a combined rate of about fifty miles per hour. A few of the American ships in the line of battle had radar. They did in fact see Abe and were ready to open fire. None of them were leading the formation but were stuck in the middle of it. Be that as it may, they saw Abe's force approaching ten or more minutes before the Japanese lookouts visually picked up the Americans. Callaghan chose to fly his flag on a ship without radar and stationed it in the middle of the line. He seems to have ignored or overlooked the reported radar sightings. He did not survive the night. In fact, he likely did not live past the opening salvoes. So we do not know just what he heard, saw, considered, and decided. Scott too left no account, having been killed before the shooting stopped.

What happened when the two forces met was a melee likened to a bar room fight with the lights shot out. It was just after midnight, early on the morning of Friday the 13th that each side's leader suddenly realized the other was there. Japanese torpedoes were launched, but American destroyers were not allowed to do so by Callaghan's order. Usually naval battles are not fought nose to nose. Rather gunshots and torpedoes are exchanged from miles apart. Not this battle: Callaghan headed his ships directly at the oncoming Japanese. He went in among Abe's fleet. For the next several hours, ships of either Navy were seen on all sides, intermingling, trying not to aim at friends but to shoot the enemy. Shots were fired by the combatants in every direction. The range was point blank, less than one thousand yards in some cases. Ships were close. Sometimes they could not lower their guns enough to bring them to bear on a nearby foe. So called friendly fire took its casualties. We know some American shells hit US ships and likely the same happened with the Japanese fleet. In the space of several hours, the US lost two cruisers and five destroyers. The Japanese lost two destroyers and had a battleship severely damaged. Both sides had other ships damaged. Shooting lasted until about three AM.

Dawn, November 13. While trying to get some rest overnight, soldiers and flyers couldn't help but see flashes and hear guns and explosions. They knew that another big gun battle raged on Ironbottom Sound, their name for Sealark Channel. They knew men were fighting and dying, but the tally, who won and who lost, would have to await the dawn. With the sun, the evidence became visible. The Sound was littered with ships dead and dying, some on fire, struggling to stay atop the sea. A few ships of each navy were making slow headway. Hundreds of men and bodies floated, coated with fuel oil. The ever present sharks roamed. American PT boats and other small vessels came out to help fight fires and offer rescue. American sailors welcomed the chance to climb or be hoisted aboard. They were grateful for another day. Not the

Emperor's sailors. Almost all Japanese refused to grasp the offered hand of rescue. Some simply swam away or dove under. There were cases of officers shooting men who were trying to surrender. They fully believed it better to die for the Emperor than live for self. A small number were taken, most against their will. They spent the rest of the war in a POW camp somewhere, probably Australia.

Admiral Abe retreated with his surviving ships and men. He failed his mission. The ships of his force ships fired not one shell towards Henderson Field that night. The bombardment that was to have been the opening salvo of the operation never occurred. No Americans were killed or stunned into inaction that night. A bombardment that was to set the stage for retaking the airfield did not occur. Scott, Callaghan, and their men paid heavily to stop it. They gave up their tomorrows so that the men ashore would not suffer bombardment and the airfield could continue to operate. The airmen, GIs and Marines would for one night not suffer a rain of six, eight, and ten inch shells.

There was more blood to be let. Each force started to head homeward. The Americans went west then south, the Japanese east and then north. Before long, both sides would inflict, and suffer, more sinkings and deaths.

The American survivors, ships and men, of Task Force 67 gathered in the waters near Tulagi. They organized a makeshift convoy under the senior surviving officer. Captain Hoover, commander of the cruiser USS Helena, stepped up and took command. The group started to limp towards safety. They could not steam at top speed but were limited to the speed of the slowest survivor. Safety in the harbor of Espiritu Santo was their goal. Almost all were damaged, some severely. Radio silence was maintained. This was standard procedure in and around combat zones to maintain secrecy. In this case it was no secret they were in the area. The Japanese certainly knew they were around. There was no air cover for the task force as it withdrew. The carrier USS Enterprise was well south and its airplanes were otherwise occupied as we will see.

TF 67's ships were hobbling and some were slowly sinking. To get to safety they had to cross the seas to the south of the

Solomon Islands. This area was known to be a hunting ground for Japanese submarines. Halsey's sailors had dubbed the area "Torpedo Junction." It had lived up to the name a few weeks earlier, in October. Then a Japanese sub had sunk the carrier USS Wasp. The sub captain had used only several torpedoes but had a big payoff. It was a real feather in his cap to sink a capital ship. Little did he know, and the US Navy didn't advertise it either, that his torpedoes reduced US carrier strength by 50%. After that sinking there was one, count it one, operable US carrier afloat in the South Pacific. As a bonus to taking the Wasp, the sub also sunk a destroyer and damaged battleship North Carolina with the one spread of three or four torpedoes. That battleship was out of commission for months.

It was not a surprise to the US sailors trying to get away from Guadalcanal that a Nipponese sub attacked them. As TF 67 slowly hobbled along the ships were sighted by Japanese submarine I-26. She sent a spread of torpedoes towards the gimping survivors. At least one hit the USS Juneau. She was a new ship, an antiaircraft cruiser. She was built to provide antiaircraft gunfire protection to the fleet, not to be in big gun fights. The fact that she was thrown into one the night before shows just how desperate Halsey was for firepower. In any event, she had been heavily damaged in the previous night's battle. She may have had her keel snapped. We'll never know for sure, but we do know she was slow and the damage made her steer sloppily. When a torpedo hit her a tremendous explosion ensued. Probably the tin fish penetrated a magazine, an ammunition storage compartment. This type of lucky shot didn't occur often. A similar fate befell the British battleship HMS Hood when it was pursuing the German battleship Bismarck in 1940. A German shell penetrated a magazine and the Hood explosively vanished. Only six of 1418 crewmen of the crew survived to be plucked out of the Atlantic. About two years later and half a world away, the Juneau explosion was similar. Certainly she suffered more than just a torpedo exploding against her side. Witnesses spoke of a gun turret flying off. This was a solid steel block twice the size of a minivan. That turret weighed many tons and was ripped from the ship like a tissue and sent flying hundreds of feet in the air. What remained of the ill fated cruiser simply disappeared in the smoke, water, and fire. All but about 100 of the 750 or so men aboard were killed outright.

The other ships of the Task Force were pretty well used up. The crews were bone tired and trying to stay afloat as they coped with the previous night's horrors. They had no weapons to use against subs, no depth charges. Almost all their ammunition was gone. None of them had working gear to track a sub underwater since their sound detection gear was damaged the previous night. The remaining ships were loath to radio for help lest that draw more Japanese, vultures to the carcass. And most of them were struggling to repair their damage and stay afloat themselves. Captain Hoover as senior officer faced an agonizing choice. Should he stop and search for survivors, thus risking the remaining ships of his group? Or should he keep going and save his ships, not risk them by stopping where he knew a hostile submarine lurked? Should he try to save a few while risking the lives of many, or save the lives of many while giving up a few? It can't have been easy, especially since he and his men were exhausted. All hands had been awake for thirty six hours. They had just escaped a horrific fight with their lives but watched friends and shipmates lose theirs. Hoover made the decision he deemed best for the fleet and the situation. He chose to save the ships, not to risk them by stopping for survivors.

The man who had had to step up and command the wretched task force did the best he could. He found a way to try to help the survivors (if any) in the water. Keeping radio silence, he had a signalman use a mirror to signal a passing B17 bomber. By this flashing Morse code, he sent word of the tragedy and a request for help. That request got delayed and rescue did not arrive for some time. Of the one hundred or so men who lived through the Juneau explosion, ten survived to be picked up days later. Sharks, thirst, and battle wounds took the rest. Sailor George Sullivan survived the explosion but did not live to be rescued. He was one of five brothers from Waterloo Iowa serving together on the ship. None of his brothers survived the blast. Their loss brought a change in Navy and Army policy: henceforth siblings could not serve on the same ship or in the same unit. Later in the war a newly launched destroyer was named for the brothers. USS The Sullivans served gallantly the last two years of the war.

Hoover's surviving ships reached the safety of Espiritu Santo with no further losses. The acting task force commander reported the battle and losses to ComSoPac. Halsey was furious that he did not stop to help the survivors of the Juneau. He sent Hoover out of the theater and saw to it that the man was never promoted. After the war, too late for the Captain, Admiral Halsey agreed that Hoover's decision had been the right one at that place and time. Halsey acknowledged that the man should not have been criticized or punished.

To the north of Guadalcanal, the Japanese found they were not yet done paying their butcher's bill. Admiral Abe was withdrawing his ships. While he was running for safety, his fleet came under the very air attack it had been sent down to curtail. The plane drivers at Henderson Field had heard the night battle and at dawn, had seen the sinking ships. On early patrol, they searched the sea that morning of Friday, November 13. Hoping to find Japanese, they wanted to finish what Callaghan and Scott had started. A shipload of planes from the carrier USS Enterprise joined the hunt. Also came a flotilla of B17s, high altitude heavy bombers flying from Espiritu Santo. It was to one of these planes that Captain Hoover sent a signal to about the survivors of the Juneau.

The Yankee planes found the remnants of Abe's fleet working north away from Guadalcanal. Hiei, a venerable Japanese battleship, had been greatly damaged the night before. The pilots from Cactus jumped her. Seventy planes attacked starting just after 0600. Twenty five Nipponese Navy planes defended her. The Emperor's Eleventh Air Fleet took down three Americans at the cost of eleven pilots and planes. Hiei hung tough as she absorbed multiple torpedo and bomb hits. At one time Abe ordered her to be beached on the Canal but this was not carried out. The planes mortally hurt her. Her escorts did their best to protect her but damage to them was mounting. Late in the day she was abandoned and scuttled. Hiei slid under sometime after dark on the 13th.

On that day, the Cactus Air Force grew markedly in size and strength. Eight US Army Air Forces P38 twin engine fighters flew in. They joined Marine and Navy fighters and bombers, and Army Aircobra fighters. While eight planes is in itself not a huge number, this addition was the starting trickle of what would become a flood of new air assets coming to Guadalcanal. The P38 was a powerful, well armed, state of the art fighter. Its addition strengthened the reach and punch of Vandegrift's air force. Also that morning, fifteen planes took off from the USS Enterprise which was cruising south of the island. They were slated to land and stay at Henderson Field. But before they touched down and officially became the latest additions to the Cactus Air Force, they found and struck at battleship Hiei. This wounded lady was to become the first of the Japanese battleships sunk by the Americans.

Late in the day on the 13th, from the north came the second act of the drama. Admiral Nishimura with three cruisers and four destroyers headed south to the Canal. His force successfully bombarded the airfield complex just after midnight, early on the 14th. He did not encounter any heavy American combatants. However he had to contend with some opposition. During his two hour bombardment the admiral had to evade sorties by light units. Two American PT boats fired torpedoes but did no damage. These were small fast wooden boats, PT for "Patrol" Boats, which were designed to harry the enemy and go into shallow waters to make trouble. In this case the boats successfully made trouble. Their attacks confused or unsettled the Admiral. He was trying to shoot up Henderson Field but in fact shelled Fighter One, a grass strip. A subsidiary air strip, it was located a mile east of Henderson. In mid September it had been made to allow dispersal of planes and operations. Nishimura's shells destroyed and damaged a number of planes there. His bombardment altogether missed the main airfield and plane storage area. Even after that, the next morning both Fighter One and Henderson were operational and sent up planes.

Admiral Yamamoto had to move Z Day back. This was not the

first time Imperial Headquarters had to postpone victory celebrations. The admirals and generals there were finding the Allies had their own plans and timetables. It was dawning on them that the world did not necessarily bend to Nipponese intentions and desires.

The point of the whole Z Day operation was to be able to send down and land soldiers unhindered by American air attacks. That is what Abe was supposed to have accomplished and Nishimura was to have reinforced. They came down to the Canal, but both failed to conquer. The Admirals' big guns were not able to neuter the air power based on the field.

Even though these two senior Japanese officers didn't play their parts, the rest of the plan continued to move forward. The transports carrying the invasion troops and their escorts had followed Abe down south. Their invasion was supposed to be the follow-on to Abe's successful bombardment. This troop carrying fleet was commanded by Admiral Tanaka. Called the Reinforcement Group, it was comprised of twenty two ships, eleven transports and eleven destroyers. All twenty two were packed with supplies and crammed with troops. Tanaka had held up, slowed and bought time, when Abe was roughly handled by Scott and Callaghan. He had actually started to beat a retreat. But after midnight, early on the 14th, Tanaka turned his transports south again and headed towards the Island. This admiral was nicknamed "Tenacious Tanaka" by Yankee intelligence. He was stubbornly determined to land his troops and supplies. His track record of delivering men and supplies was solid and reliable.

Americans sent search planes out with the morning light on the 14th. There were planes from the USS Enterprise and Cactus Air Force craft from Henderson. They first found Abe's retreating ships. Hiei had been put down the day before, but there were many other targets for the Americans fliers. Pilots and bombardiers went to work, dropping bombs and strafing. The Kinugasa, a retreating Japanese cruiser in Abe's force, was sunk about 1000 hours. Others of Abe's fleet were damaged as they ran north. He finally ran out of range of the Cactus Air Force and safely reached harbor later.

Admiral Tanaka's fleet of transports continued to come south. They were located by searchers at 0730. This was ninety minutes after Abe's fleet had been sighted. Vandegrift knew an assault force was coming and recognized these transports and destroyers as the fleet carrying the invasion troops. Better to try to sink them than wait to fight them on the beach, he reasoned. Planes were scrambled from Cactus when their location was reported. The transports were attacked starting at 0830. American pilots dug in and made the most of the opportunity to drown the invaders. Thirty or more planes at a time bombed and strafed these twenty two fat slow lightly defended targets. Tanaka's fleet put up what antiaircraft fire it could. They were overmatched and undergunned. It must have been horrific to be a Japanese Army Private stuck on a packed slow moving ship deck while being shot up and bombed. There was some Japanese fighter protection, Zeros flown by naval pilots, but they too were overmatched.

On that day, the 14th, Tanaka took a beating. The onslaught started at 0830. Between then and sunset he lost seven transports to the Cactus Air Force and the other Americans. All the supplies and many of the embarked troops followed those ships to the bottom. The cost to America to sink all of them was five planes and crews. At dusk, Tanaka still had a remnant of his reinforcements afloat, four transports and eleven destroyers. They continued doggedly towards Guadalcanal.

American B17's, long range high altitude bombers, joined the mayhem mid morning. The pilots claimed some hits. If a hit was made, it was a rare and remarkable feat. High level bomb runs yielded very few hits on ships, even stationary ones. This was proven over and over in the Pacific, the Atlantic, and the Mediterranean theaters. The high altitude big boys may have made a score or two that day. Whether or not they did well, the Cactus Air Force pilots were having their way with Tanaka and Abe. The American ground support men back on Guadalcanal kept working hard, focused on sustaining and encouraging them. Crews at Henderson scurried to keep the planes fueled, armed, and sent back in the air to hunt Japanese. Pilots made multiple runs. Stopping or eliminating the invaders was a critical task, and the Americans went all out to achieve it.

Meanwhile, on the decks of Tanaka's ships and in the water around them, Japanese sailors and soldiers were just focused on survival.

Another gun battle was building amid the confusion and excitement. Attention was on the air pursuit from Henderson that day, but more action was to come. From the north came Admiral Kondo for yet another go at bombarding the air field. On the way down, his Attack Group grabbed the battleship Kirishima. She was quickly transferred from Abe's retreating fleet and added to Kondo's force. He also had four cruisers and nine destroyers. In the other corner, from the south, came Task Force 64. Comprised of new battleships South Dakota and Washington with four destroyers, it was commanded by Admiral Willis Lee. TF 64 intended to stop Kondo. The Naval Battle of Guadalcanal was coming to a crescendo.

Before the war, conventional wisdom was you don't use big ships in tiny waters. If you had asked senior admirals of any major navy about using big ships in channels only a few miles wide and confined by islands, they would have said it should not and could not be done. It was unorthodox, to say the least, for Admiral Halsey to send battleships into confined waters to slug it out. Established doctrine, and almost every navy's plans, called for battleships to steam in the open ocean. Their job was to hit at the opposition from a distance of miles.

But Halsey was more concerned with protecting his toehold on Guadalcanal than naval theory and admirals' dogma. And he was about out of options: the Enterprise was the only usable US carrier in the Pacific. She was nursing substantial battle damage. One of hers two elevators was damaged and put out of use. The ship was usable but not in best condition. US Cruisers were being used up at a fearful rate and no more were available for deployment at the time. Destroyers, too, the workhorses of the fleet, were being used up and worn down. In fact, the destroyers assigned to Lee's TF 64 were simply those quickly available with enough fuel to accompany the battleships north. They had not previously worked together nor with Admiral Lee. Halsey knew that a battleship bombardment by Kondo was being planned. Still the Japanese needed to soften or disable the airfield before they could start to dislodge the Marines. Admiral Halsey could not let that go unchallenged.

How did Halsey know what was coming? Radio intelligence. As mentioned, the Americans had long been trying, with fair success of late, to decipher the Japanese Naval Code. There was a breakthrough in late 1941. The US Navy was able to start to read some of the Emperor's mail. The Japanese periodically changed ciphers and it took a while after each of those to regain insight. By late 1942 the high command in Washington, Nimitz in Hawaii, and MacArthur in Australia were all able to read a fair amount of Japanese Naval communications. They were able to develop a fair idea of what the Japanese Navy was planning. This insight was into both strategic matters and day to day operations. From code breaking and other sources they could also infer much of what the Emperor's Army intended and planned. US code breakers knew enough that the generals and admirals had to selectively and discreetly use those insights. Much care was taken to act only when the information could have been obtained somehow other than by breaking code. The source could not be compromised. It was imperative to keep Tokyo from knowing their naval code was not secure.

This was a very useful breach of the enemy's code. A bonus was that more than just naval stations and ships used these codes. Naval officers stationed around the world relied on them as well for communications. In fact, much of what the Allies knew about Hitler and his plans came from Japanese communications. They were reading the dispatches of Baron Oshima, Japanese ambassador to the Reich. Oshima had broad and respected contacts with high ranking Nazis. He met with them often. As the ambassador from a friendly country, he also had face to face talks with Hitler himself. Tokyo got a full and prompt account of all of these meetings and conferences, enciphered in naval code. Oshima was free with his assessments of developments in Germany and the Reich. He was privy to and reported on weapons information and inspection trips. This was a gold mine. The information and insights gained were invaluable to the Allied war effort.

The Allies were in effect a fly on the wall listening to these meetings and conferences. Knowing what the Axis leaders were thinking and planning no doubt shortened the war and saved countless lives. The theater commanders, Nimitz, MacArthur, and Eisenhower, were responsible for planning operations. They had the luxury of knowing many of the enemy's weak and strong points and could attack or hold accordingly. Each of these theater commanders made repeated good use of this intelligence.

On the other side of the fence, there are indications that the Imperial Japanese Army knew the Navy's code was compromised. There was so much animosity and competition in Imperial Headquarters that Generals apparently never told Admirals about it. The Japanese never cracked American or British codes. But they had their own successful radio intelligence efforts. They used traffic analysis to advantage. This is the study of the number, length, and source of radio traffic. Analysis can tell a lot about enemy activities, from movement of units or ships to new commanding officers to concentration or dispersal of forces. While it can give useful background and context, traffic analysis is not the same as outright reading of the enemy's messages.

For these reasons, the Americans knew what Yamamoto and his man Kondo were up to in the southern Solomon Islands. Kondo's job was to steam down and shell the field. He did not anticipate a gunnery fight with other heavies. Like Admiral Abe as he approached Guadalcanal, Kondo had his ships loaded with ammunition. The high explosive ammo would destroy planes and buildings and people. He had other ammo available in his magazines. If he got into a ship to ship scrap, he would need to use armor piercing ammunition. For this he could change the ammo out but it would not be quick or convenient. Kondo did not foresee running into heavy opposition. There had been no information about American battleships in the area. Further he doubted they would come out and fight if they were around. His focus was on bombarding the airstrip with its persistent pilots and airplanes.

As the Emperor's men would soon learn, Admiral Lee with his battleships and big guns was in fact coming out to fight. By nightfall of the 14th, he was patrolling. In waters north of the Canal he and his men were on the lookout for Kondo. Lee had his staff closely watching their radar screens. Many of the officers who appreciated its advantages were too junior to have an influence on battle strategy. Willis Lee was the first American Admiral afloat to appreciate the value of the technology. He had the seniority to compel his men and ships to use the advantages it gave. The radar let him "see" at further distances than could Kondo. That gave him the opportunity to fire the first shots and to make the most of those shots. First though, as he was prowling looking for Japanese to shoot at, he had a problem: Some American PT boats came out of their Tulagi harbor, looking to make trouble. Their commanders, aggressive and adventurous junior officers, were talking on the radio circuit about torpedoing the "heavies" they saw. Lee knew they meant him, so he got on the radio and in plain English identified himself and called them off. After some hesitation the PT commanders realized Lee was really an American and that they should not go after his ships. The PTs returned to harbor.

The shooting started at midnight or so, November 14 into the 15th. Lee and Kondo met in a brawl a little less confused and sprawling than the one with Scott, Callaghan, and Abe. There were fewer, bigger ships and they did not intermingle as much. Still it was a close in, desperate and bloody fight. Lee got in the first punches. Kondo did not expect opposition much less battleships with guns bigger than his. The Washington and South Dakota had sixteen inch guns, the Kirishima boasted fourteen inch guns. The bigger the gun the further it can shoot. The ship with the bigger gun can stand out of range and pound at the other.

The battle ebbed and flowed. Battleships were hit, lesser ships were sunk. Japanese Kirishima and USS South Dakota both took multiple shells, the Kirishima getting the worst of it. The USS Washington suffered not a scratch. The roiled waters of Ironbottom Sound closed over more brave sailors and gallant ships. The Japanese put under three of Lee's destroyers, and their heavy shells temporarily knocked power out on the South Dakota. She was ordered out of the battle. Lee stayed in and finished the fight with the Washington's big guns. All told the US ships sank a Japanese destroyer and battleship Kirishima. They hurt other Japanese units as well.

The fact of note that night was that Kondo turned back. He told his survivors to turn around and head for home just after midnight. His fleet did not fire any shells on to or towards Henderson Field. He had suffered the loss of a capital ship, a battleship, in the bargain. The pilots, bombardiers, and ground crews of the Cactus Air Force would have no cratered runways, no burning planes, no casualties to deal with and clean up. Those warriors would join the fight early and effectively the next day. But the most important achievement, the upshot of the battle, was that the US took night time control of the seas around Guadalcanal.

While the big boys, Lee's and Kondo's battleships, were slugging it out, Admiral Tanaka and his remaining transports sailed relentlessly on. Even though destroyers and battleships were nearby, firing at each other and sinking, he persevered. "Tenacious Tanaka" was a well earned nickname. He was determined to deliver his reinforcements, at least those that had survived the day's aerial onslaught. He closed Guadalcanal with his remaining four transports and eleven destroyers. The admiral decided not to have them pull near shore and unload the normal way. He didn't want to expose them to the air gauntlet while they tried to escape north. So he simply ordered the transports grounded at Tassafaronga Point. The ships ran themselves ashore within Japanese lines, less than ten miles from Henderson. With no need to unload troops or goods into small boats for transfer ashore things went quickly. His men managed to move supplies ashore and get some two thousand troops to land. This took place after dark, literally while Lee and Kondo were blasting at each other. Leaving the stranded transports, Tanaka headed his destroyers back north to safety.

The grounded ships were of course like honey to bees for the Americans. Starting at daylight, the Cactus Air Force made run after run, attacking the transports. The ships and any Japanese seen around them were bombed and strafed. American artillery crews heartily joined in. A newly arrived Army unit, the 244th Coast Artillery Battalion, unlimbered their guns and fired away. The Marine 3rd Defense Battalion put their artillery to work, sending their lead cased well wishes along too. The Navy's destroyer USS Meade cruised off shore throwing 5 inch and 40mm shells. Of the roughly two thousand of the Emperor's troops who lived to set foot on land, few reached safety. Virtually none of their supplies, foods, medicine and ammunition arrived. Starvation Island is what the Japanese troops called the place, rightly so.

By contrast every one of the US troops and all the supplies brought in the previous three days reached American lines safely.

The American victory in June at Midway marked the stopping of Japanese forward momentum in the Pacific. The three day Naval Battle Guadalcanal marked the point when America took the initiative. After that day, November 15, the US and her Allies had the Pacific War momentum going their way. This was a victory on several levels. It was not cheap, but it was significant. Americans had owned control of the air (and the most important ground in the area, Henderson Field) since they came in August. With this victory they took local control of the sea, a tactical victory. In the big picture, it was a strategic victory. America and her Pacific Allies were never on the defensive again. Japan was never on the offensive again. It would take almost three years of spilled blood and destroyed property before things were conclusively settled. The seesaw was starting to drop.

CHAPTER IX
November 13,14,15
Russia; The Home Front; New Guinea

The tide of war was starting to shift all over the globe, not just in Guadalcanal and the southern Solomon Islands. Almost everywhere, things were reaching a crescendo. Worldwide, in almost every theater, the seesaw was starting to tip. The North African campaign saw the Axis on the defensive, driven out of Egypt and having to fight for a place to hunker down in Tunisia. New Guinea was still stalemated but the Allies were gearing up to shove the Japanese out of Papua. All this was occurring in the first half of November. Another campaign was nearing a decision point on the frigid steppes of Russia, far from rainy fetid jungle and arid desert sands.

In the southern Soviet Union, the German Army was in Stalingrad. They did not hold or control it, but they were there in force. Hitler thought the Wehrmacht had a noose tight around the neck of the city. The senior commanders at OKW thought things were going their way but weren't totally convinced about the noose. They all thought that if they pulled just a little harder, fought a little more, they were sure they could choke it off and have a big victory. If won, it would be a watershed victory that would tighten their hold on southern Russia. They could then concentrate on the northern front and hopefully force a political settlement with Stalin. The Germans were putting out every effort, knowing they had to win this battle.

The city of Stalingrad had long been a strategic and industrial center. It was located along the mighty Volga River, at a westward bend which brought it about 100 miles from an eastward bend in the Don River. These rivers are lifelines of commerce and culture not unlike America's Mississippi or Europe's Rhine. Whoever dominated that land bridge and the two rivers there controlled access to the oil resources of the Caucasus and the agricultural riches of southern Russia and Ukraine. In Imperial Russia under the Tsars, the city was called Tsarytsin. That the Royal House had put their name on the city shows how important the place was even two or three hundred years ago. It was considered a strategic and important location during the Russian Revolution of 1917–c. 1920. Then, its defense was commanded by a Georgian whose birth name was Iosip Dugashvilii. As a young man he was schooled in a monastery but forsook the Church for politics. He became a Communist. As a prominent member of the Party, he took the name Josef Stalin. The English translation was Joe Steel. His (and the Communist Party's) civil war foes, the White Army, could not take the city from the forces he commanded there. He did so well that the metropolis was renamed for him.

The Nazis did in fact have the lion's share of the city. They were, however, relearning the hard lesson taken over and over again by many well armed modern armies. They found that all the latest technology was a poor match against a determined and stubborn populace ready to work together and even die to stop them. By late November, the Soviets held only a little of the city, mostly separate parcels down along the west bank of the Volga. Wehrmacht armor and infantry had possession of pretty much all the rest of the city. Actually, not a lot of city was left but there were plenty of ruins. In the urban built up area, virtually every building was destroyed or damaged. Most were useless except as a sniper hide, machine gun site, tank trap, or as a den to hide and sleep in.

Each side had to bring in gasoline, food, ammunition and all other supplies from afar. The Soviets brought supplies and fighters—men and women—down the Volga and moved them across to the downtown battle zone at night. They used barges until the river froze. For the Axis, everything came in from the west, mostly by land, some by air. Trucks, trains and horse drawn wagons delivered hundreds of tons daily. The supply lines ran through a corridor from Kharkov, a German held city three hundred miles away. The passage through that corridor was held open by a sprinkling of German units, but chiefly by Rumanian, Hungarian and Italian troops. The Germans troops were at the point of the spear, in Stalingrad or in the Caucasus.

Stalingrad had become a focal point, partly because of its name, mostly because of its location. It was the grudge match of the war in the east. This location had the city Hitler wanted to seize and Stalin wanted to keep. Even though this city held the world's attention in November 1942, it was not the only site of fighting. The theater was called the Ostfront, the Eastern Front. For the Russians it wasn't the east, it was the west. But the area was generally known as the "East." Whatever name it was known by and called, Germans were fighting Russians along an arc about one thousand miles long. The two fought battles from Finland and Leningrad in the north all the way down to the Caucasus and Crimea on the Black Sea.

The Nazis got a quick start after their June 22, 1941 invasion. It was a surprise attack against a treaty partner. By December, when Japan was overrunning the Pacific, the Wehrmacht had Panzers within sight of the Kremlin and Moscow. They were unable to go in and take the city. There were numerous reasons for this. Hitler felt it more important to take territory than to decapitate the government and take the main administrative and industrial city of the enemy. He did not reinforce the attack on Moscow. Another reason was, the Japanese had been trying to decide whether to attack Russia or the Indies. North or South were the two schools of thought, respectively advocated by the Imperial Army and Navy. The Emperor's forces turned south in their aggression, leaving Russia unharmed. They chose to go after the resources of the Netherlands East Indies. This reprieve from attack in the east allowed Stalin a breather. He was able to reduce the number of troops which had been guarding Siberia and eastern Russia, and move them to help defend Moscow. Also, the Germans were not ready for a Russian winter. Hitler had assumed he could make a quick conquest.

His planning, civilian administration, home front mobilization, and supply measures were built on taking and holding the country by fall of 1941. This did not happen. In fact, Hitler found his armies were fighting a long war in a wide, deep land with few local resources, many vengeful partisans, and a growing, strengthening foe in the Red Army. Not to mention the dreadful winters and that there was another set of enemies to fight, America and Britain.

By November winter was starting to set in on Stalingrad. Still, General Chuikov's 62nd Army held on. They contested every foot and the battle was at a standstill. Neither side was really gaining any ground. Chuikov was bleeding General Paulus' 6th German Army badly. Paulus' men were giving as good as they got, hurting the Soviets much. Like the Americans and Japanese in the Solomons, the seesaw was off the ground. Each side was determined to prevail. Both strove to get their side of the seesaw down to the ground. Try as they might, neither was able to muster the effort to evict or annihilate their enemy.

By late November the Volga had frozen. This cold weather meant misery for everyone living in a hole, that is, most every German and Russian in the area. But it also gave an advantage to the Soviets because they were physically and psychologically ready for it. It also enabled easier movement of supplies for the Soviets. They were used to moving men and goods over ice or through snow. They were geared up and equipped for the weather and they welcomed it. Snow and cold are as much a part of Russia and Russians as are the monsoons to India or the sunlight on the mesa to the Navajo. Even in 1942, a year and a half after the invasion, the Germans were still not supplied with heavy clothing, felt boots, white overcoats, skis, etc. Hitler forbade supplying them. He feared giving the troops winter gear would let them know they would be there all winter, and that would be bad for morale. One has to wonder why he thought spending the winter there in summer garb would be good for morale. But then Herr Hitler did not see things as most of the world did.

The Russian high command was planning a surprise for Hitler and the Wehrmacht. The Soviet Union was ready to spring an attack timed to take advantage of the distraction of Operation Torch. The political leadership of the Allies agreed the Red Army would attack in the east after Hitler was trying to deal with the US and British invasion of Africa. To this end, the Russians had been looking at the long enemy supply corridor. Paulus' 6th Army was at the end of a supply chain hundreds of miles long. Near Stalingrad it was only about fifty miles wide. It was held open by Axis allies not Wehrmacht troops. These forces were Italian, Romanian and Hungarian troops. They had to get by with arms and equipment inferior to what the Germans had.

The Germans thought that what they held with their Stalingrad position was a spear pointing at their enemy's chest. The Russians decided that was not the case. Rather, they determined that Hitler had stuck his head into a crocodile's mouth. And that croc was about to snap its jaws shut. The Red Army prepared quietly and carefully. No orders were put on paper. Only very senior officers knew what was planned. Most officers and all the men were kept uninformed and were not given any information. Infantry, armor, and artillery were massed but kept hidden to the east, north, and south of Stalingrad. Chuikov and his men continued to scrabble and fight amid the rubble and the cold. Each day got a little shorter and colder. Each day the crocodile got more teeth as more Soviet men and arms assembled around the city.

One quarter of the way around the world, in North Africa the Germans lost whatever diplomatic standing they might have had. The Allies and the French negotiated and inked a truce in Algiers on the 14th. US General Eisenhower signed as commander of Allied troops in the theater. The Frenchman signing was Admiral Darlan. He was the senior officer commanding and had been in charge of the region for the Vichy Government. The agreement ended the shooting by Americans, British, French, and French Colonial troops. It cleared the way for the Allies to put their full efforts towards capturing, killing, or ousting German and Italian forces on the continent.

There was another important result of the armistice. It reopened the Franco-German state of war that had been cut short by Nazi victory in June 1940. France, or at least the African part of

France, was no longer at peace with Germany. This added another enemy for Germany to contend with, and started to rebuild French martial honor. This was an important factor in French behavior. There was shame and resignation when Germany prevailed in 1940. Military and political leaders of France would joust and maneuver for primacy for several years to come. The backdrop of these efforts was the ongoing war. There was a lot of wrangling over the hows and whys of the 1940 defeat. It would be after D-Day in 1944, when the Allies saved France, before a clear national leadership team was recognized and accepted by the French people. That team was made up of men and women who had escaped France to fight the Germans or colonials who had never accepted Vichy's rule. No major leader who had cooperated with the German occupation was a factor in postwar national leadership.

The government in Vichy quickly and angrily denounced this truce signed by Darlan and Eisenhower. Germany gave up the pretense that Vichy spoke for an independent France. They sent German and Italian troops in to the hitherto unoccupied part of the country. France under Vichy had been a nominal equal to and ally of Germany with the power to administer and handle its own affairs. But French local forces in Morocco and Algeria essentially did not resist the Allied invasion of North Africa. This caused the Nazis to boil. Hitler promptly brought France under his heel just like most of Europe. It would shortly be just another occupied country.

In Africa, Americans under General George Patton and British under General Alexander pushed east respectively from Morocco and Algeria. Meantime Field Marshal Kesselring's Germans established a secure bridgehead in northern Tunisia and fended off Allied thrusts. Rommel's forces, routed from Egypt, were retreating west. Kesselring had secured the area around Tunis and Bizerte in northern Tunisia. He held it open, making sure there was a bridgehead for Rommel to retreat to. Also, he hoped or at least kept open the option to use that bridgehead to go back on the offensive and evict the Allies.

The battles Americans fought in North Africa were the first armed contact Americans had with Germans since 1918. The combat experience of the Nazis and the Americans' greenness showed. Kasserine Pass is a strategic site which controls a route of access to eastern Algeria and north Tunisia. It was one place of note where the Germans handed a defeat to the GIs. Here and on other battlefields the Americans were quickly initiated and soon hardened by the harsh school of battle. GIs learned what worked and how to use their weapons and training. Inept or old prewar vintage officers were culled. If they weren't killed in battle, they were demoted or sent home to a training or administrative job. Real life strategy and tactics were invented or remembered, practiced and perfected. Time was running out for the Axis in Africa. By mid November, there were over a million well supplied Americans, British, and other troops ashore. They were fighting against some quarter of a million Germans and Italians. The theater was a high priority for America and Britain, but it was nowhere near top priority for Hitler.

Armies and navies need people, food and clothing for them and bullets, tanks, guns, and ships to fight with. The various powers addressed these needs in their own unique ways.

By mid 1942 the American economy was starting to produce plentiful materials for war. There had been some planning and anticipation in the late 1930's and early 40's. The Selective Service Act, the "draft" was narrowly passed in 1940. Young men registered for induction to the military. The Army and Navy started taking in and training men. Industry responded by hiring people to build airplanes, ships and armaments. But it was late 1942 before production really started to pour forth. Ships were being laid down and many were coming off the ways, ready to steam the world's oceans. Boatyards in the Great Lakes and on the coasts were making submarines. Factories were converted to military production. New car production was suspended. Detroit auto assembly lines were changed over to manufacturing guns planes and tanks. Even in Denver, war industry thrived. A tire and fan belt factory in Denver was also making gas masks. The Remington Arms plant made ammunition. Components for landing ships were made and shipped by rail to the coasts for assembly In every city across the land, industry hummed. Metal fabrication shops all over the country made parts of weapons and shipped them elsewhere for assembly. This type of adaptation and innovation occurred throughout American industry. The American people were united and concentrating on war work. Housing was difficult to find in some areas with plants running three shifts every day, seven days a week.

One example of American production is the Liberty Ship. These were freighters made to a simple pattern of British design. They were welded, not riveted. Henry Kaiser organized his shipyards to quickly turn out these ships. Over twenty seven hundred Liberty Ships were made from 1941–45, in Kaiser's and many other shipyards. One was turned out, ready to steam, in five days. This was an exceptional production record. The shipyard owners wanted to see how quickly one could be completed and made every resource available to build the one ship. The average time to make a Liberty Ship was about sixty days. That is remarkable in itself. Assembling probably a million parts into a floating, mobile freighter in such a short span speaks well for the workers and businesses. These ships were not speedy but were reliable and carried freight to every theater of war. Many were sold to civilian owners and remained in use into the 1960's and 1970's. Two intact, usable Liberty Ships are left in the US, one in Baltimore and one in San Francisco. Each is now a floating museum.

Another facet of American production was mining. A case can be made that the war was run on gasoline from the Texas oilfield. As to other materials, every conceivable source of minerals was explored and many were tapped. Examples: there was a gold mine in Rock Creek Park in Washington DC and a titanium mine in the Adirondack Mountains in New York State. Old uranium mine tailings all over Colorado and the southwestern US were reworked to make material for the Manhattan Project. In October, the hardrock miners at (under?) the Climax Mine near Leadville Colorado won honors for war work. The company was awarded a "Presidential E for Excellence" in war production, for its output of tungsten, molybdenum, and zinc.

The nerve center for the US war effort was Washington DC. There was no one central military location there. The Army, the

Navy, and all the other Federal bureaus, offices, detachments, fleets, and administrations were spread out in buildings all over the region. People spent much time in just finding and getting to an office for a meeting. It was not particularly efficient. As time went on, the management and running of the war became more streamlined.

The Army took the first significant steps. Its various commands, bureaus, and detachments consolidated and moved into the Pentagon Building. This structure was located just across the Potomac from the District of Columbia itself, in the state of Virginia. This office building was the largest in the world at the time and may in fact still be. The structure itself was not complete but three of the five sides were done. Tenants could start to move in. Army Chief of Staff General George Marshall and Secretary of War Edward Stimson moved their office and staffers in on November 14.

This building is an example of how quickly Americans could adapt and get their economy behind the war. Ground was broken for this building on September 11, 1941. The whole project was planned and built at a breakneck pace. Funding was still being approved by Congress as dirt was being moved. Crews worked around the clock. They poured foundations and completed one side of the five at a time. The job was first overseen by Colonel Leslie Groves. He did not stay to see it completed as he was put in charge of the Manhattan Project, the research and building of an atomic bomb.

Having essentially all headquarters staff under one modern roof eased the management of numerous global efforts. It was a huge task to keep track and run the many parts needed to fight, much less win, the war. The American economy also had to house and feed the huge army and navy that was being trained and armed. There were scores of domestic bases built. The twelve million men and women under arms at war's end all had to be trained, supplied, moved, fed, clothed, and otherwise provided for. Bases were needed to train new army troops, teach pilots to fly, initiate sailors to the sea, and so on. Outside the US, there were air bases around the world. These were for planes on anti submarine patrols to protect the sealanes. Also they were staging points for men and planes going overseas to numerous fronts. Shipyards, steel mills, converted automobile factories, farms and ranches, textile plants, mines, all were tapped to manufacture, dig, and grow the goods and arms called for.

In America, women joined the labor force in unprecedented numbers. "Rosie the Riveter" was a logo and a slogan, but she was also a reality. Men with specialized knowledge or skills were deferred from uniformed service, kept in their civilian jobs. Manufacturing engineers and managers, miners, high tech workers and others did not necessarily don the uniform. Even so, they contributed to the war every bit as much as the rifleman, supply sergeant, or bombardier.

An agreement was made with Mexico to bring in people to work on farms and ranches, the "Bracero" program. African Americans were inducted into the military, but as a rule they were kept in non combat jobs. African American troops made up most of the construction regiments building the Alaskan Highway. They served as cargo haulers and longshoremen moving Lend Lease goods, not only in the US but also Iran and Britain. They provided drivers for the transportation of goods in Europe. Civilians worked as construction and stevedores in the US. There were a few black infantry divisions and black pilots. These units served gallantly and well. Most African Americans were steered into support jobs not combat roles.

American Indians joined the military in numbers. They served in most every role from clerk to gunner, rifleman to tanker. Native Americans made up a large part of the 163rd Infantry Regiment, part of the 41st Division which fought in New Guinea and the Philippines. Later in the war, Navajo radiomen used their native language to communicate on Pacific battlefields. The Japanese never did crack that unique "code."

Prisoners of war were put to work but not in war production. An Italian POW acting as a greenskeeper, or a German cutting logs or harvesting sugar beets freed up an American for war work. The few Japanese POWs there were contributed in similar jobs and roles.

Putting the economy on war footing took different forms in other countries.

In Russia, many factories were moved to keep them away from the German invasion. Hundreds of plants were literally taken apart piece by piece, often as the Wehrmacht approached. The parts were then put on a rail car, shipped east, and reassembled. The planning, effort, and timing required to successfully transplant a factory, much less many factories, are remarkable. Every Russian citizen worked in war factories or in the fields, seven days a week. POWs were put to work rebuilding destroyed cities, mining, logging, or in other war work.

Great Britain put its populace to work, keeping technical and managerial people at their jobs and out of the service. POWs were sent to camps in the Dominions. Kenya, Australia, Canada, South Africa and other members of the British Commonwealth took in prisoners of war. Some POWs were put to work in non war jobs. Some sat the war out doing virtually nothing.

Germany did not mobilize its economy fully in 1939. Hitler did not anticipate a long war and did not want to force privations on civilians, at least on his vaunted Aryans. It was not until about 1943 that every person and every resource was put to use in trying to support the troops and win the war. Even at the outset, Germans had a number of areas where they led the world, technologically speaking. They used their indigenous skilled labor to try to keep that technological edge. Jet engines and planes, rocketry, optics, and armor were some of many areas where the Third Reich had a technical and manufacturing lead. From the start of the war in 1939, they used slave labor taken from their newly conquered empires. This program started small but it grew. Later in the war millions of people were forced to run their factories and mines. Captured POWs from Britain, Canada and the US were not put to work at all. Germany wanted to be sure their POWS in the US or Britain were not mistreated so did not mistreat the captives they held. Russian, Ukrainian, Polish, and other central and eastern European captives were a different story. They were either starved outright or worked to death as slaves. To the Nazis, their survival was scarcely more important than an ant's.

Japan used POWs and slave labor to run their factories and mines. They put their civilians to work seven days a week as well.

Japan did not have the industrial infrastructure of a Germany, Britain, or US. They did have people working in small shops in every neighborhood in the country. As the US swept towards Nippon, they firebombed cities. Whole blocks would be burnt out. Witnesses speak of seeing ashes dotted with surviving drill presses, stamping presses, machine tools, and other manufacturing gear scattered throughout residential areas. Still, Japan was able to build planes and small boats up until the surrender in 1945.

In mid November, hundreds of miles west of the Solomon Islands another jungle struggle was playing out. US General MacArthur was protecting Australia by fighting in New Guinea. The campaign had not been decided by any means, but there was movement. By mid month, the Allies had some momentum building in New Guinea. This was started in August, about the time the Canadians raided Dieppe, the US Marines came ashore in Guadalcanal and the Germans turned towards Stalingrad. At that time an Allied force, chiefly made up of Australians, inflicted the first defeat of the war on the Japanese Army. There was a naval base with air strip on Milne Bay at the extreme eastern end of New Guinea. The Japanese tried to invade it, but were defeated by Australian infantry and American engineers.

The next month, the Allies' picture brightened a little more. On September 26, the Australian Army, militia and regular infantry, added honor, vengeance, and momentum to the campaign. They fought and turned back the Imperial Army's effort to invade overland from the north. This reversal occurred some thirty miles from Port Moresby. The Japanese had by mid November retreated almost all the way back to the north coast.

In September MacArthur had alerted the 41st Division for movement from Australia, and had actually started to send the American 32nd Division north. These were National Guard divisions, led by elected, home town officers. The 41st was from Montana and surrounding states; the 32nd from New York. The 128th Regiment of the 32nd was airlifted from Townsville in northern Australia to Port Moresby. This was a groundbreaking effort. It was the first mass airlift of troops in the entire war. MacArthur and everyone in his command were favorably impressed with its speed and efficiency. Officers and planners in Washington DC and elsewhere also took note. Air movement of Allied troops became commonplace as the war progressed.

From Moresby some elements of the Division were airlifted directly to the north coast. The other Regiments and attached units went north by various routes. One battalion, part of the 126th Regiment, marched over the Kappa Kappa Track. This was a poorly marked native trail which transited the Owen Stanley Mountains to the east of the Kokoda Track. It went over some very wild yet often barren country. Their trek lives to this day. Natives along the way remember it; the veterans certainly remember it; and it is an epic adventure and exploration story in its own right. Some GIs went around the east end of New Guinea by sea in small trawler and coastal vessels. Others were airlifted part way then lightered by sea. Some units were flown directly onto a newly built strip at Dobodura. This facility was new, really just a grass strip at the time. It was developed into a full base and was essential to the campaign. Dobodura grew to become a major base in the Southwest Pacific Theater.

Since the Japanese came ashore at Buna on the north shore in June, the Australians had been fighting them. First their militia units did a fighting retreat to within sight of Moresby. Most members of this militia were poorly trained teenagers. These Aussie citizen soldiers did a magnificent of job slowing, then stopping the Japanese thrust. Then militia and regulars pushed the Emperor's men back. In November, Australian 7th Division troops had been brought in from the Mideast. They had served and been hardened in the Egyptian desert. They were now on duty much closer to home. These veterans took over from the militia which had saved the country by stopping the Japanese invasion. The 7th troopers had thought of themselves as desert rats, but they quickly became jungle rats as they fought their way north over the Kokoda Track. Meanwhile, the soldiers of the US 32nd Division were being gathered at Pongani, a malarial village on the north coast, near the airstrip at Dobodura. The plan was for the two forces to meet and, side by side, to clear the way west. The objective was to kill or evict the Japanese from of the coastal villages of Buna, Gona, and Sanananda. These were old missionary villages which the Japanese had fortified and prepared for defense.

By November 11 the Allies were running up against those defenses. Japanese had machine gun bunkers reinforced by coconut logs and hidden by tropical growth. These were hard to see and very difficult to knock out, especially as the Emperor's men were ready and willing to die for him while defending their spot. These bunkers were sited by the defenders to give interlocking lanes of fire. GI's and Aussies found it was brutal and bloody to breach one of these. Since they all had supporting fire, taking one out did little for progress. Two or more had to be taken out before the attackers could advance. Tanks were almost useless in the swampy terrain. They simply bogged down in the mud. The Allies found that flame throwers were effective. The land and its diseases were hideous: swamps, malaria, crocodiles, dysentery, all kinds of jungle fevers. And the GIs and Aussies were also running up against the Japanese refusal to surrender. Almost every Japanese soldier fulfilled the desire of Emperor's servant to sell his life dearly: He wanted to kill as many enemies as he could before he was taken out. Clearing these three villages meant wiping out, killing, all ten thousand or so defenders. It was a savage, bloody, lengthy affair.

Changes were needed. A number of US officers were sacked, especially many of the middle and senior men of the 32nd Division. Back in the States, National Guard outfits were as much a social as a military organization. Local community leaders, especially the popular men, provided the outfits' leadership. Training was not lackadaisical but it was not intense and realistic. Discipline was not regular or severe. In war conditions, many of the officers were simply too old, too soft, or unwilling to order friends to their death. And to win this battle, someone had to give the cold and costly orders necessary to win. MacArthur sacked the Division commander and finally brought in his own man to run the battle. General Robert Eichelberger was a regular Army officer. MacArthur told him to go win the battle at all costs. His orders, literally: "Bob, Come back with your shield or on it." This was the order given by Roman Caesars to their generals—conquer or die.

Eichelberger conquered. He straightened out the supply problems and also led from the front. At last progress was made and the Japanese strongpoints were reduced one by one. He found the Japanese a more straightforward enemy than some others he made at this time. After the battle was over, he made the mistake of talking with a reporter about his role. Subsequently his picture appeared on the cover of Time Magazine. That was major, rock star exposure in early 1943. This publicity was taken by MacArthur and his inner circle as an attempt to upstage the Supreme Commander. That was not done it the SoWesPac. General Eichelberger was not banished to running an army depot in North Dakota, but close. He was put on the back burner, given a rear echelon troop training job. He did not get another combat command until 1944. By then he had learned his lesson and was very careful about talking to reporters. Other generals in the Southwest Pacific got the message: Keep your head down and your mouth shut. If there is any publicity, fame or adulation to be had, MacArthur gets it.

This publicity no-no was a dramatic lesson for the general but it was cheap when measured by things that really mattered. The real lesson of the campaign was, don't attack the Japanese directly. This lesson, this rule to live by (literally) was bought with enlisted men's blood and misery. The lesson was put to use in every campaign afterwards. It shortened the Allied casualty lists in later battles. After this campaign General MacArthur never again attacked a Japanese stronghold head on. This was the genesis of the "Hit 'em where they ain't" strategy. MacArthur put it bluntly. He said, "If you cut the Jap off, give him a way to escape, he's in the bag." So for the rest of the war, MacArthur did not attack head on. He would send his forces beyond, behind, or around a Japanese strong point. He would attack there, set up an air base, and gain local air superiority. In the meantime, the Nipponese he cut off were free to escape into the jungle or wither away. Then he would do it again. MacArthur's forces suffered more casualties in Buna-Gona than in any battle or set of battles he led for the rest of the war. He learned how to win battles, to kill or bypass Japanese, with small casualties for his men.

CHAPTER X
November 16–19
North Africa; Cactus; Stalingrad

Fighting continued in North Africa. These actions were the latest to take place on ancient battlegrounds. The Mediterranean, the "sea in the middle of the earth" has seen battles and campaigns for many centuries. Carthage is there, the city-state conquered and sacked by Rome over two thousand years ago. The Romans made sure it would not rise and threaten them again. When they salted the earth they made sure nothing would grow there for generations. In 1942, US tanks drove by and over that sterile soil. The ruins were visited by General Patton and others. The area was rife with ghosts of charioteers maneuvering for advantage, formations of spearmen marching and fighting. One can imagine nearby in the sea, ghosts of biremes and triremes ramming and boarding!

In the latest edition of war to visit the region, Allied paratroops dropped in from the sky. Tanks maneuvered to kill each other and gain ground. Artillerymen dueled, guns thudded, shells exploded, and men died. British and American troops continued to move forward, to the east, in Algeria. They advanced along the coast and inland. Some of the coastal advances were by short-hop, shore to shore boat movements. Some were overland along roads. There were also airborne troop drops at Youk Le Bains, Bone, and Soul El Arba.

Germans fought tenaciously to keep the Allies out of Tunisia. They were able to establish a solid defensive bridgehead around

Tunis and Bizerte there. They had started by feeding in troops shortly after the Allies set foot on the continent on the 8th. They defended that bridgehead stubbornly under increasing pressure by growing Allied armies. Further east, Rommel's Afrika Korps slowly but steadily pulled back along the coast. They were pursued and harried by troops coming from Egypt. Also, French troops from the colony of Chad in central Africa crossed the Sahara. They hit the German retreat in the flank. They then joined the advancing British Eighth Army. The Allies took the Libyan towns of Tobruk and Benghazi by November 19. Actually they retook both of these towns since they had had and lost possession of them several times since 1940. Now, in late 1942, there was a race on. It was between Operation Torch forces and Afrika Korps chased by the British to see who got to Tunis first. The Korps won.

German Field Marshall Kesselring, the theater commander, had air and boat lifted forces starting right after Torch. He stuffed in tens of thousands of troops. The Allies followed up the Torch landings with many thousands of their own reinforcements. These were the sides in the contest for Tunis, capital of Tunisia, located on the sea with a good harbor. The African campaigns boiled down to, whoever controlled that city would control the southern shore of the Mediterranean. The struggle for it would last until May.

This brings up the question, why work so hard to control the south side of the Mediterranean Sea? By dominating the south shore, the Allies could project power. They could protect their sea traffic and interdict Axis ships. Then they could send ships through the area. That would free up many resources otherwise tied up in sending ships around Africa. It would also open the entire area to offensive operations. Any place from Greece to the Spanish-French border could be attacked. The Axis would have to shift forces to respond. Not knowing where the blow might fall, the Axis had to be ready to defend the whole long shoreline. Hitler had said he wanted to avoid a two front war. He did not want to be fighting two enemies in two theaters. The Nazis did not take Britain down in 1940 before he invaded Russia the next year. It is not clear whether Hitler thought the English wouldn't fight on, or if he just thought he could take Russia down quickly then turn to the English. As it happened, the English stayed in the fight even if they did not immediately mount a major offensive. Now, in late 1942, they had put in a big attack. Hitler now had the two front war he hadn't wanted.

In the Solomon Islands, the Allies took local control of the air when they occupied Guadalcanal and Henderson Field. They had control of the land, as much as needed to protect the field. With their victory in the recent Naval Battle of Guadalcanal they had taken local control of the sea. That control would be tested repeatedly. Both sides would shed more blood. There would be one more night cruiser battle on Ironbottom Sound, the Battle of Tassafaronga Straight. The Americans lost more ships in that battle than did the Japanese. The Yanks still tried to fight as if they had no radar, which left them at a disadvantage against the night trained Nipponese. Old habits of not relying on radar died hard in the American Navy. But the battle's outcome did not affect the American dominance of the area. The Emperor's men would make repeated air and small ship forays in the area. Even though Japan had pulled back north they would continue to attack Guadalcanal until pushed further away in mid 1943.

Land based forces there were being reinforced and changed. On the American side, the Marines who did such a tremendous job taking and holding the island were running out of gas. Malaria and other diseases, supply shortage, and battle had worn them down. They would be rotated out soon. The Army had started sending in ground reinforcements as early as late October. Marine General Archer Vandegrift would remain in command for another several weeks.

The plan was to turn the island and "mopping up" operations over to the Army. Mopping up sounds like it should be easy, almost an afterthought. The Japanese on the Canal were not prepared to be "mopped up" like a little dust. They did not go easily or quietly. The Army GIs who replaced the Marines fought and suffered many casualties before the island was secured. Army troops on the island were members of the Army's Americal Division. This unit was unique among American infantry divisions in that it had a name but no number. Its American members were assembled on the island of New Caledonia, that is American-Caledonian, thus "Americal." The Army 25th Infantry Division was sent in from Hawaii to reinforce the Americal and continue the conquest. General Patch was serving as commander of the Americal. He would step up to take command of the island in early December. That is when Vandegrift and the rest of the original Marine contingent left. In the meantime, the ground skirmishes continued. On the 18th, Army and Marine units under Army General Sebree attacked west of the Matinakau River. This offensive was intended to clear the area of harassing Japanese artillery and sniper fire. It saw limited success and ended up a stalemate.

The Cactus Air Force continued to grow in strength and stamina. A steady stream of fresh pilots and planes were flying in. The maintenance facilities were improving. No longer were cannibalized parts being used to keep as many planes up as possible. Replacement parts were being sent in regularly. There were hardstands (earth shelters for planes), hangars were being built, and regular maintenance was being undertaken. There were new strips, grass for now but all weather runways were being planned. No longer was the place just the one short, graded dirt runway that the Marines had taken in August. Plane drivers would fly out of Henderson Field in ever growing strength. US pilots of all the Services and New Zealand Air Force pilots would contribute to the drive north from Guadalcanal.

On the Japanese side, the troops were hurting. Nipponese efforts to neutralize the airfield had come to naught. Recently, one reinforcement convoy had had more of its troops drowned than it had landed on the island. Such resupply as got through was inadequate to keep the troops alive, much less to sustain them in combat. The soldiers already there were starving. Cannibalism was starting to occur. The English name for the island is "Guadalcanal." The Japanese word for it is "Gadarukanaru." But the typical Japanese soldier, with the cynicism shown by army privates everywhere, called it Death Island.

The Japanese air campaign failed for several reasons. First was distance. The Nipponese bases were just too far from the Canal to effectively fight for it. Also, from the very start of the campaign, every Japanese plane appearing over the Canal or its approaches was from the Imperial Navy. Imperial Japanese Army pilots and planes did not contribute one iota during the first three months of the struggle for Henderson Field on Guadalcanal. Navy fliers fought the entire campaign and took the brunt of the combat. This had undesirable results. The Navy's overall flying capabilities suffered. The pilot corps was reduced in numbers and experience level. Carriers were stripped of squadrons which were then thrown into the maw of the southern Solomon Islands. For a country without a massive industrial base, the plane losses were telling. In November, the Imperial Japanese Army Air Force at last agreed to cooperate and contribute to the campaign. This was a milestone. From August to mid November not one plane from the Japanese Army had flown to, around, or over Guadalcanal. The fresh planes and combat experienced pilots helped but they came in with too little, too late.

The air staff at South Pacific Command had foreseen that Guadalcanal could become a sink for Japanese planes. They realized that if the Americans fought right they could force the Nipponese to expend planes and pilots in a losing fight. That is just what happened.

Contrast the Japanese problems with the Cactus Air Force. It was an amalgam of US Marine, Navy (both land and carrier) and Army planes. The Marines and Navy had concentrated on patrolling, air combat, and sinking ships. The Army planes, at first just a squadron of semi-obsolescent P40s, specialized in supporting the ground troops. The P40 was not fast or maneuverable but it was well suited to low altitude bombing and strafing. They were ideal for close troop support and often took the place of artillery. Planes of all services brought in supplies and troops. The CAF had been under command of Vandegrift as island commander. As the land campaign became the responsibility of the Army, command of the air forces became more flexible and sophisticated. The role of the

CAF grew. It became more than just respond to attacks on the island, to just hold the field at all costs. That is what it had to do at first. As the Americans' hold on the area got tighter, the role of air power evolved. The stage was set to use the air forces to project power north. Rather than just defend Guadalcanal, it would be used to support and enable the drive towards Tokyo. Over time the "ComAirSols" job evolved. In this, officers from each service would command the Cactus Air Force for a month at a time on a rotating basis. The officer of the month was Commander of Air in the Solomons, or in military jargon, ComAirSols. This was a flexible and fair arrangement which worked well.

The Japanese Army air force did not participate in the Solomons campaign. That part of the planet was the Navy's sphere and the Army simply did not contribute. There were arenas, like New Guinea, which were the province of the Army and the Navy did not contribute. This points up the matter of inter-service rivalry. It was not just the Emperor's forces which had jealousies and rivalries.

Every nation, even while fighting for its life, saw competition between the military services. The joke about the US Navy was that it had two enemies, the Japanese and the US Army. There is an element of truth to all humor, and it is true there was rivalry on the Allied side as well. Bomber Command, the heavy air force arm of the British Royal Air Force, was legendary for its ability to command resources and go its own strategic way. In all theaters, Generals and Admirals were constantly jousting and vying for resources among and between themselves and their areas of operations. Ships, planes, troops, and supplies were sorely needed everywhere. Within services and between services, there was also competition. For instance, the admirals in the Pacific wanted resources just like admirals in the Atlantic. Generals in Britain vied for planes and troops against generals in the Mediterranean. There was unlimited demand and limited supply of war materiel and troops.

That said, every British-American Allied theater had one senior American or British officer in charge. That Admiral or General had full authority and responsibility. He commanded all Allied operations and personnel of any service. American General Eisenhower in northwest Europe, British General Alexander in the Mediterranean, British Admiral Mountbatten in China-Burma-India, Americans General MacArthur in Southwest Pacific and Admiral Nimitz in the Pacific, all commanded multinational forces. The Russians did not share command or have other nationalities in the chain of command. They did on occasion allow a few British and American observers to accompany the advancing Red Army.

During the war, there were cases of Army Infantry Divison Commanders being sacked by an Admiral. This was for reasons of performance or nonperformance, always justifiable and never personal. Army General MacArthur replaced an admiral early in the war. This may have caused some bad blood but it did not seriously harm the war effort. Inter service lack of cooperation was felt at the working level as well. One such case was that of Army Major Al Brookes. En route from the mainland to New Caledonia for duty, he transited Hawaii. He tried to go to a Navy Officer's Club but was denied entry, being Army. His question to them was, "We're fighting the same war, aren't we?" He got no good answer and never did get in.

But this is minor bureaucratic and organizational stuff. It pales compared to the Japanese experience. Senior officers of the services routinely withheld even basic information from their counterparts. The Pearl Harbor attack was not disclosed beforehand to the Imperial Army, even to the most senior officers. The naval defeat the US gave the Imperial Navy at Midway was hidden. Word of it was kept from the population at large and from the War Minister and Army. Midway survivors who made it back to the homeland were quarantined and forbidden to contact even their families. Japanese Army activities in China were kept secret. The generals sometimes even withheld operational information from the Emperor not to mention from the Admirals. And there is reason to think that the Army knew the Navy codes were being read by the Allies, but never told the Admirals. This is hard for the western mind to understand. Perhaps the Army was reading the Navy codes too, and didn't want the Admirals to know that.

One wonders how the Guadalcanal campaign might have been different had the Japanese Army brought its air fleets to bear on Henderson Field in August. Or how differently events would have unrolled had the Emperor's Navy discovered and fixed its security leak.

In Germany, Hitler held all the reins. That said, he was happy to have his underlings both military and civilian fight it out. All the major Army and Nazi Party factions and senior individuals continually plotted and schemed for their gain and the favor of the Fuhrer. Hitler's philosophy was, if his underlings were at each other's throats they wouldn't be conspiring against him. His senior Admirals, especially Doenitz of the UBoats, had a relatively free hand. The Luftwaffe, under the wing (so to speak) of Goering, had a relatively free rein. If the admirals and airforce generals delivered and caused no problems Hitler left them alone. The Wehrmacht was another story. Hitler scorned the officer class and micro-managed the Army.

He had been a soldier in World War I, a brave and highly decorated corporal. He felt he knew strategy and tactics better than anyone. In fact that seemed to be so the first two years of the war. He overruled his generals repeatedly, and things seemed to work out to the Nazi's advantage. Further, Hitler held the officer class in contempt, thinking them arrogant know-nothings. Sometimes he bypassed the chain of command and gave direct orders even down to the Division level. Later in the war when things turned against the Nazis, he went as far down the organizational chart as to order the placement of Battalions. Rivalry and ruthless maneuvering was rife behind the Fuhrer's back, but no one dared countermand or cross him.

Similarly, in Russia, Stalin had total control. As the war progressed, he micro-managed affairs less than he did at first. He even consented to giving a unit's commanding officer true command. He pared the power of political (i.e. Communist Party) officers who had until then had an equal say in military decisions. Stalin also started to respect and utilize his Generals' professional advice. Still, no one went against Stalin's orders. Very few were willing to disagree with him, or even to appear to do so. He had purged the military of officers in the mid 1930s, executing many thousands whom he considered to be a threat. Most anyone who thought for themselves or spoke up fell into this category, and he was eliminated. This purge came back to haunt Stalin and the Communists. When war came, the lack of experienced and knowledgeable leadership was a real handicap to the Red Army. Perhaps Stalin was the only one who was surprised, but he found he could not personally command an army of millions. Between the early reverses suffered and the individual soldier's reluctance to stand out, it took quite some time for new leaders to emerge.

West of Guadalcanal, across the Coral Sea, the New Guinea theater continued to consume resources and men. The US 32nd and Australian 7th Divisions moved through disease ridden jungle and swamp. The 163rd Infantry Regiment, part of the US 41st Division, was being assembled for transit to New Guinea. This was a National Guard outfit from Montana, Washington, Idaho and Oregon. The 41st would fight honorably at Buna other battles in New Guinea and the Philippines.

Gerald Beckett was born in Montana in 1919. He was a member of the 163rd and was promoted to be a Warrant Officer in 1942. He was the assistant Regimental Supply Officer. In the Buna-Gona-Sanananda campaign the regiment saw action and was instrumental in Eichelberger's victory there. Beckett was at the tip of the spear, living in a tent or foxhole, supplying his men. He spent many a day and night dodging and evading Japanese snipers and infiltrators. In early 1943 he wrote from "Somewhere in New Guinea." He couldn't say where due to censorship but he was probably near the Dobodura Airdrome. He talked about censorship and revealed a little about his personal wartime demons. "Haven't much to write about only that which would be cut out so no use giving the censors additional work. Someday I'll give out the lowdown, maybe I'd just as soon forget most of it though I understand now why the soldiers of the last World War would rather not talk about it." He later wrote about this time,"…that first month was HELL and no punches pulled, and I hope I never have to go through it again. Our precarious position made transportation quite a problem, hence a lot of it rained from the air. Even our small arms ammo. Much of the ammo came with tracer and we had to keep a crew constantly going through it, taking the tracer out." They didn't want to expose their position by tracer fire, allowing the Japanese to precisely aim at the shooter. As this quote shows, the fight on the north coast of New Guinea for the towns of Buna, Gona, and the Sanananda beach fortifications was horrific. Beckett was awarded the Bronze Star for his leadership and bravery.

The US 41st Division and their brothers in arms were trying to take the settlements of Buna and Gona on the north coast. Disease killed hundreds and took many more out of action on the Allied side. The Japanese suffered at least as much, with starvation thrown in. They fought ferociously anyway. The individual Japanese soldier was taught the idea of "gyokusai." This concept taught the nobility and desirability of fighting to the last man, of never surrendering. They were trained to fight on until literally they had only a few rounds of ammunition left. Then they were to kill themselves, taking an enemy with them if at all possible. After Buna, Gona, and Sanananda were taken, Allied soldiers found the Japanese had stacked their corpses like protective sandbags in their bunkers. Those Nipponese soldiers knew there was no way out. Rather than surrender or escape, they used comrade's bodies as shelter to perhaps give them another day or two to try and kill more Australians or Americans. Here too, despite heroic efforts, neither side could eject or overwhelm the enemy. The seesaw was in the air.

In Russia, Operation Uranus was about to start. This is the name given the offensive Stalin and his generals had devised. If it worked exactly right and everything fell the Soviets' way, the result would be the cut off and isolation of all German troops in southern Russia. Of course they knew the Germans would react and some aspects wouldn't work. But the offensive was intended to knock the Nazis back a ways and give the Red Army a victory. The campaign was timed to take advantage of the weather and global developments. Specifically they wanted to hit the Germans while they were preoccupied with North African events. The Nazis were reacting to Operation Torch in Morocco and Algeria, and also Montgomery's El Alamein victory and subsequent pursuit.

Operation Uranus had been in the planning for some time. The time for the attack to start was fast approaching. Internal security was tight even by Soviet standards. In an army where only officers were trusted with maps, it was expected that the grunt at the front would be told nothing. Extra effort was made to keep this operation absolutely secret and a surprise. Senior generals were in the know. But in the field, troops and officers were told nothing. In an active area like Stalingrad, patrols are routinely sent out to take a few prisoners for questioning. All sides do this. This is why information on Operation Uranus was so closely held. No chances were taken that someone would be captured and start talking under "persuasion." What one doesn't know, one cannot divulge. So Stalin's staff made sure everyone outside headquarters knew nothing. Acting on blind orders, troops were moved and gathered, artillery massed, supplies stored. When it finally reached the point that operative details had to be shared and troops briefed, it was all oral. If plans were not printed out they could not be intercepted or captured. All orders on movements, goals, times, and so forth were passed orally, by word of mouth only.

The Soviet objective was the German Army in Stalingrad. They wanted to take the city back. They wanted even more to isolate the place and destroy the Nazi forces in it. Several hundred thousand German troops were in and near the city. These were the entire German Sixth Army and part of the Fourth Panzer Army. There were also Luftwaffe units, with air bases and support facilities. The Nazis were still fighting in the wreckage of the city, trying to drive the Red Army east across the Volga.

The German center of effort, their point of the spear, was equipped and armed from the rear. The Wehrmacht and Luftwaffe units were supported and supplied via a corridor some fifty miles wide and several hundred miles long. This corridor was held open by Axis troops. They were chiefly Rumanian, Hungarian, and

Italian units. There were some German troops on the south side of the corridor. All the forces allied to the Nazis, and all German units were either in Army Group A (in and around Stalingrad) or Army Group B (in the Caucasus and southern Russia).

Everything that both Army Groups A and B needed, be it supplies, access, hospital care, fuel, reinforcements, everything, had to cross the Dnieper River. And there was only one point that crossing could be made. That is, there was a grand total of one bridge which carried all the food, fuel, and ammunition for every Axis troop, tank and horse in south and southeast Russia. Like the corridor leading to Stalingrad, this crossing was protected in large part by Axis not German troops. These Axis troops were not as well trained, motivated, or armed as the Germans. Some senior German officers had seen this as their own Achille's Heel. They tried to persuade the OKW—the German equivalent of the Pentagon—to mix in some German units along the corridor. The generals wanted to stiffen the protection. Hitler would have none of it. In typical Hitlerian fashion, he forbade moving Germans from active operations to support roles. He wanted Germans up front doing the fighting. He was content to let his Italian, Rumanian, and Hungarian friends serve in static support. He felt and firmly believed that they didn't need to fight. If they would just guard the goods then his Aryan troops could take the fight to the Communists.

The Soviets too had noticed this weakness. The planners of Operation Uranus took it into account. Indeed, it was the key to the entire scheme. The opening attack was directed at the very fracture point, the non German troops, along the supply corridor to the German front. In preparation, Soviet artillery was massed wheel to wheel, with hundreds of guns per mile, over miles of front. The fact that the guns were placed without the Germans or their allies noting and reacting speaks well for the Soviet operational security.

At 0400, four in the morning, on November 19, the Soviet artillery barrage opened on German and allied positions. Being on the receiving end of a surprise barrage by hundreds of artillery pieces had to be a stunning, disorienting, and terrifying experience. The big guns fired for four hours, delivering thousands of rounds. At 0800 the Soviet infantry started to advance. Six Russian Armies attacked south and three Armies came north. The crocodile with its many sharp teeth was snapping its jaws shut. From the north and south of Stalingrad poured thousands of fresh, well equipped, motivated Red Army soldiers. They advanced over 30 miles in twenty four hours. Daily gains like that hadn't been seen in Russia for a long time. That size of advance rivaled the ones the Germans made at the start of the war, in the summer of 1941.

On the north side of the Stalingrad corridor, the Red Army virtually wiped out the 3rd Rumanian, 2nd Hungarian, and 8th Italian Armies. These armies were less prepared for winter conditions than their German masters. And they were not as well trained or armed. In the South, the Rumanian 4th Army fared little better, being killed, or routed and rounded up as prisoners. By the 22nd, in only three days, the Soviet pincers had met. They joined in the town of Kalach, about 40 miles west of Stalingrad. The Red Army poured in reinforcements and turned outward, ready to repel German counterattack or to continue their own attacks. And they turned units east, to cut off and compress the German holdings in Stalingrad.

General Paulus and his Sixth German Army were isolated. He had to move some of his forces to the west in order to fill the gap left by collapsing central European Armies. This did not help his efforts to stamp out Russian held pockets on the west side of the river. He did still enjoy air access to the friendly rear areas, and held at least two working airdromes. Hermann Goering, head of the Luftwaffe, promised Hitler that his planes could supply Paulus' 6th Army. That army would, according to the Luftwaffe plan, continue to get food, arms and fuel and could finally evict the Russians from Stalingrad. Paulus' men and horses needed some two hundred tons of supplies per day just to survive. Goering was never able to deliver more than about thirty tons per day, and that was a good day. Most days, many fewer tons of supplies were delivered. Whatever horses still survived quickly vanished, slaughtered for the troops.

Preparations for a German counteroffensive, Operation Winter Garden, were immediately started. The plan was for Army Group B to attack north and Paulus to fight his way west, away from Stalingrad. The thinking was to give up some territory but keep his army in existence. The Werhmacht was gearing up to make great effort to get him and his army free. However, Hitler intervened. The Fuhrer forbade Paulus to even try to fight his way out. His army was to continue to hold Stalingrad, and he was to let others fight their way in to him. Hitler forbade their withdrawal by even an inch. Instead, Operation Winter Storm was put on, where the Wehrmacht tried to fight into Stalingrad to relieve a stationary Paulus. They failed in this attack. Stalingrad's invaders were doomed.

Two factors converged at this time. First was the initial success of Uranus, second was Hitler's forbidding of Paulus to fight his way out. Stalingrad was in the bag for the Red Army. Also, all the Germans in the Caucasus, hundreds of thousands of men, were at risk. There was a real possibility that they would be cut off and starved or captured as well. They were able to withdraw from the Caucasus to southern Russia without capture. But the German high tide was receding.

Over a million German troops went from being predator to prey in a short time. The Soviets suddenly threatened all of German Army Group A and much of Army Group B. Over one hundred thousand German, Italian, Hungarian, and Romanian troops were killed or captured. Stalin and his generals planned and their men executed well. In a matter of three days, from the 19th to the 22nd, Operation Uranus caused the seesaw to start to drop.

CHAPTER XI
November 20–29
What if?; Burma; Tunisia; Land Battles

World War II lasted many years. For the Japanese starting in China and expanding to southeast Asia, it lasted fourteen or so years. For the British and Germans, six. For Russia and the Germans, four. For the Americans and Japanese, almost four. In any case, there were battles aplenty and deaths to satisfy the Grim Reaper many times. In the big picture of the entire war, the amount of the blood shed by all the soldiers and sailors in the last three weeks of November 1942 was small. But that flow, those sacrifices made by ordinary people, had an effect all out of proportion to its size.

During this time, five major campaigns started to unfold or came to a point of resolution. Two of them rolled along the Mediterranean coast of North Africa, one east and one west. Another took place on the steppes of Russia. Just below the equator, one played out in New Guinea and another in the southern Solomon Islands. By late November each had reached a point of decision. Of course we know how they turned out, who won and how. But at the time, the results were not apparent. At no time in 1942 was the struggle's outcome a sure thing. It was certainly not preordained that the war and the peace turned out as they did.

What if?

Each of these campaigns turned on a myriad of acts, facts, and omissions, steps taken or postponed. Of course we look chiefly at the acts of the high commanders and political leaders. Individual acts had impact as well. Soldiers, sailors, and pilots actually fought these battles out. There were no doubt many never to be known acts which were critical to the outcome of skirmishes and battles. Some of the many bullets fired, maneuvers made, planes launched or torpedoes fired caused battles and then campaigns to go in favor of one or the other party. We can never forget the acts of individuals.

What if a sniper had shot Admiral Halsey when he was visiting Guadalcanal in early November? Whoever stepped in as his successor as ComSoPac would have taken a while to take control of the job. The Japanese might have used that period to shell Henderson into submission and evict the Marines. Then they could have turned to New Guinea and MacArthur's efforts. Their southern front would have been more secure....

Or if a German shell had taken General Chuikov whose urban fighting strategy stopped the Germans in Stalingrad? Would the Russians have been able to hold on to the west side of the Volga, keeping the Germans from solidifying and expanding their hold on the region?

What if a German Uboat commander caught sight of the huge Morocco bound convoy carrying the invaders? The US transports bringing Torch troops across the Atlantic to Morocco might have been detected. Could he have called in other Uboats? Their sinkings could have seriously disrupted Torch and given Germany a chance to bring troops to Algeria and Morocco. North Africa might have remained in Axis hands.

What if the Japanese Army had sent its air forces to aggressively contest the skies over New Guinea? This could have stopped and would certainly have slowed the Allies. It could have halted or slowed the air and sea movement of Allied troops to the north. It could also have enabled the South Seas Detachment, the IJA force turned back on the Kokoda Trail, to reach and take Port Moresby. If Moresby became an active Japanese base, northern Australia would have been vulnerable. MacArthur's road back to Tokyo might have started in Queensland, not New Guinea.

What if the plane bringing Halsey to take over SoPac was

lost, shot down or crashed? Ghormley may have stayed for a while in command of the South Pacific theater. His fatigue and lack of aggressive leadership could have infected the troops. The US could have seen the Guadalcanal Marines overrun, gone to guerilla war on Guadalcanal. In fact, oral instructions were given to certain Marine officers to be ready to go to guerilla war if the Henderson Field fell. With an airfield in the southern Solomons, the Japanese could have interfered, even cut, supply lines to Australia. The US might have had to fight its way back starting in Samoa or even Hawaii.

What if Yamamoto had sent the weight of his fleet to bombard the airfield, rather than hold it back for some fantasy of a "decisive battle"? Japanese war doctrine had called for their navy to draw out the US navy. The grand plan was to find and defeat it in a big gun shootout in deep water. But what if that doctrine had been rejected by the Admirals? Instead the mighty battleship Yamato and her sister Musashi, the two largest battleships on the globe, could have gone into shallow waters around Guadalcanal. Each of these ships was larger with bigger guns than any other ship anywhere. A well timed pulverizing of the airstrip with strong land follow-up might have turned the tide. A Japanese victory in the Solomons would have prolonged the war. It might have forced a political settlement with the US.

A Japanese victory in either place, Solomons or New Guinea, would have enabled them to shift resources to the remaining campaign. Then it would have been the Allies having to respond to two separate fronts, not Japan. That would have been that much more demanding of resources at the end of a very long supply chain.

What if Hitler had ordered Paulus to break out of Stalingrad? Rather than give the order "do not retreat even one meter," he could have ordered the army to fall back, regroup and try again to destroy the Red Army. If Paulus had fought out and joined up with the Wehrmacht, would the Soviets have been able to eject Germany from their homeland? Perhaps so over time, but it is possible a political settlement would have been reached. This would have freed up Germans in other areas. They could have taken on the Anglo Saxons in the west, or gone south to take the Mideast oilfields, or gone in other directions. This would have changed the balance and focus of the war.

What if the French had not surrendered in North Africa after a token resistance? They could have stopped or made it very costly for the Allies to get to and seize Tunis. This would have given Rommel a safe haven for launching another try at the Suez and eastern Mediterranean. Or, it could have seen Africa become a major theater of war. This would have been to Germany's advantage, keeping the war far from the homeland.

To find how things actually turned out, we need to read the histories and look at casualty figures and an atlas. In late November 1942 the Axis drives seemed to be stopped or blunted with momentum shifting to the Allies. But it didn't have to happen that way.

The war swept on.

In Europe, the Allied bombing campaign was stepping up. On the 20th, Britain's Royal Air Force bombed the northern Italian city of Turin, causing heavy damage. Everything is relative. Damage that was considered heavy in 1942 likely would have been shrugged off in 1944 as a nuisance. But this RAF raid was merely a precursor. It was a foretaste of coming nightmares. Before too long, the American Army Air Forces would send daily raids and the British RAF would send nightly raids over Germany. Thousand plane raids would become commonplace as would multiple raids on multiple cities. German cities and citizens in particular would suffer. The Japanese, too, would feel the wrath of repeated bombing attacks. Firebombing would destroy whole cities in both countries.

November 20 saw winter setting in to northwestern Canada. That day, on the border of the Yukon Territory and British Columbia, the Alcan Highway was dedicated. This road was started the previous summer. In mere months it was pushed through thousands of miles of wilderness. The American and Canadian engineers and troops built it through a roadless region. The area was literally untracked and it was big enough to swallow New England AND Texas. Builders worked through forests, bogs, and mountains. They fought moose, bears, mosquitoes, snow and cold, and permafrost. Some bogs were big and deep enough to literally swallow a bulldozer or truck. When the road was done, supplies and troops could reach the Alaskan and northwest Canadian areas.

It was also used for moving Lend Lease supplies going to the USSR. Alaska was a portal for Lend Lease supplies and expertise sent to the Russians. Trucks, guns, and planes all came through from the continental US. Russian citizens would come to Fairbanks and Nome where American pilots delivered warplanes. They flew them up, stopping at airfields along the Highway. The Russians would then fly them across Siberia to the front. Approximately 5000 planes were sent to the USSR by this route. Trucks and guns were shipped to Russia where they were sent, usually by rail, to the front.

In Alaska, the Russians were also trained in the use of sonar, a high tech instrument which allowed the detection of submarines while they were submerged. Lieutenant Frederick Henderson was born in Colorado Springs and graduated MIT. His job in the Navy was to train men in the use of sonar. He was stationed in the Aleutian Islands. Working with Russian naval officers and men, he expedited the transfer of lend lease ships and arms. He also made sure the Russians knew how to use the arms and equipment the US was "lending" them.

This happened all over the globe—the US was not only providing arms and goods to its allies, it was teaching the recipients how to use those arms to defeat Hitler, Hirohito and Mussolini.

In Italy later in the war, the US provided the arms and equipment for a French Army to participate in the invasion of southern France in August 1944. Major Al Brookes, a graduate of Colorado School of Mines, was an Ordnance officer AFHQ, Allied Forces Headquarters for the Mediterranean. Brookes made sure the right equipment was provided to the French and saw to it that they were trained. The troops were primarily colonials, that is North and Saharan Africans. No matter, they learned the equipment and fought quite well.

21 The fight for the north coast of New Guinea continued. US 32nd Division troops attacked towards Cape Endairadere that

day. The Australian 7th Division fought towards Gona and Sanananda Point. As ever the terrain was as much an enemy as the Japanese. American work to build and improve an airdrome at nearby Dobodura continued.

22–23 The Soviet counterattack gained momentum. Whole Rumanian, Italian, and Hungarian divisions and armies were wiped out as the Soviet pincers met. Six Soviet Armies had sprung from the north of Stalingrad; they met three Armies coming from the south on the 22nd and 23rd. The meeting point was Kalach, some 40 miles west of Stalingrad. The southern prong also aimed to cut off German Army Group B in the south. Germany would counter in turn (Operation Winter Storm), trying to relieve Army Group A in Stalingrad but did not succeed. Ultimately 90,000 or so surviving Axis troops surrendered there. Many were put to work rebuilding the city of Stalingrad. Only about 10,000 of those 90,000 survived to return to western Europe in the mid 1950s.

23 On Guadalcanal, the Cactus Air Force was growing: On this day it had 84 operational aircraft, from both US and New Zealand air forces. This was a far cry from September. Then the US was struggling to hang on to the field. Some days would start with as few as twenty or twenty five planes. The Americans would lose eight or ten to combat, and have an additional five or so destroyed by bombardment. Replacements trickled in, not every day, but often enough. The logistics picture changed when the US gained command of the seas. Supplies and troops could come in greater numbers. Docks, new airfields, buildings, antiaircraft guns, repair facilities, all started to make appearance. But for the Japanese, supplying those already ashore, much less bringing in reinforcements, was becoming costly and difficult. The Emperor's Navy was reduced to making runs at night with destroyers which tossed off floating barrels to be retrieved by soldiers on shore. This innovation was not particularly successful. The plane fliers from Henderson used those barrels as targets and shot them up at first light.

24 In Burma, the 14th Indian Division had been fighting south down the Arakan Peninsula. From Cox's Bazar and Tumbru, they fought to open up a new Japanese flank, to give the

Emperor another front to have to fight on. The objective was to obtain defensible sites for forward airfields. The ultimate aim was to clear Burma by invading Akyab and then south to Rangoon. There were never enough landing craft to allow this, much less planes and troops. The China Burma India theater was even further down the supply chain than MacArthur's Southwest Pacific. It was not a strategically significant area.

In the Guadalcanal arena, Japanese belatedly realized the value of local air cover. They saw that they needed better air cover for their troops and ships than they had been providing. It was decided to build an airdrome at Munda, New Georgia. It was much closer to the action than Rabaul or Bougainville. Too late, they realized the need to give solid and uninterrupted air cover for naval reinforcement and attack. Construction at Munda started on the 24th of November. Even though the construction effort was camouflaged, it was soon discovered. The Allies bombed this new field daily, even as it was being built. It was never put to full use by the Nipponese nor was it a factor for them in the Guadalcanal campaign. Its value was apparent to the Allies and it became a takeover target as the Allies moved north. Army and Marine forces took it after a prolonged struggle in summer of 1943.

Also on the twenty fourth, Admiral Thomas Kinkaid arrived at Espiritu Santo to take charge of a cruiser force. He had orders to stop night landings by the IJN and developed a plan to do so. But he never got to work his plan. Just before the fight he was sent north to command in Alaska. He did well there, overseeing the campaign to eject the Japanese from Alaska. He went on to command the 7th Fleet, "MacArthur's Navy," in the Southwest Pacific Theater. The force he would have commanded near the Canal was taken over by Admiral Carleton Wright. The force took a beating at the Battle of Tassafaronga on the 30th. American reluctance to trust the radar and expert Japanese use of their torpedoes both contributed to the loss of a cruiser and many American lives. Admiral Wright disappeared from Guadalcanal and went somewhere into the Navy's global network of minor commands and bases.

26th, Thanksgiving Day in the US. Halsey made sure his

Guadalcanal and other troops got turkey and cranberry sauce. To the GIs sailors and Marines this was tangible proof of Halsey's promise that "I'll give you all the support I can." Most US troops around the world had similar meals. For the Japanese, Russians, Germans, British, Indians, Canadians, Italians, Hungarians, French, and Romanians it was just another day at war. Also on this day, the Admiral had something else to be thankful for: He was promoted to full admiral as of the 26th in recognition of his leadership and the importance of the theater. He earned his four stars.

27 The French Fleet was anchored at Toulon. It had been inactive since Vichy took France out of the war in June, 1940. The Wehrmacht occupied Toulon in late November, the twenty seventh. The same day, French sailors scuttled their own fleet.

In the summer of 1940, as France fell, French General Weygand promised the British Government and Winston Churchill that the French fleet would not fall into German hands. Churchill wanted it to sail for British ports but the French would not allow it. Said Weygand, they would scuttle themselves before any foreign power took them. He promised Churchill he would not let the Germans have the French ships. But Churchill and the British had their backs to the wall, barely able to stand up to Nazi Germany. They simply could not take the risk that Germany might take over and use the firepower of the French Navy. Especially they could not risk that Hitler might use it to help invade England. In July 1940 the Royal Navy acted, on Churchill's cold but understandable orders. His Majesty's ships approached Mers El Kebir, Algeria where the French Fleet was at anchor. They demanded the fleet sail to Britain or a neutral port for demilitarization, or be sunk. The French refused and after a short time, a few hours, the British Royal Navy opened fire. They sunk or disabled the majority of the fleet, especially the capital ships. This signaled to the world that Britain would ruthlessly fight on. It also angered the French and complicated later political dealings. But in late November 1942 the sailors of the French Navy, by their own hands, honored their commitment not to fall into German hands.

CHAPTER XII

The Future Defined

November 1942 was the fulcrum of the war. At that point the balance started changing from Advantage: Axis to Advantage: Allies.

That month the Axis tide was at its high point. At the start, German troops and their allies ruled North Africa from Morocco almost to Suez. They stood astride all of Europe except for Spain, Portugal, Sweden and Switzerland. They occupied the Soviet Union from north of Leningrad almost to the northern border of Turkey, as far east as the Volga River, fully half of European Russia. The Japanese ruled from the Aleutian Islands in Alaska to the Andaman Islands off of Burma in the Indian Ocean, from Manchuria in the north to Bali and New Guinea in the south. They briefly presided over fully one eighth of the planet. These two countries had conquered these immense prizes with alarming ease. Whatever their opponents tried to do, it didn't really seem to slow the Axis forces much in 1940, 1941, and early 1942.

Allied offensives would roll that tide back. It would take many lives and much time. As the Axis' empires reached their zenith, it became apparent there were chinks, weak points in their armor. In other words, there were places where they could be attacked which offered at least a prospect of success for the Allies. Troops of the US, the USSR, and the UK started slowly. First it was simply nibbling at the edges of the Axis' conquests. They did this in widely spaced, diverse locations. These nibbles soon developed into big bites. The Allies' strides towards Berlin and Tokyo got bigger and faster as time went on. There was ebb and flow, but once the Allies started winning, they did not stop. The few setbacks they faced were temporary and relatively small.

The change of momentum, the time when balance shifted and the seesaw started going the Allies' way took place definitively in the twenty one days from November 8 to 29 1942. The campaigns and sacrifices in the first years of the war, of course, cleared the way for this turn. But the change of that time is evident in every theater we have looked at. In New Guinea, Stalingrad, Northeast Africa, Guadalcanal, and Northwest Africa during these three weeks, the Allies experienced a turning point. In one case, Northeast Africa, the very recent victory at El Alamein gave the British great momentum. In New Guinea, the Australians and Americans were gathering strength and would very soon spring on the Japanese and eliminate them at the northern towns of Buna, Gona, and Sanananda. In the other three, Stalingrad, Guadalcanal, and Northwest Africa, the climactic, turning point battle took place during these three weeks.

The Russians at Stalingrad made the Germans fight house to house, rubble pile to rubble pile. The British and Americans in Northeast and Northwest Africa made the German overextend himself and then cut him off and chewed him up. The Americans at Guadalcanal made the Japanese come to them through the jungle while enduring the air power projected from Henderson Field. In New Guinea the Yanks proved willing to slug it out toe to toe to in order take a physical objective, and won quickly and convincingly.

Results of these decisive moments were apparent by January 1943. After months or years of reverses and surrenders by the allies, the turn to consistent and decisive victories was quick.

The battles fought in these days caused major changes in the global military picture. Among the changes which soon became evident:

In North Africa: The Afrika Korps retreated safely to Tunis. The British 8th Army and Desert Air Force converged from the east and joined with the British-American Torch Expedition coming from the west. They forced the surrender of over two hundred thousand Axis troops in May. This was in addition to some fifty thousand prisoners taken by the 8th Army from October to December. This was a major blow to the Nazis in terms of manpower, materiel, and morale. It opened the Mediterranean to Allied shipping. The entire north side of the Mediterranean Sea was suddenly opened to Allied attack. Hitler had his dreaded two front war; he had to divert troops and resources to the theater. Mussolini's Fascist Italian government tottered but did not fall, yet.

The countries of the Mediterranean basin would return to pre-war status for twenty or more years: Colonies on the south and east sides of the sea would remain so, other than the creation of Israel. Those nations on the north side would return to their parliamentary democracies, with the exceptions of the Balkans which would become communist dictatorships. Many of these economies and political states stand today. Those which ended the war behind the Iron Curtain reinvented themselves in the 1990's.

In Russia: The remains of the German 6th Army in Stalingrad surrendered in early February. Some 90,000 German, Italian, Rumanian, and Hungarian men went into captivity. Only a fraction of them survived to return home in the mid 1950s. The German Army was forced to retreat from Stalingrad and the Caucasus. The Red Army had the initiative, never to lose it. The Wehrmacht was in permanent retreat until the surrender in May 1945.

The Russian Empire would extend from the Pacific on the east to central Europe. Half of Germany and all of Poland, Hungary, Czechoslovakia, and the Balkans came under the sway of Moscow. This is the opposite of what Hitler desired. It is also the opposite of the prewar conditions—those nations were independent in 1939. The Soviet Union fed on the Lend Lease aid from the US and the wealth of these conquests to become a superpower. That status lasted for two generations before external competition, internal frictions, and inherent economic contradictions caused it to implode. The impetus of events stemming from Stalingrad and the other fronts carried through and shaped Russian political and economic thinking until nearly the turn of the century.

In New Guinea: The Japanese garrison in northern Papua was destroyed by January. Australians and Americans paid a heavy price for the small amount of real estate they conquered. The Japanese troops paid a horrific price before giving it up. The area became a springboard for General MacArthur's attacks along New Guinea and the Philippines towards Tokyo. The Emperor's forces were in perpetual retreat from this point of the war. Even so, they fought savagely and sold dearly every inch they gave up.

New Guinea returned to colonial status as the Japanese vacated. The Dutch held the west end, the Australians created a dependency on the east end of the island. These lasted a matter of a few years before the local populace threw off the colonial yoke and declared independence as Indonesia and Papua New Guinea, respectively. Today, the world's most populous Muslim country is Indonesia. That nation as well as other southeast Asian and south Pacific nations owe their birth and early development to events directly stemming from the decisive November days of the Pacific War.

In Guadalcanal: In Tokyo, Imperial Headquarters decided to pull back to strong points in the middle Solomon Islands. During the previous six months they had written the book on the use of destroyers and fast transport ships to supply and send reinforcements. For lack of alternatives they used the same technique to evacuate the island. By timing the run of their destroyers in to Guadalcanal they were able to pull out their surviving troops. Every man who could walk or hobble to the beach got put onto a ship and taken north to fight again. This difficult maneuver was completed by the end of January, and it got done in secret. The Americans soon discovered their absence but did not know about the evacuations as they occurred. General Patch declared the island secure in early February. The Japanese Army and Navy lost about twenty four ships and easily twenty five thousand men. The US Marines and Army lost less than two thousand men. The US Navy lost more than three times as many men, and also about twenty four ships. It is no wonder that the compass dances when ships go over the graveyard in Ironbottom Sound.

The Americans developed the island as a major base for their northward advances. Most of the men who served in the Solomon Islands were just anonymous citizen-soldiers doing their part, men like Al Brookes and Bill Stevenson. Some who passed through or were stationed there enjoyed prominence later in life: John Kennedy (US President, 1961–63), Byron White (Associate Justice of the Supreme Court, early 1960's–mid 1980's), and John Mitchell (Attorney General for Richard Nixon) were all based there as Naval officers.

The Solomon Islands returned to British dependency for several years but became an independent nation in the 1960's.

At sea, this time was a turning point as well. The critical point in November seemed to favor the Axis, thanks to the German Uboats. In fact, in November 1942 the Allies suffered the most monthly tonnage sunk by Uboats during the war. Had the boats kept up that rate of sinking the Allies would have had to divert resources. They couldn't ignore that threat to their supply lines. Those diverted resources otherwise could have gone to one of the land theaters. Had that happened perhaps some of the turning point battles we have explored would not have occurred, or would have had different outcomes. In any case, March 1943 saw the Battle of the Atlantic turn the Allies' way. By that time, antisub resources and knowledge had been mobilized and developed. Starting that month, there were sharp and continuing reductions in Allied ship tonnage sunk and sharp increases in Uboats destroyed. The Nazi submarines continued to prey on shipping until May 1945. Boats were at sea and stalking freighters literally until the last days of the war. But they were never again a substantial threat to the Allied war effort.

The outcome of these campaigns lined out the strategies and tactics that the Allies used to win the war. In all but Northwest Africa, logistical challenges played a big part. In Russia, the Pacific, and Egypt the Allies' logistic support had to travel less far than did the opponent's. Russia truly had interior lines. In the Pacific and Egypt, the Allies had long logistic support lines but they were shorter and better protected than the lines of the Japanese or Germans. Lessons learned: see to your supplies and do what you can to disrupt the enemy's.

Lessons learned in specific campaigns, which were put to general use, include:

- Stalingrad: Don't let your enemy fight on his terms. Make him fight on yours.

- Northwest Africa, do what you can to bring the foe to your side using political means. Soften the foe's resolve and give advantage to those who help you. This may outweigh your supply problems if you approach from a great distance. Also, much was learned from Operation Torch about staging shore to shore amphibious assaults.

- Guadalcanal: Air reigns supreme. If you have control of the air you will ultimately have control of the ground and the sea surface. This reinforced the lesson the Royal Air Force taught the Luftwaffe over England in 1940.

- New Guinea: Don't attack the Japanese head on. Bypass them if at all possible. MacArthur took this to heart. Unfortunately for the US Marines and many GIs, some of their objectives across the Pacific couldn't be bypassed. Islands such as Tarawa, Iwo Jima, and Okinawa reinforced the lesson that the Japanese taught MacArthur and the Australians at Buna.

So these five campaigns, Northeast Africa, Northwest Africa, Stalingrad/southern Russia, New Guinea, and Guadalcanal, were formative on a grand strategic level. Their outcomes set the foundation for the world we now have, and their lessons and results were formative on the war fighting level until late 1945.

In early December 1942, American researchers were able to start and control an atomic chain reaction. This practical proof of theory was crucial to the success of the Manhattan Project. This was the super secret effort to build the atomic bomb before anyone else got one. In November, plans were already being made. In December, land was bought or appropriated and buildings were constructed for that immense effort. The whole effort went ahead full speed as soon as the theory was proved. We all know the use and effect of the bombs Manhattan Project produced. This effort would likely never have happened had not the war and fear of Hitler prompted the effort.

« »

Winston Churchill is reputed to have said, "Before 1942 almost nothing went right for us; after 1942 almost nothing went wrong."

As 1942 was the turning point of World War II, November was the turning point of 1942.

At the end of that month the Allies went from losing and retreating to advancing and winning. Those victories started small and slowly, but they set the tone and built the foundation for winning the war and defining the shape of the peace.

Those victories that were won or set up in November 1942 shaped the thinking and politics of the rest of the twentieth century and our world of today.

BIBLIOGRAPHY

A Brief History of India, Alain Danielou, Inner Traditions International, 2003
Alaska, A History, Claus-M Naske & Herman Slotnick, University Oklahoma Press 1979, 2011
Battle of the Atlantic, Terry Hughes & John Costello, Dial Press, 1977
Bloody Buna, Lida Mayo, Doubleday & Co, 1974
Boarding Party: Last Action of the Calcutta Light Horse, James Leasor, Bluejacket Books, 1979
Dear Miss Em, General Eichelberger's War in the Pacific 1942–1945, Robt Eichelberger, Greenwood Press
Encounters with the Arch Druid, John Mc Phee, Ballantine Books, 1971
Field Marshall Von Manstein: the Janus Head, Marcel Stein, Helion &Co, 2007
Finest Hour, The Journal of Winston Churchill, Numbers 152 & 154
For Five Shillings A Day, Personal Histories of World War II, R. Campbell & P Liddle, Harper Collins, 2002
Ghost Mountain Boys, James Campbell, Crown Publishers 2007
Glory Road, Robert A Heinlein, Berkeley Publishing 1963
Green Hell, The Battle for Guadalcanal, William Owens, Hellgate Press, 1999
Guadalcanal Diary, Richard Tregaskis, Random House, 1943
Guadalcanal, The Definitive Account of the Landmark Battle, Richard B Frank, Penguin Books, 1990
History of US Naval Operations in World War II, Samuel Eliot Morison, Atlantic Monthly Press 1959
    Vol. I: Battle of The Atlantic Sept 1939–May 1943
    Vol. V: The Struggle For Guadalcanal, August 1942–February 1943
    Vol. VII: Aleutians, Gilberts and Marshalls June 1942–April 1944
Horror in the East, Laurence Rees, Random House 2001
Intelligence in War, John Keegan, Alfred A. Knopf 2003
Japan at War, An Oral History, H.T. & T.F. Cook, The New Press, 1992
Lonely Vigil, Coastwatchers in the Solomons, Walter Lord, Viking Press 1977
Neptune's Inferno, The US Navy at Guadalcanal, James D Hornsfischer, Bantam Books 2011
Once Upon a Town, The Miracle of the North Platte Canteen, Bob Greene, Harper Collins 2002

Oral Histories, American Patriot's History Association, Veteran's Oral History Project, Library of Congress:
    Mike Negri, May 26 2010
Ostkrieg, Hitler's War of Extermination in the East, Stephen G. Fritz, University Press of Kentucky, 2011
Pacific Legacy, Rex Smith & Gerald Meehl, Abbeville Press, 2002
Pentagon, A History, Steve Vogel, Random House, 2007
Personal Letters and Papers:
    Gerald Beckett
    Frederick Henderson
    Wilmer Rawie
    William D Stevenson
Personal Reminiscences:
    Ed Bennett
    Albert Brookes
    Charles Fields
    John Harrison
    Stan Holtan
    Charles Moore
Raj, The Making and Unmaking of British India, Lawrence James, St Martin's Press, 1998
Reader's Digest Illustrated History of WWII, Reader's Digest, 1989
Resource Guide for Teachers and Students, Alaska at War, NPS, 2000
Second World War, Winston S Churchill, Houghton Mifflin, 1951
    Vol. IV: The Hinge of Fate
    Vol. V: Closing the Ring
Stalingrad: Point of Return, Ronald Seth, Coward-McCann, 1959
Survival in Shanghai, Journals/Fred Marcus 1939–49, Audrey Friedman Marcus Pacific View Press 2008
Three Came Home, Agnes Newton Keith, Atlantic Little Brown, 1946
Trail of '42, A Pictorial History of the Alaska Highway, Stan Cohen, Pictorial Histories Publishing, 1979
War In The Far East 1941–45, Basil Collier, William Morrow & Co, 1968
Websites:
    AmericanHistoricalSociety.org
    Guadalcanal.Homestead.com
    U-S-History.com
    1stmarinedivisionassociation.org
    Stalingrad.net
    Wikipedia

GLOSSARY
Who Is Raj and What Is a Tin Fish?

Afrika Korps: The German forces in North Africa in 1941 and 1942. Commanded by General Erwin Rommel, it comprised German motorized and infantry troops and air forces, and Italian infantry.

Allies: Great Britain, the Soviet Union, and the United States along with smaller countries (Australia, Brazil, China, France, Norway, Poland, and others) banded together to fight the war. Collectively known as the Allies, also known as The Grand Alliance. The English speaking powers consulted often and had a very high degree of operational cooperation. They consulted regularly with the Soviet Union. There was only general coordination of operations between Russia and the English speaking countries.

Amphibious invasion: An invasion from the sea. This is historically difficult since the shoreline is easily defended and the attacker is a long way from his base and must send supplies over the beaches.

Armor: Tanks and similar armored **fighting** vehicles. Usually used in large formations.

Artillery: Large land based guns. Usually too big to be self propelled.

Axis: Germany, Italy, and Japan banded together in treaty of common defense. Hitler invoked this treaty when he declared war on the US on December 11, 1941. Some other countries also contributed troops (chiefly Hungary and Romania, fighting at Germany's direction). Italy followed Germany's lead and provided troops and support. There was little consultation and no coordination or common planning between Germany and Japan.

Battle of the Atlantic: Every day from September 1939 to May 1945 German Uboats, or submarines, tried to sink freighters sending supplies to Britain. The Allies devoted many ships, planes, women, and men to stop them. This was the longest battle fought over the biggest area of the entire war.

Blitzkrieg: A method of war devised by the Nazis. German for "lightning war." It entailed devastating air attack then fast exploitation of the confusion by movement of tanks behind the lines then follow up and taking captives with infantry.

It was very effective for the Nazis in conquering huge swathes of territory.

Bombardment: Shelling enemy lines or beaches with big guns. The guns can be ship mounted or land based artillery. In either case a bombardment kills and destroys, and stuns the survivors.

Bushido: The Japanese warrior philosophy which held that will and spirit can overcome superior material, that is that armament and firepower is no match for a determined Japanese soldier.

Cactus: The code name the Allies used for the island of Guadalcanal.

CAF: Cactus Air Force, the airplanes flying from Guadalcanal.

CO: The Commanding Officer. The person in charge of a platoon, company, ship, squadron, or any military or naval unit or detachment. Sometimes called "The Old Man."

Code Names:
    Barbarossa: The German invasion of Russia, June 22 1941.
    Drumbeat: The German submarine offensive off the eastern US, spring 1942. Also called "Operation Paukenschlag."
    Go: The Japanese plan to retake Guadalcanal, Fall 1942.
    Lightfoot: The British attack on El Alamein, Egypt, October 23 1942.
    Neptune: The naval portion of Overlord.
    Overlord: The Allied invasion of France, June 6 1944.
    Supercharge: The British pursuit and destruction of the Afrika Korps in Egypt, starting November 4 1942.
    Torch: The Allied invasion of Morocco and Algeria, November 8 1942.
    Uranus: The Russian counterattack to isolate Stalingrad and southern Russia, November 19 1942.
    Watchtower: The American invasion of Guadalcanal, August 7 1942.
    Winter Garden: The aborted plan for the surrounded German 6th Army in Stalingrad to fight its way out and meet other German forces fighting in to relieve them.
    Winter Storm: The unsuccessful plan for German forces to fight their way in to Stalingrad and relieve the 6th Army which was surrounded there.
    Z Day: The day Henderson Field was supposed to be taken by Japanese troops, November 13 1942 and others as delayed.

Doolittle Raid: A raid in April 1942 which launched heavy bombers (usually land based) off of a carrier near Tokyo. The raid caused minimal physical harm but damaged the prestige of the Japanese military. It caused them to quickly seek a revenge battle to destroy the US fleet. That battle was Midway which did not turn out well for Japan.

Defeat in detail: The practice of meeting a dispersed enemy and defeating each of the dispersed units before they can unite to attack you.

GI: Slang for an American soldier. It is a play on the phrase "Government Issue."

Grand Alliance: See "Allies."

Greater East Asian Co-Prosperity Sphere: The name the Japanese Government gave to its newly conquered empire.

Henderson Field: The airfield on Guadalcanal. America's "unsinkable aircraft carrier." Named after Major Lofton Henderson, a Marine flier killed in the Battle of Midway.

Infantry: The guys who carry rifles and whose job is to take and hold ground. If a battle is to be won, sooner or later the infantry has to come do its work.

IJA: Imperial Japanese Army

IJN: Imperial Japanese Navy

Ironbottom Sound: The name given the waters between Guadalcanal and Tulagi. It was so named because about fifty ships were sunk there during the campaign. It was later found that when surface units transited those waters, their compasses actually veered due to the magnetic anomaly from all the iron on the bottom of the sea.

KIA: Killed in action.

Kokoda Trail: A footpath which goes between the north and south coasts of the Papuan peninsula of New Guinea. Site of a major struggle between Australian and Japanese armies.

Kreigsmarine: The German Navy.

Luftwaffe: The German Air Force.

Manhattan Project: The secret American project to try to build the atom bomb. It entailed thousands of people, hundreds of millions of dollars, three big bases and scores of minor bases.

Midway, Battle of: A carrier battle in June 1942. The Japanese intended to attack the island of Midway near Hawaii, thus drawing out the US Fleet. Due to intelligence obtained three US carriers were waiting. They sunk four Japanese carriers for the loss of one. This battle stopped Japanese expansion and set the stage for the South Pacific struggles. This may have been the most important battle for western civilization since the Battle of Tours in 732 when the Moorish invasion of France was turned back.

NCO: Non commissioned officer. Corporals, Sergeants, Petty Officers are all NCOs. A NCO is roughly equivalent to a foreman or supervisor in the civilian world.

Nisei: A person of pure Japanese descent, born outside of Japan.

OKW: The German High Command, short for Ober Kommando der Werhmacht.

Ostfront: The Eastern Front, the German war with Russia.

Panzer: German for panther, what they called their tanks.

POW: Prisoner of War. A soldier captured by the enemy. Not a civilian or refugee caught up in the war, but a captured, uniformed member of the military.

Raj: The name of the British Colonial Government of India.

Red Army: The army of the USSR, the Russian Army.

Reich: German for government or empire. Hitler's government called itself the Third Reich.

SS: A Nazi army under command of Heinrich Himmler. It was separate from and in many ways, competing with the German Army. Short for Schutzstaffel. It was selective and prestigious. One had to be of "pure Aryan stock" to get in. It took on many ideological or "racial purity" tasks such as Hitler's bodyguard detail and running the death camps.

Ships:

Battleship: a large ship built for bombardment and ship to ship combat.
Carrier: a ship built to be a floating, mobile air base. Slangily, a flattop.
Cruiser: a mid sized ship built for bombardment and ship to ship combat.
Destroyer: a small ship built to screen and protect other ships, to destroy submarines, and to accomplish other tasks and escort duties.
PT Boat: a speedy, wooden or light metal boat designed to go into shallow waters on patrol and to harass and sink larger ships. John Kennedy commanded one in 1943; General MacArthur and his party escaped the Philippines in 1942 on PT boats.
Submarine: a submersible ship built to destroy other ships.
Suez Canal: The canal which linked the Mediterranean Sea with the Indian Ocean. It was an artery of trade in a strategic position. Who held the Canal controlled the Mediterranean Sea and access to India.
Swastika: The bent cross symbol prominent on the German flag and on most all Nazi banners, armbands, uniforms, etc. This is actually an ancient symbol found in Celtic relics and American Indian Navajo rugs. It has a long and until 1933 honorable history.
Tin Fish: Slang for torpedo, the underwater guided missile/bomb submarines used to sink ships.
Theater: Large geographical area of operations under one command.
Tommy: Slang for a British soldier, not unlike the American GI.
UBoat: German submarine, short for "unterseeboot."
Vichy France: The government of the part of France that Hitler did not occupy after his 1940 victory. It was based in the town of Vichy. It was a satellite government owing its existence to Berlin.
Wehrmacht: The German Army.

DAILY BREAKDOWN

NOVEMBER 8
In northeast Africa: The German Afrika Korps continued its retreat, pursued by British and Allied forces.

In northwest Africa: In a totally separate action, Operation Torch started. This was the Allied invasion of Morocco and Algeria. American and British troops landed to mixed receptions, from open arms to vigorous opposition with deadly shooting.

Russia: Germans batter at what was left of Stalingrad, having already taken most of the city. In south Russia, Wehrmacht Caucasus forces continue their advance as well.

New Guinea: The Japanese continued their retreat north across the Papua Peninsula. They were pursued by Australian regular infantry and militia forces.

NOVEMBER 9
In northeast Africa: In response to Torch, Germans started sending reinforcements in to Tunisia. Allied troops advanced in Morocco and Algeria.

NOVEMBER 10
A Uboat sowing mines forced authorities to close New York harbor for a day. Worldwide, November had more tons of shipping sunk by Uboats than any month of the war. More tonnage was sunk than the Allies could build in a month. The Germans wanted to continue this trend while the Allies tried to stop it.

NOVEMBER 11
In France, Italian and German troops invaded and started to occupy Vichy France in retaliation for weak French resistance to Torch. The pretense that the Vichy Government had any power and authority over the French people was abandoned.

NOVEMBER 12
In Guadalcanal: The three day Naval Battle of Guadalcanal opened. A multi-pronged Japanese attack to retake the airstrip started. American Admirals Callaghan and Scott along with thousands of American and Japanese sailors were killed; many ships were sunk. The Japanese task force set to deliver the battle's opening bombardment of Henderson Field was turned back.

In New Guinea, Australians continued the overland pursuit of retreating Japanese. American troops were being air and sea lifted to the north coast to fight them. Some Americans were marching across the peninsula.

NOVEMBER 13
In North Africa: American General Eisenhower, Allied commander, and French Admiral Darlan, French commander in North Africa, met and reached a truce. They also made an agreement for local Frenchmen to help the Allies.

The Naval Battle of Guadalcanal continued. Despite air inflicted losses to the Japanese Navy, Admiral Nishimura was able to get through to bombard the airfield.

NOVEMBER 14
Guadalcanal: Japanese invasion troops were being ferried south. They were attacked by planes from the airfield and a carrier. Many were the ships sunk and soldiers drowned at a low cost to American pilots. The Naval Battle of Guadalcanal ended. American battleships under Admiral Lee sunk Japanese ships and prevented a bombardment of the airfield. Local control of the sea and the strategic initiative passed to the Americans.

In Washington DC the Secretary of War and Chief of Staff of the Army moved into the Pentagon building, thus streamlining management of the war. The Navy remained in old offices throughout the area.

NOVEMBER 15
In Russia: German troops took control of oilfields in the Caucasus. But the oil machinery was destroyed by retreating Russians and very little oil was ever extracted or put to Nazi use.

NOVEMBER 16
In North Africa the Germans secured a bridgehead in Tunisia. This gave them a base to fight from and a safe haven for the Afrika Korps which was retreating in from Egypt.

Guadalcanal: Land offensives were planned and started by Americans on the island. Plans were made to rotate the Marines out and put Army troops in charge.

NOVEMBER 17
New Guinea: American troops were lifted by air and boat, and marched towards Buna and Gona in New Guinea while Australians fought towards these towns on foot. They would fight bitter battles to clear these small towns of Japanese.

NOVEMBER 18
The Soviet Army prepared a counteroffensive, called Operation Uranus. Its goal was to relieve Stalingrad and destroy German units. Germans continued to pound at the remains of Stalingrad trying to push the Russians out.

NOVEMBER 19
In Russia: The Red Army launched Operation Uranus. This plan aimed to cut off

and isolate the approximately 100,000 Germans in Stalingrad and destroy their allied armies which supported them. It also aimed to threaten or even cut off and isolate the German armies operating in southern Russia.

NOVEMBER 20
Land offensives continued throughout the African, Russian, and Pacific theaters.

In Yukon Territory, Canada, the Alaskan Highway was completed after a concentrated six month effort. It was used to move troops and goods to Alaska, and Lend Lease goods to Russia.

NOVEMBER 21
Americans started to build an airstrip at Dobodura in northern New Guinea. It would support operations in the area and was destined to become a major base used the remainder of the war.

NOVEMBER 22
Soviet pincers of Operation Uranus met some forty miles west of Stalingrad, successfully cutting off the many Germans and their allies behind them. All German armies in southern Russia were also in danger of being isolated. The strategic initiative passed to the Red Army.

NOVEMBER 23
The American and Allied air forces on Guadalcanal were growing. Japanese could not adequately resupply their forces. They were reduced to throwing barrels full of supplies off of speeding destroyers in the dark, hoping they would drift to the hungry troops ashore.

NOVEMBER 24
In Burma, The Indian Army was fighting in the Akyab region of northwest Burma. The goal was to reach and isolate Rangoon. This theater remained secondary for the entire war.

Guadalcanal: The Japanese started to build an airfield on the island of New Georgia. It was much nearer to Guadalcanal than their other main base. The Allies found and bombed it. It would become operational for the Japanese but they did not make it a major base. The Allies would take it in the summer of 1943 and use it against the Emperor's men.

NOVEMBER 25
The Red Army continued to run over and destroy German and Axis armies. Hitler forbade the Stalingrad forces to fight their way out or even consolidate their lines. He ordered them not to surrender even an inch, rather to hold and await relief.

NOVEMBER 26
For the fighting man, this was Thanksgiving Day for American troops. Turkey and cranberry sauce were to be had by all hands. Also this day Admiral Halsey got his fourth star as he was promoted to full Admiral. This was in recognition of the importance of the South Pacific Theater and his positive leadership.

NOVEMBER 27
The French fleet anchored at Toulon in southern France was scuttled. The ships' own sailors sunk them rather than let them fall into German hands.

NOVEMBER 28
New land offensives were planned on Guadalcanal. The Marines were relieved and sent to Australia. A US Army General takes arrived to take command.

DISCUSSION QUESTIONS

Which major political leader had the most effect on the outcome of these five campaigns? The least effect? Why?

How important were high command personalities (military commanders, not civilian political leaders) in the campaigns described?

Do you think either Japan or Germany could have won their war? How?

Japanese Admiral Mikawa was criticized for not finishing the job in early August, by shelling the transports and Marines after he sunk much of the US fleet. If he had, how different might the war's outcome have been?

The book speaks several times about "citizen soldiers." How did they contribute to the war effort?

Which of the five campaigns was most critical to the outcome of the war? Why?

Which of the five campaigns was least critical to the outcome of the war? Why?

Was there another military campaign or civilian effort which should have been included in this book? What and why?

Stalin is quoted as saying "The war was won with British courage, Russian blood, and American money." Agree/disagree? Why?

Documents released after the collapse of the USSR seemed to show that Stalin was preparing to attack Germany in 1939. Hitler beat him to the punch. If Stalin had struck first, how might the map of Europe and the story of the 20th century be different?

What if Hitler had been killed in a plane crash in early 1942?

There seems to be no one dominant personality behind Japan's war: no Hitler, FDR, Stalin or Churchill. Each of these men put their imprint on their nation's efforts. Why did Japan lack one strong, visible leader? Is this important?

ABOUT THE AUTHOR

Stan Moore is an avid reader of books, magazines, websites, and historical papers. A third generation Coloradan, he is a Vietnam veteran. When not reading up on today's and tomorrow's past, he is traveling, or more likely is outdoors. Exploring mountains in Colorado and canyons in Utah are among his favorite activities. Another favorite pastime is enjoying family, wife, children and spouses, grandchildren, and friends. He makes his home west of Denver with his long suffering spouse and the two cats who let them stay there.

www.ingramcontent.com/pod-product-compliance
Lightning Source LLC
Chambersburg PA
CBHW032032290426
44110CB00012B/765